Philip Kennedy teaches theology in the University of Oxford, where he is a Senior Research Fellow at Mansfield College. He is the author of *A Modern Introduction to Theology: New Questions for Old Beliefs* (2006) and *Twentieth Century Theologians: A New Introduction to Modern Christian Thought* (2010), both published by I.B.Tauris.

'Christianity is such a complex, diverse phenomenon that an introduction must simplify, but without simplification: and this Philip Kennedy achieves with admirable success. His book captures Christianity in all its allure and diversity. Kennedy's prose is limpid, but his judgments sharp and challenging. For the rich Christianity offers the divine, cosmic Christ, but for the poor there is the human Jesus, humiliated but triumphant in his blessings; and in the interplay between these two images, Kennedy finds reason for the success and conflicts of the Christian story. This is a simply superb introduction to Christianity in all its contradictions and variety.' – *Gerard Loughlin, Professor of Theology and Religion, Durham University*

'What an epic and what a read! From the Babylonian Empire to the banking crisis at the end of the first decade of the third millennium; from messianic stirrings to the Four Horsemen of the Apocalypse – Kennedy combs times and geographies like a contemporary Faust. His prose is lucid, his observations deft and the figuring of events, cultural achievements and people masterly. This is not a summary and it is not just an overview. It is a magnificent story about divine longing and human frailty. Anyone interested in Christianity past and present will learn immensely from this panoramic odyssey.' – *Graham Ward, Professor of Contextual Theology and Ethics, University of Manchester*

D0630345

I.B.TAURIS INTRODUCTIONS TO RELIGION

In recent years there has been a surge of interest in religion and in the motivations behind religious belief and commitment. Avoiding over-simplification, jargon or unhelpful stereotypes, I.B.Tauris Introductions to Religion embraces the opportunity to explore religious tradition in a sensitive, objective and nuanced manner. A specially commissioned series for undergraduate students, it offers concise, clearly written overviews, by leading experts in the field, of the world's major religious faiths, and of the challenges posed to all the religions by progress, globalization and diaspora. Covering the fundamentals of history, theology, ritual and worship, these books place an emphasis above all on the modern world, and on the lived faiths of contemporary believers. They explore, in a way that will engage followers and non-believers alike, the fascinating and sometimes difficult contradictions or reconciling ancient tradition with headlong cultural and technological change.

'I.B.Tauris Introductions to Religion offers students of religion something fresh, intelligent and accessible. Without dumbing down the issues, or making complex matters seem more simple than they need to be, the series manages to be both conceptually challenging while also providing beginning undergraduates with the complete portfolio of books that they need to grasp the fundamentals of each tradition. To be religious is in the end to be human. The I.B.Tauris series looks to be an ideal starting point for anyone interested in this vital and often elusive component of all our societies and cultures.' – *John M. Hull, Emeritus Professor of Religious Education, University of Birmingham*

'The I.B.Tauris Introductions to Religion series promises to be just what busy teachers and students need: a batch of high-quality, highly accessible books by leading scholars that are thoroughly geared towards pedagogical needs and student course use. Achieving a proper understanding of the role of religion in the world is, more than ever, an urgent necessity. This attractive-looking series will contribute towards that vital task.' – *Christopher Partridge, Professor of Religious Studies, Lancaster University*

'The I.B.Tauris series promises to offer more than the usual kind of humdrum introduction. The volumes will seek to explain and not merely to describe religions, will consider religions as ways of life and not merely as sets of beliefs and practices, and will explore differences as well as similarities among specific communities of adherents worldwide. Strongly recommended.' – *Robert A. Segal, Professor of Religious Studies, University of Aberdeen*

Please see the back of the book for the full series list

I.B.TAURIS INTRODUCTIONS TO RELIGION

Christianity

An Introduction

by

Philip Kennedy

I.B. TAURIS

LONDON · NEW YORK

Published in 2011 by I.B.Tauris & Co Ltd
6 Salem Road, London W2 4BU
175 Fifth Avenue, New York NY 10010
www.ibtauris.com

Distributed in the United States and Canada Exclusively by Palgrave Macmillan
175 Fifth Avenue, New York NY 10010

I.B.Tauris Introductions to Religion

ISBN: 978 1 84885 382 9 (HB)
ISBN: 978 1 84885 383 6 (PB)

A full CIP record for this book is available from the British Library
A full CIP record is available from the Library of Congress

Library of Congress Catalog Card Number: available

Designed and Typeset by 4word Ltd, Bristol, UK
Printed and bound in Great Britain by TJ International, Padstow, Cornwall

To Diarmaid MacCulloch, a compassionate friend,
and creative son of Christianity

Contents

Preface

Christianity is the largest religion the world has ever known. This book introduces it by sketching its origins, history and principal features. It offers an impressionistic interpretation like any other text far removed in time from Christianity's beginnings. It is neither encyclopaedic in its details nor all-encompassing in its reach. It passes over some of Christianity's historical manifestations in silence, and ignores many Christians eminently worthy of note. That is not as a result of a wilfully maintained act of bias or negligence, but because the text seeks to focus throughout on the core characteristics of Christianity, rather than to provide an exhaustive account of its detailed history and panoply of personalities. While discussions of historical movements and colourful people abound in ensuing pages, *Christianity: An Introduction* is driven from beginning to end to explain why Christianity is a religion according to which billions of human beings have wished to live in a remote past, and continue to do so now.

Conventions

There is much to instruct, astonish and unsettle by an investigation of Christianity in its former and present forms. Before perusing or reading this book further, the reader may be helped by an explanation of conventions adopted in its writing. All dates are specified according to a distinction between BCE and CE. The former designates 'Before the Common Era' and is an alternative to using BC ('Before Christ'). CE refers to the Common Era: the period in which Christianity was born and co-existed with other world-views. The principal reason for adopting such a convention is not to be newfangled, but to avoid obliging people to designate human history by acknowledging Jesus Christ as 'their Lord', as in AD (*Anno*

Domini, 'the year of the Lord', or 'the year of our Lord'). There are Christians who insist that the aristocratic or plutocratic category of lordship is inappropriately applied to Jesus; and there are others who have never heard of Jesus or dislike what is remembered of him. For them, lordship predicated of Jesus is to mischaracterize him.

Translations from the Bible are normally those of the New Revised Standard Version, unless otherwise indicated.

The word 'God' is used hereafter as a proper name for a single deity. 'Gods' refer to more than one deity. The word 'god', without a capital 'G', is avoided so as not to assume or give the impression that deities worshipped by people apart from Christians are surreal or unreal: hence, 'the Roman Gods'; 'the Gods of the pagans'. No human enjoys the ability to dictate or define decisively what constitutes a God. This is why God is never referred to in the following pages with pronouns denoting gender. Such an avoidance serves as a reminder that whoever or whatever God might be, God is at least not an instance of the animal species, *Homo sapiens* – unless it is thought that all language about God is disguised chatter about those animals which are human.

The word 'Church' when capitalized refers to an international commonwealth of Christian assemblies (denominations), such as the Catholic Church or the Baptist Church. Written entirely in lower case, the term designates either a building ('the church next to the Post Office') or a local community of worshippers, as in 'the Anglican church of the neighbouring suburb'.

Christianity is a complex confection. It is a large religion with a long history. It can be baffling to anyone observing or trying to understand it. Its own members can be uncertain of its purpose, forgetful of its past, and confused about its present. To render this book more readily accessible to any interested reader, its Preface is followed by three lists that provide short overviews of Christianity's historical development and peculiar terminology, including: (a) an X-ray of Christianity's evolution; (b) a broad time-frame for Christianity; and (c) a quick guide to terms commonly used by Christians. The reader may wish to scan these overviews, or refer back to them from time to time, in order to situate in a particular period passages, people or topics discussed in the text.

Presenting a peep into Christianity's past and present, as this book does, is to invite oversight rather than accuracy. To prevent that as much as possible, I have relied on conversations over many years with family members, friends, students and academic colleagues. The question I have put to them all over time has been invariably: What is the pith of Christianity? Answers have been as varied as the types of Christianity that are manifest today. The counsel and kindness of my interlocutors over umpteen years have been endlessly instructive and constructive. Particularly, I ought and want to thank Stephen, my father, for his sustained interest and encouragement of me and my work; Margaret Kennedy King, similarly endlessly kind; my sisters and brothers and their families; Diarmaid MacCulloch; Jennifer Cooper; Bernard Green; Philip McCosker; Judith Maltby; Tom Nickalls; Richard Saynor; Andy Dunn; Leon Thompson; Simon Cuff; Peter Groves; Helga and Willi Kaufman; Yvan Mudry; Angel Maestro; Joël-Alexis Iseli von Jegenstorf; and Dennis Kehrberg. While I was writing these pages I heard of the death of a great theological mentor, Edward Schillebeeckx. I am unable to thank him enough for his formative influence on my life. Finally, I am especially grateful to Alex Wright of I.B.Tauris for his patient guidance, wise insights and endlessly constructive suggestions.

Philip Kennedy, Oxford

An X-ray of Christianity's Evolution

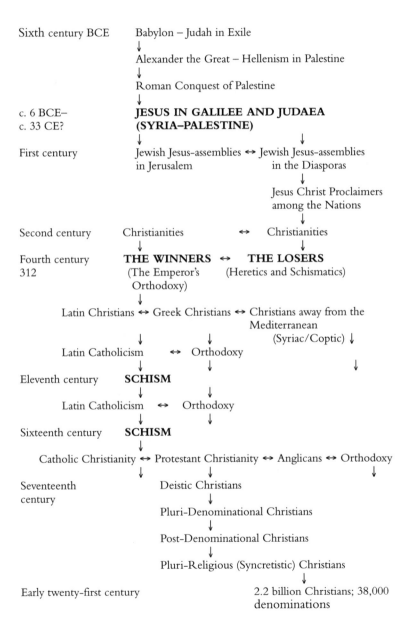

Sixth century BCE — Babylon – Judah in Exile
↓
Alexander the Great – Hellenism in Palestine
↓
Roman Conquest of Palestine
↓

c. 6 BCE–
c. 33 CE? — **JESUS IN GALILEE AND JUDAEA (SYRIA–PALESTINE)**
↓   ↓

First century — Jewish Jesus-assemblies ↔ Jewish Jesus-assemblies
in Jerusalem   in the Diasporas
↓
Jesus Christ Proclaimers
among the Nations
↓

Second century — Christianities ↔ Christianities
↓   ↓

Fourth century
312 — **THE WINNERS** ↔ **THE LOSERS**
(The Emperor's   (Heretics and Schismatics)
Orthodoxy)
↓

Latin Christians ↔ Greek Christians ↔ Christians away from the
Mediterranean
(Syriac/Coptic) ↓
↓   ↓

Latin Catholicism ↔ Orthodoxy
↓   ↓   ↓

Eleventh century — **SCHISM**
↓   ↓

Latin Catholicism ↔ Orthodoxy
↓   ↓

Sixteenth century — **SCHISM**
↓

Catholic Christianity ↔ Protestant Christianity ↔ Anglicans ↔ Orthodoxy
↓   ↓   ↓

Seventeenth
century — Deistic Christians
↓
Pluri-Denominational Christians
↓
Post-Denominational Christians
↓
Pluri-Religious (Syncretistic) Christians
↓

Early twenty-first century — 2.2 billion Christians; 38,000
denominations

Time-frame for Christianity

605–562	Nebuchadnezzar II (Ruler of the Babylonian Empire)
587 BCE	Destruction of Jerusalem and deportation of Judaeans to Babylon
539	The Persian King Cyrus allows Jews in Babylon to return to Judah. Some remain as a diaspora
520–515	Reconstruction of Jerusalem's Temple
Late sixth century–70 CE	Period of the Second Temple in Jerusalem
509	The beginning of the Roman Republic
480–479 BCE	The Persian Wars
431–404	The Peloponnesian War
334–333	Alexander the Great enters Asia Minor from Greece and conquers the Persian Empire
332	Alexander the Great gains control of Palestine (a name coined by Herodotus) and conquers Egypt
323	Death of Alexander the Great. Jewish lands fall under the control of the Egyptian Ptolemaic dynasty
198	Palestine succumbs to Seleucid (Syrian) control
167	Antiochos IV, the Seleucid king, installs an altar to Zeus in Jerusalem's Temple
166–160	Maccabean (Hasmonean) uprising in Palestine against Rome (led by Judas Maccabeus, 'the hammer')
164	Judas Maccabeus rededicates the Temple in Jerusalem
164–163	Under the Hasmoneans or Maccabeans, Israel becomes an independent state. Beginning of the emergence among Israelites of Sadducees, Pharisees and Essenes
160–142	Jonathan, Hasmonean ruler in Palestine
63	The Roman general Pompey conquers Jerusalem

63–40	Hyrcanus II, High Priest of Jerusalem
55	Antipater (father of Herod the King), governor of Palestine
37–34	Herod (an Idumaean) rules Palestine as King of the Jews
27 BCE–14 CE	Augustus (formerly Octavian) reigns as Roman emperor
c. 7–4 BCE	Birth of Jesus
4 BCE	On the death of King Herod, Varus, the Roman governor of Syria, dispatches legions of soldiers who attack Sepphoris (across a valley from Nazareth)
4 BCE–6 CE	Herod's son Archelaus rules Judaea, Idumaea and Samaria as ethnarch. Deposed by Rome
4 BCE–34 CE	Herod's son Philip is tetrarch of Gaulanitis, Auranitis, Batanea, Trachonitis, Paneas and Ituraea
4 BCE–39 CE	Herod's son Antipas rules as tetrarch of Galilee and Peraea
c. 6–9 CE	Coponius appointed Roman Prefect over Judaea, Idumaea and Samaria
6–15	Annas, High Priest of Jerusalem
14–37	Tiberius, emperor
c. 18–37	The High Priesthood of Joseph Caiaphas
26–36	Prefecture of Pontius Pilate
c. 30	Crucifixion of Jesus outside Jerusalem in Judaea
c. 36	Religious conversion of Saul who becomes Paul
37–41	Caligula, emperor
c. 49	Conference/Council in Jerusalem, including Peter, James and Paul
50s	Composition of Paul's letters
54–68	Nero, emperor
62	Stoning of Jesus' brother James
64	Neronian persecution of some Christ-followers begins
	Peter thought by many to be executed in Rome
c. 65/70–100	Composition of the synoptic gospels
66–73	Jewish Revolt against Rome
c. 67	Paul executed in Rome
68–69	Galba takes over from Nero as emperor

69–79	Vespasian, emperor
70 CE	The Roman general, Titus (son of Vespasian), destroys the Temple in Jerusalem
79–81	Titus reigns as emperor
132–35	Bar Kokhba Uprising against Rome
135	Rome razes Jerusalem and rebuilds it as Aelia Capitolina
c. 160–225	Tertullian in North Africa
185–c. 254	Origen
249	Edict of the Emperor Decius directs persecution of Christians in the Roman Empire
Late third century	Manichaeism develops (Mani c. 216–76)
303	The Emperor Diocletian begins a persecution of Christians (ends in 311)
311	Beginning of the Donatist schism in North Africa
312	Constantine adopts Christian symbolism
313	Edict of Milan tolerates Christianity
325	Council of Nicaea The Nicene Creed
330	Byzantium, renamed Constantinople/the New Rome, becomes the capital of the Roman Empire
c. 339–97	Ambrose of Milan
c. 345–420	Jerome
c. 350–428	Theodore of Mopsuestia
354–430	Augustine of Hippo
361–63	Julian, final emperor who was not a Christian
379–95	Theodosius I, emperor
381	First Council of Constantinople The Nicene–Constantinopolitan Creed
395	Death of Theodosius, final emperor to rule both Western and Eastern Empires Roman Empire divides into West and East
400–900	Early Middle (or Dark) Ages
410	Sack of Rome by the Visigoth king Alaric
428–31	Nestorius, Patriarch of Constantinople
431	Council of Ephesus
From 431	Formation of the Syriac-speaking Church of the East (wrongly called the Nestorian Church) under

	the control of Persian Sassanids in Mesopotamia (roughly modern Iraq)
451	Council of Chalcedon
496	Baptism of Clovis, King of the Franks
553	Second Council of Constance
From late fifth century	Irish and Roman missionaries evangelize Anglo-Saxons

Sixth & seventh centuries	Eastern Christianity divides into three principal groups:
	(a) The Church of the East
	(b) Oriental Orthodox Churches, which today include:
	    1. The Syrian Orthodox Church
	    2. The Syrian Orthodox Church of India
	    3. The Coptic Orthodox Church (Egypt)
	    4. The Ethiopian Orthodox Church
	    5. The Eritrean Orthodox Church (separated from the Ethiopian in 1994)
	(c) The Byzantine (or Eastern Orthodox) Church

570–632	Muhammad
638	A Christian church is built in China
680–81	Third Council of Constantinople
From c. 700	British Christians begin to evangelize inhabitants of central and northern Germany
716	Boniface begins missionary work in Frisia
726–843	The Iconoclast Controversy
768–814	Charlemagne
787	Second Council of Nicaea
800	Pope Leo III crowns Charlemagne as Emperor of the West/Holy Roman Emperor
From mid-ninth century	The Patriarchate of Constantinople begins evangelization of Slavs
900–1400	The High Middle Ages
910	Establishment of the abbey of Cluny
959–1022	Symeon the New Theologian
963	Foundation of Mount Athos monastery
988	Baptism of Vladimir of Kiev
1054	Michael Cerularius, Patriarch of Constantinople, and Cardinal Humbert, papal legate, anathematize

	each other as part of a long process of separation between Rome and Constantinople
Eleventh & twelfth centuries	Holy Roman Empire
1095–99	First Crusade
1098	The abbey of Cîteaux and the Cistercian Order are established
1145	Pope Eugenius III proclaims the Second Crusade
c. 1172–1221	Dominic of Caleruega
1181/2–1226	Francis of Assisi
1187–88	Jerusalem, and Crusaders' control of it, fall to Saladin
1189	The beginning of the Third Crusade
1137–44	Construction of the abbey of St-Denis (near Paris) begins Gothic architecture
1194–1220	Construction of Chartres Cathedral
From twelfth century	Aristotle's writings disseminated and translated in the West
1208–9	Innocent III proclaims a crusade against Albigensians
1215	Fourth Lateran Council
1224/5–74	Thomas Aquinas
1232	Pope Gregory IX launches the Inquisition
Early fourteenth century	Papacy settles in Avignon
1348–49	The Black Death in Europe
1350–1600	The Renaissance
1377–78	Papacy returns to Rome
1438–39	Council of Florence–Ferrara
1453	Turks capture Constantinople
1469–1536	Erasmus
1483–1546	Martin Luther
1484–1531	Huldrych Zwingli
1489–1556	Thomas Cranmer
1498	Savonarola burnt at the stake in Florence
1500–1650	The Reformations
1505–72	John Knox
1506	Pope Julius II begins rebuilding St Peter's Basilica in Rome

1509–64	John Calvin
1512–82	Teresa of Avila
1517	Martin Luther proclaims *95 Theses Against Indulgences*
1521	Luther refuses to recant his views before the imperial assembly in Worms
	Fernando Magallanes brings Christianity to the Philippines
	Martin Luther excommunicated
1524	Franciscan friars begin a mission in Mexico
1529	Protestants so named at the Diet of Speyer
1534	King Henry VIII becomes head of the Church of England by the Act of Supremacy
	Society of Jesus (Jesuits) established
1542–91	John of the Cross
1545–63	Council of Trent
1549	Francis Xavier begins missionary work in Japan
1560	John Knox establishes the Presbyterian Church in Scotland
1563	The 39 Articles are published
1566	Publication of the Roman Catechism
From late sixteenth century	Beginning of the formation of Eastern Catholic Churches (in Syria, Lebanon, Romania, Ukraine and Slovakia)
1600	Giordano Bruno burnt at the stake in Rome
1612	King James Bible
1616	Galileo Galilei tried by the Inquisition for the first time
1618–48	Thirty Years War
1620	Pilgrim Fathers
1630s	English Puritans emigrate to Massachusetts Bay
1647	Emergence of the Quakers
1648	The Peace of Westphalia, ending the Thirty Years War
1650–1800	The Enlightenment
1703–91	John Wesley
1738	Johann Sebastian Bach composes his Mass in B minor
1768–1834	Friedrich Schleiermacher
1770–1831	Georg Wilhelm Friedrich Hegel

1773	First Methodist Conference held in North America
1778	Colonizers and Christians arrive in Australia
1789	The beginning of the French Revolution and dechristianization in France
Eighteenth & nineteenth centuries	Christianity introduced to Australia, New Zealand, Polynesia and the Melanesian Islands
1799	The Church Missionary Society established
Late eighteenth –early nineteenth centuries	Growth of autonomous African–American Protestant churches
1804–72	Ludwig Feuerbach
1806	Abdication of Francis II, last of the Holy Roman Emperors
1830s–40s	Oxford Tractarians
1863	Emergence of the Seventh-Day Adventist Church
1865	Foundation of the Salvation Army
1869–70	First Vatican Council
1879	Mary Baker Eddy establishes the Church of Christ, Scientist
1881–1963	Angelo Giuseppe Roncalli
1884	Missionaries arrive in Korea for the first time
1886	Christians martyred in Uganda
1893	World's Parliament of Religions meets in Chicago
1901	Modern Pentecostalism begins, typified by students at Bethel Bible School in Topeka, Texas
1906	Beginning of the Azusa Street Pentecostal revivals in Los Angeles, California
1906–7	Church and State separate in France
1907	Modernism condemned by Pope Pius XI
1910	World Missionary Conference held in Edinburgh
1910–15	Publication of *The Fundamentals*
1917–43	c. 300 bishops and 45,000 priests killed in Russia
1914–18	First World War
1918	Lenin declares the subjugation of the Church to the State
	Foundation of the Pentecostal Assemblies of God

1927	Faith and Order Movement begins in Lausanne
1934	Foundation of the German Confessing Church
1939	All monasteries closed in Russia
1939–45	Second World War
1945–46	Discovery of the Nag Hammadi texts
1948	Establishment of the World Council of Churches
	Discovery of the Dead Sea Scrolls
1949	Communists attack Chinese Christians
1950	Pope Pius XII proclaims the dogma of the bodily assumption to heaven of Mary, the mother of Jesus
1951	Salvador Dali paints *Christ of St John of the Cross*
1952	Publication of the Revised Standard Version of the Bible
1958–63	Pontificate of John XXIII
1960s & 1970s	Spread of the Charismatic Renewal
1962–65	Second Vatican Council
1966	Emergence of an international charismatic renewal
1968	Pope Paul VI issues the encyclical, *Humanae vitae*
1972	Foundation of the United Reformed Church
1977	The Uniting Church is formed in Australia, aligning Methodists, Congregationalists and the majority of Presbyterians
1978	Three popes hold office in succession: Paul VI, John Paul I and John Paul II
1980	Archbishop Oscar Romero assassinated in San Salvador
1986	Desmond Tutu becomes Archbishop of Cape Town
1987	General Synod of the Church of England debates homosexuality
1989	Communist governments begin to lose power in Europe
	Barbara Harris is ordained to the episcopate in the Episcopal Church of Massachusetts
	Publication of the New Revised Standard Version of the Bible
1994	12 March: The first women are ordained to the priesthood within the Church of England in Bristol Cathedral

1998	The Thirteenth Lambeth Conference of Bishops rules that homosexuality is incompatible with the Bible
2005	Cardinal Joseph Ratzinger becomes Pope Benedict XVI
2009	On 1 April in London, with 20 International Heads of State present there, demonstrators attack and damage a branch of the Royal Bank of Scotland, next to the Bank of England, assuming the ancient biblical name, and Christian imagery, of the Four Horses of the Apocalypse. This transpires amid a severe international fiscal crisis
May 2010	Scientists led by Craig Venter in Maryland, USA, announce that they have created a single-cell life form with synthetic DNA. Its parent was a computer

Quick Guide to Common Terms

Angel	A creature lacking a fleshly body who acts as a messenger between Gods and humans; from the Greek, *angelos*, meaning 'messenger'.
Apostasy	The renunciation of Christianity by a baptized person.
Archbishop	The principal preacher and overseer of a large cluster of local churches, normally based in a metropolis.
Archdiocese	The area over which an archbishop exercises oversight, such as the Archdiocese of Rio de Janeiro.
Baptism	A ritual by which a person is initiated into the Church.
Bishop	The principal preacher and overseer of a cluster of local churches.
Catholic	Considered as a noun, 'Catholic' refers to a Christian with a sense of belonging to the entire community of Christians; from the Greek, *kata* ('according to') and *holos* ('the entirety' or 'whole'). Used as an adjective, 'Catholic' means 'universally inclusive', the opposite of 'sectarian'.
church	An assembly of Christians or a building that houses them when they meet.
Church	A denomination encompassing many local churches, or the totality of Christians.
Cleric	An ordained Christian.
Council	An assembly of bishops and their collaborators convened to discuss issues of faith, worship, organization or morals.

Creation	The act by which all finite reality is brought into existence and thereafter sustained by God.
Curia	The administrative offices of the Vatican; a term borrowed from imperial Rome.
Deacon	A Christian ordained to preach and baptize as well as to assist bishops and presbyters.
Deists	Those who believe God originally created the world, thereafter declining to tamper with it.
Denomination	A large, often international, constellation of churches professing similar beliefs and adopting common practices of worship.
Devil	An angel who has rebelled against God.
Doctrine	A teaching that for the moment appears to depict the way things are.
Dogma	A teaching solemnly proclaimed by a council and/or a pope, and believed widely among Christians over a long period of time.
Ecclesiastical	That which relates to the Church.
Elder	A venerable member of a church trusted to guide its affairs.
Election	God's sovereign choice to favour an individual or group.
Faith	A decision to trust; in a Christian setting, to trust that there is a God and to live accordingly.
God	The unnameable, unknowable Creator of the universe, manifest to human beings as love.
Gospel	Literally, 'Good News', constituted either by Jesus Christ himself or ancient narratives about him.
Grace	The unmerited benevolent disposition of God towards human beings.
Heaven	The post-terrestrial abode of those God judges worthy of God's presence in perpetuity.
Hell	The abode of those God condemns to suffer in perpetuity because of their sins.
Heresy	A teaching deemed false by a regnant Church.
Icon	An image of a person revered by others as holy or saintly.
Indulgence	A prayer or payment offered to reduce the time of souls in purgatory.

Laity	The people (from Greek, *laos*, 'the people', and *laos tou theou*, 'the people of God').
Liturgy	The officially sanctioned forms of a Church's public worship.
Mass	A name for the liturgical commemoration of the last meal of Jesus; from the Latin, *Ite Missa Est*, 'This [is] the sending'.
Minister	A person called forth and publicly instituted to serve a local assembly of Christians.
Ministry	Actions undertaken by any Christian to preach the Gospel and serve those in need.
Ordination	A ritual by which Christians are publicly recognized ('ordained') to preach the Gospel, serve a church, and minister to its members.
Orthodoxy	Either the form of Christianity adopted by Christians that has its historical roots in the Eastern Roman Empire, or a teaching considered correct by a dominant Church.
Pastor	A person sanctioned to care for the needs of a church.
Patriarch	A male ruler of a family or social group, or a senior bishop of a church.
Pentecostalism	An internationally dispersed community of Christians according priority to God's Holy Spirit in their lives.
Pluridenominational Christians	Those Christians who worship in different denominations.
Plurireligious Christians	Those Christians who incorporate into their lives beliefs and customs of more than one religion.
Pope	Popular title (from *papa*, 'father') for the Bishop of Rome and the principal prelates of some other Churches.
Postdenominational Christians	Those people who are content to count themselves as Christian without expressed allegiance to a Church.
Predestination	The state of being elected or chosen by God to be saved while others will be damned.
Presbyter	A priest or elder in a church.

Priest	A presbyter ordained to preach, lead the worship of a church, officiate during sacraments, and minister to a church's members.
Protestant	A Christian belonging to a Church that originated by: (a) *protesting for* a Church in which individual believers take responsibility for their relations to God; and (b) *protesting against* beliefs and practices of Catholics.
Purgatory	An unseen abode of souls separated from their bodies after death, and in the process of being purified before entry into heaven and reunification with their bodies.
Religious Order	An institute whose members live in communities, and take vows so as to order their lives witnessing to God and serving people.
Roman Catholic	Belonging to the Church of the Roman Rite; an alternative term to 'Catholic'.
Sacrament	A ritual that relies on material symbols to express the intangible presence of God among a worshipping assembly.
Saint	Four possible meanings obtain among Christians: a person who is (a) regarded as set apart or holy; (b) baptized; (c) in heaven; or (d) canonized (declared by a Church to be holy).
See	The site of work and authority of a bishop, archbishop or pope.
Soul	The life-force animating a person that survives the death of the body and is created by God.
Synod	A synonym for 'council'; an assembly of bishops and/or general believers (laity).
Theology	A discourse about God in any form of language.
Worship	Human actions and rituals expressing recognition of God's worth.

List of Abbreviations

Acts	The Acts of the Apostles
AD	*Anno Domini*, 'the year of the Lord'/'the year of our Lord'
Ant.	*Jewish Antiquities*, by Josephus
b.	born
BC	Before Christ
BCE	Before the Common Era (an alternative to BC)
c.	*circa* (around)
CE	The Common Era (an alternative to AD)
1 Cor	1 Corinthians (The First Letter of Paul to the Corinthians)
2 Cor	2 Corinthians (The Second Letter of Paul to the Corinthians)
d.	died
Deut	Deuteronomy
Eccl	Ecclesiastes
ed.	editor/edited by
edn	edition
eds	editors
Eph	Ephesians (The Letter of Paul to the Ephesians)
esp.	especially
Ex	Exodus
Gal	Galatians (The Letter of Paul to the Galatians)
Gen	Genesis
Hab	Habakkuk
Hos	Hosea
Jer	Jeremiah
Isa	Isaiah
James	The Letter of James
Jn	John (The Gospel According to John)

1 Jn	1 John (The First Letter of John)
JW	*Jewish War*, by Josephus
2 Kings	Second Kings
Lev	Leviticus
Lk	Luke (The Gospel According to Luke)
Mk	Mark (The Gospel According to Mark)
Mt	Matthew (The Gospel According to Matthew)
n	number or note
nn	numbers
Num	Numbers
1 Pet	1 Peter (The First Letter of Peter)
Phil	Philippians (The Letter of Paul to the Philippians)
Ps	Psalm
Rom	Romans (The Letter of Paul to the Romans)
1 Sam	1 Samuel
Sir	Sirach (Ecclesiasticus, or the Wisdom of Jesus, Son of Sirach)
Tanakh	Acronym for the Hebrew terms: *Torah* ('Law'), *Neviim* ('Prophets') and *Ketuvim* ('Writings')
1 Thess	Thessalonians (The First Letter of Paul to the Thessalonians)
1 Tim	1 Timothy (The First Letter of Paul to Timothy)
Titus	The Letter of Paul to Titus
trans.	translated by
UNESCO	United Nations Educational, Scientific and Cultural Organization
US	United States (adjective)
USA	United States of America

Introduction

Christianity is a large intercontinental religion. Christians populate the planet from Colombia to Vanuatu. They now number 2.2 billion, and form a third of humanity. Christianity is the largest of the world's religions, manifest in 38,000 denominations. It is not the oldest among religions, but compared with many conquering empires, it has lived longer with a more intricate story. This book tells that tale for anyone intrigued or baffled by Christianity, and the question of how such a large religion sprouted in the footsteps of an ancient executed Jew – Jesus from Nazareth in Galilee, also called Christ.[1] The book is intended for readers and students of Christianity who seek an account of its origins, many aspects (beliefs, doctrines, pieties and practices), as well as its convoluted history.

Christianity is not a monochrome monolith. It is a pluriform collection of people spanning almost 20 centuries. Its history is the story of these people, who included not simply emperors and aristocrats, but hard-pressed farmers, enslaved labourers, house-bound mothers, playful children and gelid fanatics. Christianity is a colourful gallery of beggars, bishops, scholars and soldiers. It is a tale of many of the ablest geniuses ever known, and of some of the vilest villains imaginable. Over time it has served both as an instrument of inspiration, and an engine of terror.

The story of Christianity is anything but dry-as-dust. The Christian religion provided the fulcrum for the creation of an enormous repertoire of enthralling music. Palestrina, Monteverdi, Handel, Bach, Mozart, Beethoven, Elvis Presley and Michael Jackson were all Christians, although vastly varied in their skills as composers and performers.

Apart from musicians, art galleries girdle the globe housing paintings and sculptures devoted to Christian themes. Caravaggio, Zubarán, Tintoretto, Titian, Raphael, Rubens, Rembrandt, Rothko, Velázquez and Dalí all produced canvases that are visual Christian testimonies and non-verbal theologies. One motive for studying Christianity and its past is that many of these works are impossible to decipher without a familiarity with the religious ideas that impelled their inception. Another is that to engage with Christianity is to encounter some of the ablest intellectual colossi of Western civilization – Augustine, Aquinas, Luther, Copernicus, Descartes, Dante, Newton, Kant, Hegel and Darwin (who late in life was troubled by disbelief). These share the title 'Christian' with crusaders, torturers, inquisitors and adventurers.

As for the Christian shape of architecture, even those who never set foot in cathedrals or art galleries are often confronted with eye-catching buildings that structurally express aspects of Christian thought and devotion. The cathedrals of Paris, London, Spain and Italy are age-old and beautiful. To the names of Christian composers and painters can easily be appended a long list of eminent architects who designed buildings for Christian communities and their worship. Pugin, Gaudi, Corbusier and Frank Lloyd Wright all come to mind.

Literature too testifies to the fecundity of Christian imaginations, witnessed in the musings of authors as varied as Dickens, Dostoyesvky, George Elliot, T.S. Eliot and Flannery O'Connor.

Even so, to portray Christianity only by highlighting its beauty-spots would furnish a deceptively skewed sketch. The ugliest wart on its body has been its lethal religious intolerance, which frequently found expression in previous centuries through homicidal violence, coupled with verbal demonizing of religiously different people. Jews, Muslims, homosexuals, and people besmirched as heretics or witches often met their deaths through the agency of rabid Christians. Specific stories will be encountered in subsequent pages. Another blemish has been an all-too-common readiness of Christians to form cosy alliances with wealthy monarchs and plutocrats to the lamentable neglect of poor and subjugated peoples.

To be curious about Christianity is to be lured into a maze of people, places, ideas, actions and doctrines. This book broaches it by tracing the historical network of its origins and development. The basic contours of Christianity's polychromatic story can be outlined in barest detail: it sprang from Judaism; grew in the regions of the eastern Mediterranean; was adopted as the religion of the Roman Empire; was then divided along the lines of Western and Eastern

Empires, with pockets elsewhere; expanded through missionary work to two continents of the globe – and much later to the Americas and Australasia; dominated medieval Europe; survived Reformations and the Renaissance; and then bumped headlong into modernity. That was a rude shock. Christianity's creeds and practices were severely tested during the Enlightenment, and it has endured a long struggle thereafter to cope with political democracies, science, fascism, feminism, indifference, the burgeoning of other religions and eliminative postmodernism (a twentieth-century belief that there is nothing ultimately true, stable or estimable).

Christianity has been so culturally pervasive in human history that people today are heavily influenced by it, even when they are blithely unaware of the ways it has entered their lives. Consider the case of contemporary English usage. The following expressions and words, widely used in English, all stem from the King James translation of the Bible: 'Out of the mouths of babes' (Ps 8: 2); 'an eye for an eye' (Ex 21: 23–24; Mt 5; 38–39); 'filthy lucre' (Titus 1: 7); 'holier than thou' (Isa 65: 5); 'the prodigal son' (Lk 15: 11–32); 'a time and a place for everything' (Eccl 3: 1–8); 'count the cost' (Lk 14: 28); 'botch' (Deut 28: 27); 'bravery' (Isa 3: 18); and 'advertise' (Num 24: 14). Judges and lawyers around the world regularly use terms that are also linked to the King James translation: 'evidence' (Jer 32: 16); 'addicted' (1 Cor 16: 15); 'a thief in the night' (1 Thess 5: 2–3); and 'the straight and narrow' (Mt 7: 14).[2] The King James translation is a high water mark in the history of the English language, and a product of Christianity's more civilizing side.

Christianity Transformed

The study of Christianity can be ceaselessly fascinating, astounding and sobering, as well as endlessly instructive. Ponder the instance of Christianity's transformation over the past century or so. Statistics are not infallible, but they can occasionally provide a general impression of broad situations.

In 1900, there were roughly 558 million Christians on the earth – 34.5 per cent of the world's population: 68 per cent of these lived in Europe; 2 per cent in South America; 14 per cent in North America; 1 per cent in Oceania; 2 per cent in Africa; and 4 per cent in Asia. By 2005, Christianity had undergone a momentous mutation in its make-up. In that year there were 2.124 billion Christians alive – 33 per cent of the world's population. Of these, 26 per cent lived in Europe, less than half the figure a hundred years before. What explains this decrease? 24 per cent of Christians lived in South America; 19 per cent in Africa; 17 per cent in Asia; 13 per cent in North America; and 1 per cent in Oceania. By 2009, just four years later, there were reckoned to be 2.2 billion Christians in the world.[3]

This much is clear: in the course of the twentieth century, the numbers of Christians decreased in Europe and North America (less significantly in the latter), and massively increased in Asia, Africa and South America. How is such a change best explained? That question will need to be engaged in due course below.

Christianity's metamorphosis in the twentieth century can be stated succinctly in geographic, economic and ethnographic terms as a fundamental shift from North to South, rich to poor and white to black, or more aptly, from European to South American, African and Asian.

Diversity Among Christians

The kinds of people who have lived as Christians, and the ways they spent their time, can also be surprising. Charlemagne, the most significant ruler of medieval Europe, was an ardent Christian with an enormous influence, but he could not read or write.[4] Sarah Grimké devoted her energies to preaching against slavery in the USA at a time when it was thought unseemly for women to speak in churches. Inquiring into Christianity uncovers more than a few unanticipated findings. There are more Lusophone (Portuguese-speaking) Christians in the world today than there are people living in Germany, France, Belgium, the Netherlands and the UK combined. Most of the citizens of Denmark, Norway and Sweden were ritually initiated into Christianity in the early stages of their lives, but only 3 per cent of them bother to worship in churches.[5] There are Christians who express their faith by babbling in catatonic trances; others who charm snakes; and still more who whip themselves until they bleed. Equally fervent Christians embark on pilgrimages, staff hospitals and hospices, and publicly demonstrate against nuclear weapons.

It is difficult to exaggerate the vast variety of Christians who have ever lived. This diverse spectrum can be very taxing to grasp for anyone trying to comprehend Christianity. In addition, Christians throughout 20 centuries have never managed to agree on what constitutes their religion. There are many among them who prefer not to be aligned at all with a particular worshipping community or church. Contemporary acrimonious disputes among Christians render attempts by observers wishing to understand their religious lives all the more daunting. This book is intended as an aid to anyone trying to come to grips with the Christian religion. Confusion about Christianity easily arises because disagreements among Christians, coupled with its long history in disparate cultures, spawn a chain of perplexing questions: who counts as a Christian? Is Christianity a way of living or consent to a body of beliefs? Can an eternal essence of Christianity be reliably specified? Was Jesus the founder of Christianity or had he never heard of it? Who was Jesus anyway? Might he have been the Son of the Most High God, as the ancient text of Mark's Gospel would have its readers believe, or a failed, executed religious enthusiast? Is Protestantism a perversion of Christianity or its reformed rejuvenescence? Do Christians believe in three Gods or one? Does contemporary Catholicism, the largest of all Christian groups, need a papacy? Are there Christians in Mongolia? Is Christianity truer than all other religions? Since Jesus was an Israelite, and if Christians are serious about emulating him, what prevents them from becoming Jews? In the ranks of Christians, do women stand in an inferior position to men?

The terminology peculiar to the Christian religion can also easily confound inquirers. Christianity is like a lively river coursing over long distances and taking a prolonged time to do so. It has accrued terminological sediment as it has unfolded over the centuries. As a consequence, people reading about it can be confronted with language about Carthusian canonesses, Cathars, Manichees, Premonstratensians, Anabaptists and Pentecostals. The writings of Christians can be liberally peppered with talk of trentals, purgatury, chantries, iconostases, predestination, and that most ubiquitous of all Christian words – salvation.

Indeed, the monosyllabic words regularly vocalized by Christians can be the most intractable to clear comprehension – God, life, faith, hope, sin, grace, guilt, love, wrath, death and hell. All of these terms will be encountered in later pages, as well as attempts to tease out their possible meanings and referents.

Christianity and Christianities

It is still possible to speak of Christianity as a unitary phenomenon despite the vast array of forms (Christianities) it has assumed. This is so because of two intertwined foci common to Christians now and previously. Christianity's first focus is God, though it is variously understood. The second is Jesus, also interpreted diversely. It is misleading to depict Christianity exclusively as devotion to the figure of Jesus because it involves a specific way of imagining God. For observers, potentially the most baffling aspect of Christians is that they profess that God decided to be enfleshed, manifested or revealed in the body of Jesus, a male human living in Galilee 20 centuries ago. Some Christians insist that God literally became incarnate in Jesus. Others interpret this doctrine of incarnation in symbolic or metaphorical terms. For them Jesus was a cipher, story, parable or refraction of God in history. All Christians tie their understandings of God to Jesus Christ. Hence the word 'Christian', used to describe them as a whole and as individuals. 'Christ' is an ancient honorific title meaning 'messiah'.

A Thesis Concerning Jesus

Jesus is a highly enigmatic figure. What historical factor most convincingly explains the situation that he has been variously remembered, venerated, celebrated and worshipped since the first century? Was he God incarnate? Could he have been the wisest person in human history? Did he secretly plan for a Church to perpetuate his legacy?

This book proposes the thesis that Jesus proved to be a figure of fascination and devotion in a vast array of cultures since his death because of a simple yet arresting combination. In his life and actions he combined imperfection and perceived perfection. The interplay between these two factors explains the allure of many historical figures. Giotto, for instance, was remembered as a peasant boy who could draw a perfect circle. Despite limitations in his material resources he enjoyed the sublime skill of artistry. The same interplay is found in Jesus – limitation/excellence; simplicity/profundity; and humility/greatness. Transposed into a theological register, Jesus came to be worshipped as human and divine.

People often love rags-to-riches stories and naturally imagine: could this happen to me? Would this happen to me? Paupers loved Jesus by all accounts because he led an unencumbered life like them. Later, kings admired him because he was like them – so they thought – in their grandeur and excellence. Thus a dialectic of imperfection and perfection, with regard to Jesus, came to be interpreted and reinterpreted by generations of people after Pilate had killed him.

Tied to a dialectic of imperfection/perfection is a second factor that explains a large variety of sustained responses to Jesus over many centuries. The factor lies in the mechanism of human interpretation itself. The perceived attractive yet elusive defining aspect of Jesus has been constantly reinterpreted as successive generations adapt their readings of him to their historical circumstances. Every human interpretation involves an objective and subjective pole. There can no more be an object interpreted without an interpreting subject as there can be an interpreting person without a phenomenon to be interpreted. In the case of Jesus, he is the object to be interpreted, and any person seeking to comprehend him is an interpreting agent. Because of people's individual and unique personal experiences, pasts and preferences, they inevitably draw on categories familiar to them (and often unfamiliar to others elsewhere) in order to articulate what is for them Jesus' identity and superlativeness. Whenever and wherever there is interpretation, there is also a clash of interpretations because of the perspectival, and hence limited and potentially fallible, dimension of any interpretation. Thus the situation that declaring Jesus to be God clashes unavoidably with the conviction that he died as a prophet long ago. God, by definition, does not die. Despite this clash, it is the same object of Jesus involved in both construals. The task of articulating the phenomenon of Jesus in a rationally cogent and convincing manner is an ongoing industry around the world today, among Christians and their onlookers alike.

Method

Many introductions to Christianity consider roughly 5 per cent of Christians who have ever lived. That is, they concentrate mostly on monarchs, theologians, intellectuals, philosophers, monks, bishops and celibate saints. The 95 per cent of the rest – the nameless, faceless and mostly illiterate majority of Christians over nearly 20 centuries are frequently accorded scant attention. Every chapter of this book will attend to both groups – the kings, clerics and prelates, as well as ragamuffins, villagers and wanderers. At any stage of history, both groups could believe and behave in starkly different ways. While avoiding an exclusively patrician view of Christianity, the book will mix a people's perspective with a consideration of the views of the powerful, which so regularly held sway over the lives of the majority of Christians. The net result will be a story of free-thinkers, fanatics, mystics, prophets, crusaders, hermits, firebrands, enslaved workers, friars, brutes, martyrs, scholars, artisans, emperors and children.

Otherwise stated, the method adopted for presenting Christianity in these pages is bipolar: first, it casts an eye on how the vast majority of unlettered Christians over 20 centuries regarded their religious lives; while second, not neglecting to attend to intellectuals and sovereigns. To shun the ideas of academics in Christian history is to underestimate the way ideas generated by intellectuals can powerfully seize the imagination of entire populations and civilizations. Take the idea of Charles Darwin, who earned a degree in theology as a young man, that species evolve according to a process of natural selection: 150 years after the publication of his *On the Origin of Species* (1859), people were still debating internationally the scientific and religious implications of his notion.[6]

What is Religion?

This book is fundamentally neither a treatise in theology or philosophy, nor an exercise in Church history. While it certainly addresses theology, ecclesiastical history and philosophers, its primary task is to introduce Christianity considered as a religion among other religions. It is thus basically an account of people who call themselves Christian. It looks at what they believe and have countenanced; how they live and what they have done; and the multitudinous ways in which they have varied among themselves.

Christianity: An Introduction is part of a larger series of books devoted to religions of the world. It shares with the other volumes an interest in the question of what constitutes a religion. Responses to this question differ starkly among those who bother to pose and investigate it. One approach is to define religion as adherence to beliefs in a divine Creator, or deities conceived otherwise. Another regards it as a daily terrestrial pilgrimage in quest of an as-yet unknown, but much better, supramundane world. A third view likens religion to an escapist narcotic used to dull the debilitating effects of suffering.

The understanding of religion adopted in these pages is that it is fundamentally a way of living based on a decision to believe in a particular world-view. Religion is viewed in people's *actions* that are indivisible from *thoughts* and *beliefs* that guide the actions. A belief is an intellectual and emotional assent to a proposition, such as 'God created the universe'. Religious faith is a decision to live as if there is more to reality than first meets the eye, and that the unseen dimensions of reality, whether these be termed as God's abode in heaven, angels or ultimate blessedness, are eminently worthy of someone's love, faith and hope.

The stance on religion just stated in a nutshell is tied to the etymology of the word 'religion', which stems from both Latin (*religare*, 'to bind together') and Greek (*ligo*, 'to attach'). Religion is thereby a pattern of living that unites groups of people in espousing a conviction that this world is not all there is, and in acting accordingly. Most religious people regard themselves as ultimately accountable not only to themselves and others, but also to hidden deities, powers or desirable realms.

Religions and Anachronistic Thinking

It is worth noting at the outset of this book that for most of Christianity's history it was not understood either by its adherents or by its observers in ways it is today, especially in Western cultures that have been seared by the Enlightenment and have happily embraced major defining features of modernity. Such marks of Western modernity have involved legally guaranteed freedoms of speech and conscience, the personal liberty to renounce religion, the prevalence of democratic forms of government, and enthusiasm for human capacities to improve the world by harnessing the instruments of reason, science and technologies. To appreciate how Christianity has exhibited itself in the past, it is important to avoid thinking of it anachronistically as if it functioned in the same ways it and other religions are often expected to take their place in contemporary cultures. Anachronistic thinking is an ever-present trap for the unwary when pondering the span of Christianity's existence. To think anachronistically is to attribute to past people and periods customs, beliefs and assumptions that were unknown to them.

At least six commonly entertained though misleading assumptions about religion need to be evacuated from the mind when inquiring into Christianity, or any other long-standing religion. The first is that religions now are similar to their manifestations in the past. Nothing could be further from the truth. The word 'religion' is of modern coinage. In Western countries tinctured by the legacy of the Enlightenment, democracy and social individualistic atomization, religion is frequently understood as a private consumer option. Viewed thus, it becomes an attachable or detachable accessory that can be either uncoupled or fused with one's essential personal identity. Religion is thereby added or subtracted freely and causally from aspects of its surrounding culture that are economic, political, social and artistic: religion can be dismissed at will, like a disdained political party, a business plan or club membership. Such was not the case at all with ancient and premodern understandings of religion. In previous cultures after the Neolithic age, religion was suffused through every pore of cultures. It was inconceivable and impossible for the ancients to carve reality into religious and irreligious zones. Their air and space was aflutter (so they thought) with interfering Gods; malign demons; witches, warlocks and werewolves; ghostly spirits; mischievous sprites; and sword-wielding avenging angels.[7]

The ancient Roman Empire illustrates a striking dissimilarity between contemporary and bygone construals of religion. In imperial Rome and its provinces, what is now called religion was then (before the fifth century CE) normally known as *pietas*, a word which gave birth to the contemporary term 'piety'. *Pietas* did not mean espousing doctrines or defending beliefs. It involved a social duty to worship the Gods of the empire. If that worship were neglected or forgotten, Roman citizens and their underlings could only expect the Gods to turn mean and exact revenge. Gods were to be feared and placated in all matters relating to politics, education, military exploits and commercial exchange. Such was the climate in which Christianity was born.

A second common preunderstanding among present-day Westerners in need of expunction is the readily accepted assumption that towns and cities are secular spaces. Metropolises and their suburbs might well tolerate religious buildings and practices, as long as it is generally agreed by citizens that urban landscapes with their governments, educational institutions and constitutions are integral in themselves, with no *need* of religions. One instance of this view is the modern political catch-cry of the separation of Church and State. For inhabitants of all ancient civilizations, it was unthinkable to conceive of a non-sacred or religiously neutral conurbation. Even those called 'atheists' in bygone Rome were not devoid of beliefs in Gods. They simply worshipped divinities apart from those forming the Roman pantheon. Such was the world in which Christianity came to be.

A third assumption that now needs to be excreted with particular reference to Christianity is the ready assumption that God is understood univocally by Christians. There has never been a uniformly held picture of God shared by all Christians. There are Christians who conceive of God in Trinitarian categories – as a Father, Son and Spirit – and others who think of God as a Spirit. Still others imagine God as external to the cosmos, and others who insist God is in human beings.

The Christian religion involves, and has involved, many different conceptions of God. These will be discussed as the book progresses. The question of how God is conceived is not an innocent matter and is a subtle issue to grasp. There have been Christian societies in the Middle Ages wherein God was imagined as a proximate, concerned, intervening Parent–Creator who oversaw people's lives. In these societies, individuals were generally poor and illiterate. Somewhat surprisingly, their shared poverty simultaneously endowed them with a human equity – they were all equal in their status and situation. As serfs, they were certainly subservient to their lords, but among themselves they were generally equal. They also shared with each other and with ancient religious peoples a conviction that Gods and God could smite, punish or impede them at any instant, especially if they did not take actions to appease deities with prayers and sacrifices. Often the intimate proximity with God was imagined as a benign affair, but fear also drove many people's religious lives in expectation of divinely wrought retribution. Later in history, God was frequently conceived as remote, unapproachable, stern, reproachful and potentially punitive. Punishment from God in this view might be meted out at the end of history before which enterprising individuals were generally left unhampered. Such an understanding, typical among Deists, became more prevalent in the West precisely at a time when modern capitalism and social inequality grew in relation to a widening chasm between the rich and the poor. Deists believe God created the world and left it to its own devices. Such a view coincided with the emergence of capitalism – a form of monetary exchange unknown to the ancients and throughout the Middle Ages. Capitalism developed gradually after 1650, but became a prevalent economic system by the eighteenth century. The rise of capitalism in the seventeenth century 'coincided with the demise of equitable relations among persons in society'.[8] Just as people *felt* remote from God as modernity developed, they also *behaved* as if they were remote from their neighbours in terms of social equality. It was easy for them to make an unconscious link between a far-away God who leaves humans to manage their own lives with a tendency not to care for those in need: if God is remote and leaves people alone, why should anyone seeking wealth be proximate to a needy neighbour? This very double-sided separation (God from humans and humans from each other) enabled and bred financial exploitation in the modern West because it is easier to lack compunction for those suffering or imperilled if they are kept out of sight and mind. Capitalism is unable to flourish in economically egalitarian settings: 'Only through the development of inequalities, through the normatization of asymmetrical relationships of wealth and power, could the accumulation of property necessary for capitalism take place.'[9] A God conceived as distant easily served a progression to the awareness that it is possible to live without reference to God, hence the prevalence and growth of atheism in modern-to-postmodern cultures. Atheism is here understood as the human decision and disposition *to live without* countenancing *any* religious beliefs, or *intellectually to deny* that there could be deities. It was not common among human beings before the last three centuries.

A fourth anachronistically unsafe assumption about religion is to conclude that what defined the religiosity of premodern peoples was their belief in, and worship of, a God. As in any age, it was perfectly possible then to live religiously without attachment to God conceived as a personal agent who cares for and acts among human beings. Religion is older than veneration of Gods. Palaeolithic peoples have left no signs that they were theists, or people who thought there is an omnipotent and omnipresent God.[10]

In the fifth place, it is a mistake when pondering religion to assume that texts revered as sacred or divinely inspired are indispensable to religion. This has not always been the case in the past, despite the ages of the Bible, Vedic texts and the Qur'an. Ancient Greek religion did not have sacred scriptures; nor do the religions of Australian Aborigines.[11]

Finally, the notion frequently encountered today that beliefs form the pivot of religion is an unstable assumption. In Second Temple Judaism, ritual purity was religiously uppermost in the religious lives of Judaeans.[12] People would not dare enter the inner precincts of Jerusalem's Temple if they had rendered themselves ritually impure by, for example, touching a corpse or as a consequence of menstruation.

The Past Unsettling the Present

A scrutiny of Christianity and its past uncovers practices and customs regarded as normal and obligatory among Christians currently, which were often alien or unknown to many previous generations. Pondering the differences between then and now can both undermine the belief that contemporary patterns of behaviour are absolute and unable to be changed, and uncover past customs that can challenge fixed and taken-for-granted arrangements among Christians. For instance, for most of Christianity's history, priests could marry. Even when attempts were made by the papacy to enforce obligatory celibacy amongst clergy, the papal edicts were widely ignored. One estimate judges that in England towards the end of the twelfth century almost all parish priests lived with a concubine, who cooked and looked after them. Such a woman was known as a *focaria* ('a hearthmate', from the Latin *focus*, 'hearth' or 'fire-place').[13] Marriage in Christianity's ancient past was normally regarded as either a private or civil matter that had nothing to do with the Church. Another discrepancy between bygone eras and contemporary frames of mind is that while the ownership of private property is currently commonly accepted as normal among Christians, in the early Church it was roundly condemned as a crime against justice if some enjoyed wealth while others were impecunious.[14]

Christians in previous centuries were often frequently more pious than their contemporary cousins, and lived in cultures wherein daily life pulsated with Christian observances. To this day, there are 900 surviving medieval church buildings on the island of Crete alone. In Constantinople of the sixth century, local Christians enjoyed the benefits of 73 imperially decreed annual religious holidays.[15]

Christians in the past could also be much stricter and more punitive of recalcitrants in their observance of biblical teachings. The Bible forbids bestiality. In 1662, William Potter was hanged for breaking this proscription. His teenage son discovered him engaging in sexual practices with a sow. The setting for such activity was the Christian colony of New Haven, Connecticut, in which bestiality was a civil as well as an ecclesiastical crime. So strictly was the Bible respected by Mr Potter's contemporaries that all the animals he had sexually engaged were executed along with him. This involved the deaths of a cow, two sows, three sheep and two heifers.[16] The sentence prescribed by the Book of Leviticus (20:15) had thus been dutifully observed. In sixteenth-century Scotland, boys were fined if they played golf on Sundays instead of attending church worship as part of a biblical command to keep holy one appointed day a week.[17]

Past punishments meted out by Christians on Christians can seriously unsettle their contemporary progeny. People who commit suicide nowadays are generally remembered with compassionate understanding mixed with acute sorrow and profound regret. Not so during the Middle Ages. People then who died by their own hand could be condemned for the sin of despair, and buried face down, often at a crossroad, with stakes driven through their bodies to pin them to the ground. On the last day of history when God raises the dead from their graves, people who killed themselves would be unable to rise because they were face down. Their souls would be incapable of moving anywhere, having been rendered immobile by stakes. If their souls did escape their bodies, they would be thoroughly disorientated, since they were poised at a crossroad.[18] All this is hardly loving treatment of those who have lost the desire to live.

Looking back, Christians of the past can appear as behaving in startlingly bizarre ways. Luke the Stylite (column inhabitant) sat on top of a pillar for 42 years, and Symeon the Stylite attracted international visitors. Gorgonia, the sister of Gregory of Nazianzus, is said by her brother to have smothered her body with blessed wine, mixed with water, in an attempt to cure herself. Thus soaked, she slept in a church throughout the night. Other Christians frequently practised incubation; that is, they slept all night near an entombed body of a venerated Christian.[19] They hoped proximity to the body would help and heal them. When imperial Rome held sway in Asia Minor (modern Turkey), 40 men in Sebasteia froze to death standing completely naked on a frozen lake as they were watched by Roman soldiers, who forced them to do so if they did not renounce their Christian beliefs.[20] The men without exception chose to die rather than betray their shared faith. Fifteenth-century Florence boasted 42 flagellant confraternities – associations of men who practised self-flagellation in penance for their sins.[21] In the Middle Ages, some fretful people paid for as many as 50,000 Masses to be said for them after they had died to ensure that they, or rather their souls, were not consigned by God to hell.[22] Churches and their worship in the first few of Christianity's many centuries were often based in homes, and organized by women who preached. The medieval confraternity of St Paul in Paris devoted itself to burying the dead, caring for the sick, tending to the poor, feeding the hungry, and ensuring that young women were dowered. More than that, its members organized an annual feast, invited the poor to attend, seated them in the most coveted places, and served them the finest foods available.[23] Now, in the USA, Christians can drive cars to megachurches. Far from holding banquets for beggars, the primary preoccupation of some of them is shopping in Christian supermarkets. There they can buy and bedeck themselves in items of fashion all emblazoned with Christian logos. If they dislike visiting Christian megamarkets, they can go on-line with their personal computers and buy rings, necklaces, earrings, hats, wallets, leather jackets and T-shirts, all embossed with Christian symbols.[24] Festooned fashionably, no Christian need feel out of place in cultures transfixed by the acquisition of commodities.

Basic Structure

This volume contains eight chapters divided between four larger parts. The chapters unfold according to a straightforward chronological pattern, beginning in the sixth century BCE, so as to set ancient Christianity in its much broader historical context related to ancient Mesopotamia and directed from Babylon (in contemporary Iraq). It is not possible adequately to grasp the emergence and features of either Jesus or Christianity without attending to Judaism of the Second Temple Period, and this period begins with the end of the Babylonian captivity of Judaeans in the late sixth century BCE. Jesus and Christianity emerged from the Judaism that was forged when the Jerusalem Temple was rebuilt in the early fifth century BCE, and which grew in lands dominated by Hellenism – a form of Greek culture exported from ancient Greece, especially by Alexander the Great.

The first chapter concentrates on Jesus in his historical setting of the eastern territories of the Mediterranean Sea. It explains the long and complicated history of political dynasties that successively ruled the areas in which Jesus lived, and contains a portrait of him that relies on recent historical and archaeological research. The book's opening chapter does not associate Jesus directly with Christianity. This is because Christianity was entirely unknown to him and his family. It could not possibly have been. It formed and grew after he died – in memory of him. After his death, Jesus became the most significant figure of Western civilization and its beneficiaries.

The second chapter of the book turns its attention to Christianity. It charts the decades-long process, beginning most clearly in the late first century CE, whereby the new religion that came to be called Christianity distanced itself from Judaism. It illustrates that the major geographical and historical divisions that arose among Christians, and still obtain, stem from the way the Roman Empire was constituted. The Empire included two fundamental types of territory: senatorial and imperial provinces.[25] Rome itself lay in a senatorial province in that it came under the direct control of its senate. Christianity did not emerge there, but in the imperial province of Syria–Palestine, where Greek was spoken by many educated peoples. Imperial provinces, since they were distant from Rome, could be more politically volatile, and were directed by local client rulers of Rome, or by Roman citizens who were appointed as governors. The chapter explains that within the East Roman or Byzantine Empire, there emerged a Greek-speaking church, centred on the imperial city of Constantinople, involving hubs in Alexandria (with most members speaking Coptic, not Greek) and Antioch (Syriac-speaking). Up until the fifth century, these groups were roughly unified. Greek-speaking churches evolved in parallel with Latin-speaking communities. Considered as a whole, Christianity during the first few centuries of its gestation was mainly Eastern and Greek in its patterns of thought. A major burden of this chapter will be to elucidate the cardinal Christian dogmas concerning God (the Trinity) and Jesus (articulating his relation to God), which eventually led to permanent divisions between Churches of the East and West. These divisions have never been overcome. The chapter will also explain how Christianity came to enjoy imperial favour and protection, thus beginning a long history of Christendom, the consequences of which were far from beneficial for other religions.

Part 1 is the pivot of the book, sketching the stage setting against which the later drama of Christianity's development was enacted. Part 2, involving two chapters, is devoted to the medieval period, which was chronologically extensive, covering at least a thousand years. This leads to Part 3's consideration of the European Renaissance and the radical sixteenth-century Reformations of Christianity that produced a new type of Christianity in the sixteenth century, collectively called Protestantism. Part 4 attends to the fortunes and fate of Christianity during the Modern-to-Postmodern Age. The historical period roughly encompassed by the fifth to the nineteenth centuries could loosely be called the Age of Christianity in the West. During the last two centuries, Christianity gradually lost its cultural and political hegemony in most nations of the world. Many Christians today no longer allow their lives to be controlled by beliefs that held sway among their ancient and medieval ancestors. Among such beliefs were fear of a punitive, wrathful God, the prospect of everlasting painful torment in hell, and wariness of malicious people-possessing demons.

As a whole, the book paints Christianity as a kaleidoscope of experiences rather than a unitary institutional phenomenon. It concludes by commenting on the current situation of Christianity and tentatively reflects on its future prospects. Since its beginnings, Christianity has never ceased to mutate into thousands of forms, each with evolving customs and creeds. *Christianity: An Introduction* assumes throughout that it is possible to speak of Christianity in the singular, as well as a myriad of Christianities, because all groups, sects, and churches that style themselves as 'Christian' share one attribute – an identifying reference to the specific historical individual, Jesus Christ. For this reason, the first chapter dwells on him.

Part 1
Origins and Growth

Chapter I

Jesus and the Mediterranean World

'Can anything good come out of Nazareth?'
John 1: 46

'... not much happened while Tiberius was emperor'
Tacitus

Christianity takes its name from a Semite – Jesus Christ – who lived 20 centuries ago. As a boy, he was known simply as Jesus rather than Jesus Christ. The second part of his name as it is now remembered comes from the Greek word, *christos*, a title for someone who is especially favoured by God. 'Christ' has the same meaning in Greek as a messiah does in Hebrew or Aramaic. 'Jesus' is originally an Aramaic term meaning 'God (Yahweh) saves'. The very combination of two languages in Jesus' name and honorific designation (Aramaic and Greek) is a symptom that this man, who came to be remembered as one of the greatest figures in human history, lived in, and was formed by, a cultural amalgam of very different cultures and peoples. The more that is known of the amalgam, the more can be ascertained about Jesus and the origins of Christianity. This chapter sets out to introduce his life considered in its setting, and in view of a particular history that formed him. It does so in two stages. First, it sketches aspects of the Eastern Mediterranean world before either Jesus or Christianity made their presences felt there; second, it focuses on the historical figure and fortunes of Jesus. The second stage is crucial: if Jesus is mischaracterized or caricatured in any way, all that is subsequently said about Christianity is skewed; if discourses about God (theologies) are composed with Jesus at their centre, and major historical characteristics of Jesus' life are misconstrued or ignored, the discourses more easily turn into legends or mythical flights of fancy. The next chapter considers how the Christian religion grew and

diversified in the wake of Jesus. It outlines the way groups of Jesus'
enthusiasts began to disperse in the Roman Empire beyond Palestine,
where Jesus spent his entire life. The first chapter contains a good
deal of historical detail which may seem a tedious distraction. For
anyone wishing to understand Jesus it is indispensable at best, and an
advisable hurdle at worst, because the religious idea that dominated
his life, the kingdom of God, is incomprehensible in abstraction from
the human kingdoms of which Jesus was acutely aware.

With regard to Christianity, it needs to be said at the outset
that Jesus was not a Christian. The religion of his allegiance, from his
childhood to his death, was Judaism as it was practised in Galilee and
Judaea of the first century CE. He was a Nazarene and a manual
worker, and hence known for a life spent among agrarian labourers
in the small village of Nazareth, in Lower Galilee of the Roman
imperial province of Syria–Palestine. While Christianity would
never have arisen without him, he was not its devisor or founder.
None of the people who met him while he was alive was a Christian,
unless one means by 'a Christian' a person who knew, liked and
believed in his goodness. A Christianity familiar to later centuries
began to take shape in the closing years of the first century, once
enthusiasts of Jesus, decades after his death, finally stopped attending
synagogues.

One of the greatest historical puzzles concerning Jesus' life was
not the issue of whether he founded Christianity. It lies with the
manner of his death. He was executed by torture and crucifixion on
the order of a Roman prefect. The word 'prefect' (Latin: *Praefectus*)
was a Roman military title. Why would a soldier–governor of the
Roman Equestrian Order crucify a manual-working Nazarene?[1] Any
attempt to answer that question needs to consider Jesus' times, life
and locality.

The Near East

Jesus spent his life in the hinterland of the eastern Mediterranean Sea.
He and his friends were conquered people. They spent all of their
existence under the heel of the Roman Empire. Jesus lived under
two emperors: Octavian, who took the name 'Augustus', and
Tiberius. He was born under the first, and killed during the reign of
the second. His ancestors over many generations had endured the

hardship of political subjugation, stymied by a succession of imperial dynasties that had conquered their lands.

The geographical setting of Jesus' life and the later emergence of Christianity was the ancient Near East. Referring to the East, Near (Middle) East or Far East belies a European perspective, but even so, it has become a commonplace in historical studies. In such a view, Europe enjoys a globally central position, and all other regions are labelled according to points of the compass, with the Near East regarded as those regions to the south or south-east of Europe, including Syria, Palestine, Asia Minor (modern Turkey), Iraq, Iran and Egypt.

It all Began in Iraq

The story of Christianity begins with the story of Jesus, and the story of Jesus begins with the story of Iraq. One way of charting the historical emergence of Christianity is to focus on the ancient city of

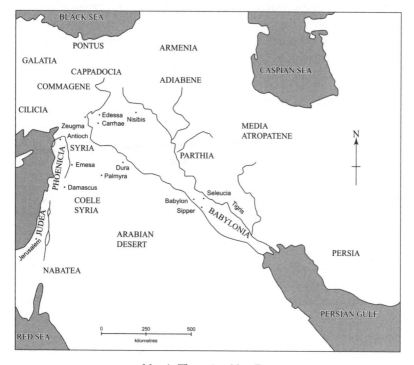

Map 1: The ancient Near East

the Near East called Babylon, and its surrounding territories of
Mesopotamia. There is still a city in Iraq called Babylon. It was once
an imperially powerful site, and is remembered as the hub of the
Babylonian Empire. It was in Babylon that many of the most important Hebrew texts of the Bible were edited in their final form. The
Bible begins with two stories of creation (in the Book of Genesis)
that were joined together by editors in Babylon around 2600 years
ago. A primary point of these narratives, which are focused on God,
not cosmology or biological evolution, is to reassure exiled Jews from
Judaea that despite their current circumstances, God will remain
faithful to them. Hebrew texts redacted in Babylon and regarded as
sacred by Jews, ancient and contemporary, are writings that heavily
influenced the mind and life of Jesus. They are also venerated by
Christians. Of the historically remote origin of Christianity, it is not
misleading to conclude that 'it all began in Iraq'. Christianity issued
from Judaism, and the Judaism familiar to Jesus was forged in
Babylon. What is now called Iraq provided the setting which helped
form the Temple-centred religion known to Jesus, commonly called
Second Temple Judaism. The Temple at the hub of his religion was
destroyed by the Fretensis (Xth) Roman legion in the year 70 CE. It
has never been rebuilt.

The Judaism of Jesus

Jesus lived nearly all of his life in Galilee, a northern territory of
Palestine. By far the majority of Galileans of his time were Jews.
Before describing the regions in which he grew up and that moulded
his religious outlook, the larger issue of considering the religion to
which he gave his life presents itself.

Jesus lived in a land that has been named differently in successive
stages of history. It has been variously called Canaan, Israel, Judaea
(Roman spelling), Judah or Palestine. When Jesus was alive, his land
was known in the Roman Empire as Palestine. This word was coined
by the ancient Greek writer, Herodotus (fifth century BCE), and
designates the territories of the people called Philistines. In the time
of Jesus, Palestine included three major territories: Galilee to its
north, Judaea in the south, and Samaria in between. It hugged the
eastern Mediterranean Sea on its west, had Syria to its north, bordered the Syrian desert in its east, with the Negeb desert on its most

southern region. The Jordan River flows through it on a north–south axis.[2]

Palestine has long been a region of chronic tribal conflict, and its inhabitants have lived under the control of many dynastic empires. The Palestinians known to Jesus, whether they were Galilean, Samaritan or Judaean, were all Jews who worshipped according to the laws and customs of Judaism. Jews of Jesus' Palestine had a vivid memory of their people's suffering under an extensive line of imperial rulers. Their history was not exclusively a tale of woes, for they enjoyed benefits of Hellenism, a form of exported Greek culture that was spread throughout the eastern Mediterranean by the young Macedonian king, Alexander the Great.

The word 'Jew' is modern.[3] It derives from the Greek, *ioudaios*, and Latin, *judaeus*, which translate the Hebrew term, *yĕhûdî*, meaning 'Judaean'. So, formerly, a Jew was an inhabitant of the land of Judah. The first textual reference to such a person is found in the Second Book of Kings (16: 6). Whereas 'Jew' describes a specific individual, Judaism connotes a more general feature of several people: Judaism means 'Jewishness' or, more strictly, 'Judaeanness'. It is now used to name the religion of Jews. The original coinage of the term 'Judaism' seems to have been in the Second Book of Maccabees (2: 21).

The historical origins of ancient Jews are remote and obscure, and are traced by contemporary Jews to the figure of Abraham, who features prominently in the opening stages of the Bible (Gen 12–25). Judaism, Christianity and Islam are often called Abrahamic religions because they trace their views of God to Abraham as a common ancestor. Not much is known assuredly of Abraham, but he is often thought to have originated in the territory of Ur in the Fertile Crescent (broadly the eastern Mediterranean) around 39 centuries ago. It is difficult to ascertain the origins and identity of the figure remembered as Abraham because there was no written form of Hebrew in the age during which he is said to have lived. Prophets in Israel before roughly the sixth century BCE collectively show no knowledge of him. The personage of Abraham in the history of Israel became prominent in written sources among Jews especially during the sixth century.[4]

More approximate origins to the Judaism known to Jesus can be traced to a period late in the thirteenth century BCE, when tribes of

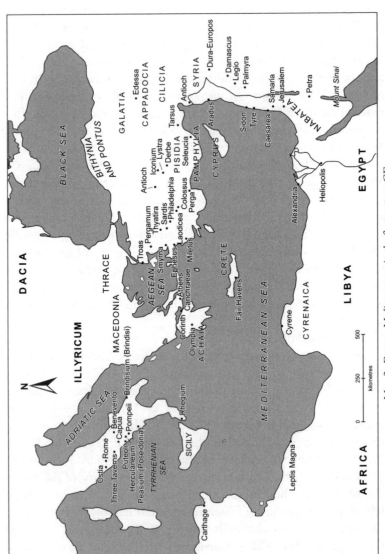

Map 2: *Eastern Mediterranean in the first century CE*

Semites made Canaan their home. Semites are people believed to have been descended from Shem, the son of Noah (Gen 10: 21ff.). Semites included Arabs, Jews, Babylonians, Assyrians and Phoenicians. Canaan was the coastal plain between the eastern Mediterranean Sea and the Jordan River that was later included in Palestine by Herodotus. Philistines and Ammonites were neighbours to Canaanites. Some of the original tribes who settled in Canaan, not without armed conflict, appear to have spent time in Egypt. Their experiences inspired the great biblical saga of Moses, who is described in the Bible as an enslaved man in Egypt who led his people in escaping from the fetters of an Egyptian Pharaoh. To this day, Jews celebrate the Passover – the night which commemorates escape from Egyptian subjugation. Moses was arguably more an historical figure than Abraham. 'Moses' is an Egyptian name, which lends credence to a Moses who was known to Egyptians and who led captive tribes in escaping vassalage under Egypt's Pharaoh.[5]

The life-blood of Judaism is the belief that God delivered a series of instructions (Torah) to Moses while he was staying on Mt Sinai. The Hebrew word for this divine teaching is tôrâ, which has come to be rendered in English as 'law', or 'the Torah'. In discussions of Judaism it is often simply designated as 'the Mosaic Law'. Included in the Torah are admonitions not to kill or steal, and to have no other Gods apart from the God of the Israelites.

As traced thus far, the history of Judaism involved violent subjugation in Egypt and violent conflict in Canaan. The Bible recounts that Jacob, Abraham's grandson, led his family into Egypt. God so favoured Jacob, the Book of Genesis declares, that God gave him the new name of Israel (Gen 32: 28). The biblical narrative also records that Jacob had 12 sons who generated what became known as the Twelve Tribes of Israel. It was these tribes that Moses is described as leading from bondage and into a wilderness east of the Jordan River. The next plot in the story concerns Joshua, who was well known to Moses and is said to have led the tribes from wandering in wilderness into Canaan.

After incessant struggles with local and neighbouring tribes, the clans of Israel agreed to unite. The mechanism for their unification was a monarchy. The first of their kings was Saul (c. 1020–1000 BCE). He was followed by David (c. 1000–961), who was succeeded by Solomon (c. 961–922). When Solomon was king, he decided to build a temple in Jerusalem, which was to be the centre of the religious cult of the Israelites. The Temple (spelled hereafter with a capital letter to distinguish it from all other temples) was so pivotal in the life of Israelites that any region located beyond its threshold was called profane (*pro-fano*).[6] The primary purpose of the Temple was to serve as a place in which Jews could worship the God of Israel.

As an act of reverence, many Jews – ancient and modern – will not vocalize their God's name. They spell it by omitting vowels. It thus becomes YHWH. Others dare to pronounce the name by including the letter 'A' between 'Y' and 'H', and 'E' between 'W' and the second 'H'. In English, this produces 'YAHWEH'. The abbreviated form, 'YHWH', is called the Tetragrammaton ('word of four letters'). Pronouncing the divine name can be entirely avoided by substituting it with 'God' or 'the Lord' ('Adonai').

Solomon was a greatly loved king. When he died, so too did the unity he served to symbolize. His kingdom split. It was divided into two regions: Judah in the south and Israel in the north. These realms were often at odds with each other, and each suffered a different fate. The northern realm of Israel was conquered by the Assyrian Empire in 722 BCE. Much of its population was deported eastwards closer to Babylon (2 Kings 17). It became known as the 'ten lost tribes of Israel'.

Judah survived for roughly another century and a half until it was subjugated by the Chaldean Empire. Chaldeans are also known as neo-Babylonians because they made Babylon the centre of their rule. They were formed by an alliance of five tribes who gained control of Babylonia late in the sixth century BCE. Assyrians ruled the region before Chaldeans. Of many successive imperial dynasties that dominated Babylon, the Chaldean was one of the strongest, and is occasionally called the Tenth Babylonian Dynasty, lasting from 625 to 539 BCE.[7]

In 587–586 BCE, the armies of a Chaldean king, Nebuchadrezzer (or Nebuchadnezzar), invaded the southern realm of Judah, with calamitous results for the Judaeans. Nebuchadrezzer's armies destroyed Solomon's Temple and deported the population of Jerusalem to Babylon. The history of these captured and deported Judaeans bears directly on the life of Jesus and, because of him, the history of Christianity.

The Chaldean Empire was subsequently overrun by Persians, whose dynasty was based in what is now called Iran. The Persian king Cyrus conquered Babylon in 535 BCE and allowed Judaean exiles in Mesopotamia to return to Judaea in 538 (Ezra 1: 2–4; 6: 2–5).[8] Those who remained in Babylon formed part of what came to be known as a Diaspora (Judaeans living outside their original homeland). Those who resettled in Jerusalem were permitted by Cyrus to rebuild their Temple.[9] Thus began the period of the Second Temple. This Temple in an enlarged form was visited by Jesus.

Alexander the Great

Despite resettlement and a rebuilt Temple, the social stability, cohesiveness and relative peacefulness enjoyed by Israelites (descendents of Joshua), under the monarchies of Saul, David and Solomon, never became entrenched again. This was so largely because of Alexander the Great's conquest of the Near East, and of the vanquishing dynasties that succeeded him in the region.

During November of 332 BCE, the young king Alexander unexpectedly defeated the army of the Persian king, Darius III Codomanos, in a battle on the Issos plain. The result was that Alexander became the new master of Syria, and thence of Palestine. In antiquity, Syria was a locality of capital importance. It was a geographical territory encompassing the western Semitic Near East.[10] It was bordered to its west by the north-eastern edges of the Mediterranean Sea, with the Euphrates River on its eastern boundary and Palestine to its immediate south. Its principal cities were Damascus and Antioch on the Orontes.[11] According to the biblical book, the Acts of the Apostles, written towards the end of the first century CE, people were first called 'Christians' in Antioch (Acts 11: 26).

For contemporary Westerners, Alexander died while still a young man. For his contemporaries, to die at the age of 33, as he did, was perfectly commonplace. After his death in Babylon in June of 232, his generals began squabbling heatedly. As a result, they descended into a lengthy phase of armed conflicts. Ptolemy I, based in Egypt, seized control of southern Syria, as Seleucos I was given control of all of Syria by his allies. These Greek rulers were friends and did not fight with each other. Ptolemy died in 283, and Seleucos in 281. The Ptolemies (rulers of southern Syria) were forced out of Syria in 200–198 BCE by Antiochos III, but the Seleucid Dynasty in Syria did not remain unchallenged for long.[12] It was eventually threatened and unseated by a new Jewish dynasty, that of the Hasmonaeans or Maccabees, between roughly 150 and 140 BCE.

The legacy of Alexander and the Hellenistic dynasties that succeeded him in the territories of the Near East had two major consequences for Palestinians, including Jesus and his family. First, following Alexander, large numbers of colonizers moved from Greece and settled in Syria, bringing with them Greek forms of social control and education. And second, the colonizers established what are now called city-states. Antioch was one such city in the Seleucid Empire. As people who could speak Greek began to live in Syria and Palestine, they were called 'Hellenes'. The process by which they transformed their new homes was 'Hellenization'. The Greek verb, *hellenizein*, means 'to speak Greek'.[13]

Unlike many ancient empires, the Greek conquerors of Syria did not force anyone to accept their ways. People were largely left free to adopt their language and customs or not. While they were content to allow people to go about their daily activities as they had previously done if they so wished, they proceeded to introduce a host of new practices in their new homes, such as distinct styles of clothing, practising sports while naked, worshipping Greek Gods and educating boys in gymnasia (girls were not accorded the same privilege).[14]

Not all the inhabitants of Palestine were content with an encroaching Hellenistic culture, and antagonism came to a head in the second century BCE. In 167, closer now to the time of Jesus, the Syrian king Antiochos IV desecrated the Temple in Jerusalem and, violating a typical Greek principal of tolerance, tried to forbid the Jewish practice of male circumcision. In the same year, the Jewish family of Hasmoneans rebelled. Led by the priest Mattathias and his son, Judas Maccabeus, Hasmoneans rose up against Seleucid control of the lands. The sons of Judas Maccabeus, Jonathan and Simon, continued the struggle and succeeded in severing Syrian control. They then proceeded to establish a Hasmonean dynasty in Israel.[15] Finally, after centuries of foreign imperial rule, Palestinians could once again boast an Israelite leadership.

Roman Rule of Palestine

Well might it be wondered just what the point is of recounting Assyrian, Chaldean, Persian, Ptolemaic, Seleucid and Hasmonean military exploits in a book devoted to Christianity. Simply put, the world in which Jesus lived and Christianity was born was a Near Eastern environment shaped over many centuries by a baneful history of dynastic conflict, imperial subjugation, military slaughter, and the enslavement of peoples that regularly followed battles. The rule of oppressive overlords must have deeply seared the mind of Jesus because it is frequently mentioned overtly in many teachings that are accorded to him in the Bible. When Christianity became a more highly structured religion in the fourth century CE, it adopted patterns of leadership, building and dress that were borrowed from the Empire that brought to an end Hasmonean rule of Palestine. That Empire was Rome, and Jesus was born into it.

During the first century, Rome controlled the people and territories surrounding the Mediterranean Sea. The Empire of Rome at this time stretched from Britain in its northwest, throughout (contemporary) Spain and France to its west, included Europe, extended to Syria and Turkey in the east, and encompassed North Africa in the south.[16]

It is a mistake to conclude, as is often the case, that Palestine in the time of Jesus was occupied by Romans. Occupation implies residence by armies.[17] Palestine was controlled by Rome, but not occupied by it. Rome ruled discretely from a distance unless it was resisted. Then it unleashed its legions to kill, burn, destroy and subdue. Rome ruled by terror – from a distance. When Jesus lived, Rome relied on Herodian tetrarchs (local princes) and Roman prefects to maintain peace and prevent uprisings in Palestine. The prefects did not command legions.

The legion (Latin: *legio, legiones*) was the driving force behind the Roman Empire and its armies. No legions, no Empire. A legion was the basic tactical unit of the army. It comprised ten cohorts (*cohortes*), with double strength of numbers in the first cohort. Each cohort contained 480 soldiers (*milites*), divided into six sub-units (*centuriae*) of 80 legionaries. A century (the sub-unit) was commanded by a centurion (*centurio*).[18] Sometimes legions grew as large as 6000 legionaries – heavily trained and highly skilled infantryman. Each legion included 120 mounted soldiers (*equites legionis*).[19] The numbers of legions were swelled by auxiliary soldiers (*auxilia*) – today called mercenaries. The members of legions were all Roman citizens. Auxiliaries were not, but were recruited as freeborn people

*Figure 1: Statue of a centurion with his prized ear-to-ear headdress and the
cane used to beat slovenly legionaries*

(*peregrini*) from around the Empire. Each legion was commanded by a legate (*legatus*) assisted by five tribunes. The Roman army boasted about 25 legions in the first century CE[20] – 47 were deployed at the battle of Actium. The combined fighting force of legions was ferocious. While Jesus was alive, he was never hurt directly by them. Four were kept in Antioch then, but none was garrisoned in Palestine.[21] They constituted an ever-present menace to Palestinians, who knew that they had been deployed in Palestine before (63 BCE), and could be again were Rome irked.

The Mediterranean region in which Jesus spent his life was a perilous place, even for powerful rulers. Of the 79 Roman emperors who reigned from Augustus to Romulus Augustus (deposed in 479 CE), 31 were murdered, six committed suicide under duress, and four were deposed violently.[22]

Palestine remained largely free from foreign rule under its Hasmonean leadership between 166 and 63 BCE. The last Hasmonean queen was Salome Alexandra. When she died in 67 BCE, her two sons, Hyrcanus II and Aristobulus, began bickering over which of them would succeed their mother as ruler. It transpired that neither of them did. They made the unwitting mistake of asking for their dispute to be heard and settled in Rome.

The man appointed to resolve the sibling rivalry was the Roman general, Pompey. Settle the dispute he did, by invading Judaea. He calculated that Jews would not resist his imposition of power over them if he moved against them on the Sabbath, the seventh day of the week during which Jews did not work. On a Sabbath in 63 BCE, he violated Jerusalem's Temple by entering it with soldiers and going into its most sacred precinct, the Holy of Holies. He imprisoned Aristobulus (son of Salome Alexandra) in exile and allowed Hyrcanus to operate as High Priest of Jerusalem.[23] Pompey thereby included Palestine in the strategically vital Roman province of Syria, a province known in Latin as Syria–Palestina.

In 60 BCE, Rome came to be ruled by an alliance of three men; that is, the triumvirate of Pompey, Crassus and the famous Julius Caesar. Pompey and Caesar eventually fell out with each other and ended up facing each other as rivals in 48 BCE at the battle of Pharsalus. Caesar won. He became the dictator of Rome in 47 BCE and appointed the ruler of Idumaea, Antipater, to govern Palestine under the eyes of Rome. Antipater was succeeded by two sons,

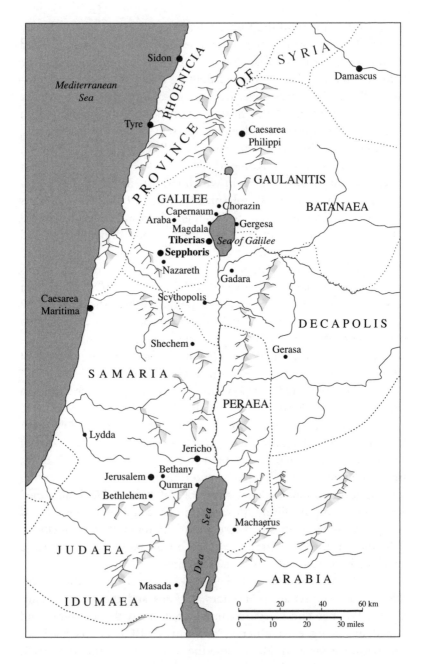

Map 3: Palestine in the time of Jesus

Figure 2: Marble bust of General Pompey, Conqueror of Palestine

Phasael and Herod. When Jesus was born, Herod was the Roman-appointed king of the Judaeans who exercised control over Judaea, Samaria and Galilee, and hence the life of Jesus.

Stability in the region did not last long. A son of the exiled Aristobulus, called Antigonous, managed to persuade Parthians (an Iranian tribe) to help him. He succeeded in unseating Herod and re-establishing Hasmonean rule in Palestine. Herod fled to Rome, where he was welcomed by Julius Caesar and Octavian (Caesar's adopted son). In 40 BCE, the Roman Senate conferred on Herod the title of 'King of Judaea', and in 37 BCE dispatched the Roman army to settle him in Jerusalem as its ruler.

King Herod

By ancient standards, Herod was a great king. He launched massive building programmes throughout Palestine and ruled for three decades. His greatest achievement in construction was ambitiously to extend the size and splendour of the Temple. He was also a brutal king. One story will suffice to illustrate his ruthlessness. Herod enjoyed the power of appointing the High Priest of Jerusalem. In the transition of the year 36 to 35 BCE, Herod appointed a very young High Priest called Aristobulus III. Aristobulus was a Hasmonean and the son of a former High Priest, Hyrcanus II (the son of Salome Alexandra). When he was appointed, Aristobulus III was only 17. The Jewish historian Flavius Josephus (37/8 CE–c. 100 CE) records that Aristobulus was tall for his age and exceedingly handsome, so much so that he enamoured the people of Jerusalem. Herod saw immediately how popular the attractive High Priest was, and decided to act. Herod witnessed the people acclaiming Aristobulus in the Temple during the festival of Sukkot.[24] He subsequently arranged for Aristobulus to relax with him by the side of a swimming pool. The boy was enticed to go swimming, and once in the water was held under by Herod's henchmen who pretended to play with him. They murdered him by drowning (*JW* 1.22.2 § 434; and *Ant.* 15.3.3 § 50–56).

Herod was an Idumaean who was born in 73 BCE. He died a horrific death by disease in 4 BCE. The son of Julius Caesar, Octavian, confirmed Herod in his place as king of Judaea in 30 BCE. On 16 January, the Senate in Rome declared Octavian Imperator Caesar Augustus; that is, Emperor of Rome and its vanquished territories. He reigned as such when Jesus was born towards the end of Herod's life.

Even though Herod was appointed king in the year 40 BCE, he really only managed to exercise control from about 37 BCE onwards. Once settled, he destroyed or oppressed all opposition to his rule. In the course of his life, Herod had nine wives.[25] He forced one of them, Mariamme I, to kill herself. In all, he had 15 children. His first six sons were Antipater, Alexander, Aristobulus, Archelaus, Antipas and Philip. The last three listed came to be well known in Palestine while Jesus was alive. Of the six sons, Herod executed the first three. Alexander and Aristobulus were strangled at Sebaste in 7 BCE on suspicion of treason.[26] Antipater was executed in 4 BCE, just five days

Figure 3: Model of the Temple as extended by Herod

before Herod died.[27] After the first six sons, Herod proceeded to have seven more boys and five daughters. All of these survived him.

The emperor honoured most wishes in the seventh and last will of Herod and trifurcated Herod's kingdom by implanting three of the king's sons as client rulers in Palestine. None of the sons was accorded the title of 'king' like their father. The sons Herod named as his successors were the three of his first six sons he did not kill: Archelaus, Antipas and Philip. As boys they had been educated in Rome. They were well acquainted with Roman customs and forms of government.

When Herod died, Augustus installed Archelaus as an ethnarch ('ruler of the peoples') in Palestine. Archelaus thus became the ethnarch of Judaea, Samaritis, Idumaea, Caesarea and Sebaste. Philip became tetrarch ('ruler of a fourth of a territory') of Trachonitis, Batanea, Gaulanitis, Auranitis and Panias, while Herod Antipas was appointed the tetrarch of Galilee and Peraea.[28] As Jesus grew up in Nazareth, the person who exercised proximate and direct political rule over him was Antipas.

Antipas was only a boy of 16 when he became tetrarch.[29] He was still able to assume political control of Galilee because boys in his family were regarded as adults from the age of 12 or 13 onwards. Antipas proved to be a less brutal person than his father, and despite his youthfulness and inexperience when he came to live in Galilee, he proved to be an efficient ruler whose reign lasted for 40 years. In Luke's Gospel, Jesus refers to him as 'that fox' (Lk 13: 32). He must have been shrewd to have survived so long in power.

The Eastern Mediterranean World in the First Century

While much has been said thus far in the narrative of this chapter about potentates and their empires, a guiding principle of this book is to present Christianity and its historical origins with a combined focus on hard-working anonymous local people *as well as* their rulers. The former formed a massive majority of ancient people in the Near East. A good deal of attention has been paid to rulers so far because their decisions directly shaped the socio-cultural circumstances that impinged on Jesus' life. The masses of the people they ruled deserve equal attention because Christians first emerged among them.

The people Jesus lived among, and the localities in which they lived, differed strikingly from the settings of most contemporary Christians who try to interpret Jesus. Present-day Christians of the West risk a constant danger of depicting him anachronistically in terms more applicable to them than to him. Growing up in Galilee, Jesus found himself in a society in which most people were illiterate. They lived at or just above a subsistence level, trying to find enough food to survive. His contemporaries were not free to marry at will, and unmarried people could not choose partners or spouses as they wished. Children were betrothed by their parents under contractual terms between families. Technically, most people who lived as couples in the Roman Empire of the first century CE were not married at all according to Roman law because they were not Roman citizens, but conquered subjects of the emperor. They married according to their own local traditions, not Roman law. In Roman law, just marriage (*matrimonium iustum*) was only recognized between Roman citizens or Junian Latins (former enslaved people). All other human partnerships were called concubinage (*contubernium*).[30]

Jesus and his contemporaries were not free to speak publicly as they wished, act as they pleased, or go where they liked when they wanted. They were yoked to labour, in agriculture or craft, and at all times were obliged to submit to the rule of Rome and its local client governors.

Throughout the Mediterranean territories of the first century, life expectancy at birth for 97–98 per cent of the population lay between 20 and 30 years for most adults.[31] Wealthy people could live longer because of the better nutrition that was available to them. Infant mortality was very high, with as many as 50 per cent of neonates and infants not surviving to the age of ten.[32] Adults could expect to have poor eyesight, little head-hair and rotten teeth if they reached the age of 30.[33] They were old by the time they were 30. The lives of infants and adults alike were plagued by malnutrition and consequent ill-health. For those who lived in urban Mediterranean clusters (5–10 per cent of the population), life was smelly, crowded, dirty and dogged by fires, floods, animal excrement, human household waste, infectious diseases that spread rapidly and lethally, sporadic work, and ethnic frictions. Further misery was caused by the constant obligation to pay taxes, tithes and (financial) tribute to the emperor.[34]

In the Bible it is striking how often Jesus is recorded talking about food, drink, crops and animals. This is not at all surprising when it is realized that the lives of his contemporaries were dominated by fretfulness about food. Life for his contemporaries in Galilee and the Roman Empire was not unrelievedly imperilled, but it was certainly harsh. For most, living involved a ceaseless struggle to survive by gathering or cultivating food: 'In antiquity, as in all pre-industrial societies, most people were of necessity engaged in food production.'[35] Meat was rarely consumed by most of the Mediterranean population, and certainly not on a daily basis. Staples taken for granted nowadays, such as sugar and potatoes, were entirely unknown around the Mediterranean in the first century. Crises revolving around scarcities of foodstuffs occurred frequently in the Mediterranean communities of the first century CE, causing for the populace recurring periods of chronic malnutrition or endemic undernourishment.[36] Diseases related to the lack of basic nutrition, such as blindness, rickets and hypovitiminosis (vitamin deficiency), blighted the lives Mediterranean populations.[37]

So too did the practice of imperial tribute. After Pompey took Palestine for Rome in 63 BCE, its entire population was laid under tribute. This meant, if Josephus is to be trusted, that Rome demanded a constant supply of revenue from Palestinians, paid in the form of harvests. Josephus tells his readers that Roman tribute demanded about 25 per cent of a region's harvest every second year (*Ant.* 14: 202–3). Added to that, the people had to pay tithes (a tenth of an income) and taxes to the Temple in Jerusalem. Paying tribute is a demeaning and punitive practice for anyone.[38] It is still widely practised by another name around the world today. It is normally called extortion, and is witnessed in the all-too-common scenario of a local gang or thug extracting regular financial payments from a hard-working shop owner by threatening to smash the shop's windows and contents, or to violate the owner's children if payment is not forthcoming.

Palestinians normally did not dare to refuse to pay tribute to the emperor because they knew that Roman legions in Syria, or Herodian soldiers in Palestine, would squelch them if they did.

When Jesus was alive, there was no such cluster of people as a middle class. The Mediterranean world was governed by oligarchies – small bands of powerful people. Oligarchies included the emperor and his retainers, Herodian court officials, the High Priesthood in Jerusalem, urban princes and governors, and wealthy merchants; 2–3 per cent of the Mediterranean population in the age of Jesus constituted oligarchies, often called ruling elites. The rest of the people, 97–98 per cent of the population, were poor, enslaved or laboured with their hands to make a living;[39] 90–95 per cent of people lived in rural areas and spent their days working the land. Enslaved people were a prominent segment of the population in the first-century Mediterranean territories ruled by Rome.[40]

The Life of Jesus

The people known to Jesus in Galilee had recently been a rebellious lot. The fact that Galileans stood up to Rome just before Jesus was born is an historical key for comprehending much of what he is recorded as saying later in his life.[41] His first allegiance and that of his people was to the God of Israel, not to Imperator Caesar Augustus.

Jesus was born into an exceedingly dangerous environment. Upon Herod's death, Galileans and Judaeans revolted against Roman overlordship. Trouble flared up in 4 BCE in both the Galilean fortress town of Sepphoris and Jerusalem, when the ethnarch Archelaus proved to be less than a prudent ruler. He acted violently when the local populace demanded privileges for their feast of Pentecost. According to Josephus, Archelaus saw to it that 3000 worshippers in Jerusalem were slaughtered (*Ant.* 17.8 4–9.3; *JW* 2.1–3: 1–13).

He then travelled to Rome, leaving General Varus, the Roman *legatus* (military legate/governor) of Syria, to deal with the continuing uprising in Palestine. During the period of the early Julio–Claudian emperors – that is, while Jesus was alive – the four legions garrisoned in Syria were Legions III (nicknamed Gallica), VI (Ferrata), X (Fretensis) and XII (Fulminata).[42] At the beginning of the first century, there were no Roman legions further south in Palestine. Varus dispatched a legion downwards to Jerusalem at the feast of Pentecost, but Jerusalem's populace laid siege to it. He reacted swiftly and brutally. He dispatched two more legions, auxiliary soldiers and cavalry, put down the revolt, destroyed the fortress town of Sepphoris, enslaved its inhabitants, crucified 2000 others, and imprisoned scattered trouble-makers. He then withdrew to Syria.[43] Such was the world in which Jesus was an infant. Sepphoris can be seen from Nazareth across a valley.

Sources for Depicting Jesus

It is not possible now to describe Jesus' life with untroubled assurance and complete accuracy because of his historical inaccessibility. After 20 centuries, he is far removed geographically, temporally and experientially from anyone living today. He is no longer available for direct observation, and nothing written (if he could write) or made by him has survived. It is only possible in current circumstances to gain an impression and construct a portrait of him, on the bases of tangential or indirect indications. Of these, there are at least five principal sources: (a) his physical environment; (b) the *kinds* of people he knew, loved and reacted against, considered in association with the *types* who were set against him; (c) his religion of Palestinian Judaism; (d) orally transmitted stories about him remembered by people who knew him; and (e) the four Gospels of Mark, Matthew,

Luke and John, which are written theological proclamations focused on him, composed during the first century based on historical reminiscences of him, and articulating earlier stories passed on by his associates and their descendents. The best known written sources are the Gospels of the section of the Bible that Christians call the New Testament. They distinguish the New Testament from the biblical writings of the Israelites which they call the Old Testament and contemporary Jews designate as the Tanakh. The New Testament also contains writings by Paul, an early devotee of Jesus, some of which were written a little more than a decade after Jesus' death. Apart from the Bible, there are a few brief references to Jesus in the works of Flavius Josephus, Tacitus and Pliny the Younger.[44]

The New Testament

The last segment of the Bible that Christians call the New Testament is the primary repository for historical information and theological comment about Jesus. It contains 27 writings, composed in Greek with some Aramaic words. It begins with four Gospels, labelled Matthew, Mark, Luke and John. The first three are known as Synoptic Gospels because they are so similar in respects that their verses can be arranged in parallel columns and viewed together at a glance ('synoptically'/'with one eye'). Mark is usually held to be the first to be written around the year 70 CE. It was known to the authors of Matthew and Luke, who used it as a basis for their texts. Matthew wrote shortly before Luke. Both penned their Gospels around 85–90 CE. John's Gospel was the last to be composed, towards the end of the century. The Gospels are followed by the Acts of the Apostles, which have the same author as Luke's Gospel. They recount the deeds of Jesus' closest followers, called apostles ('messengers'). Then come letters written by Paul to communities in the Diaspora or dispersal of Jews outside Palestine. Some bear his name in the New Testament, but were most likely not actually written by him because they use a vocabulary and ideas that are not his. Thirteen letters are attributed to him. The seven that are generally accepted as authentic are Romans, 1 and 2 Corinthians, Galatians, 1 Thessalonians, Philippians, and Philemon. The authorship of six others is unclear. Three are possibly pseudonymous (using the name 'Paul', but written by someone else): Ephesians, Colossians and 2 Thessalonians; and three more are most likely to be pseudonymous: 1 and 2 Timothy, and Titus. The New Testament ends with an apocalypse (a Greek word for 'revelation'), a type of literature envisaging the revelation of God to people at history's end.

Even though the Gospels speak about Jesus, they are not the primary witnesses to his existence. They record experiences and memories of people who met and knew him before the New Testament was composed. Any comment on Jesus now is only possible because of recorded reminiscences of those who new him. The Gospels were composed several decades after Jesus' crucifixion by authors who are now anonymous. Names were appended to them (Matthew, Mark, Luke and John) in the second century to give the impression that they were written by followers of Jesus, which was not the case.

Since Jesus' friends and enthusiasts spoke of him with terminology drawn from their region, still more be can be ascertained of his life obliquely by focusing on the places in which he and his associates lived. The more that is known of the geography, topography, archaeology, politics, financial mechanisms and religious temper of Palestine, the easier it becomes to gain an impression of the kind of territory and culture in which he lived, and the type of existence he must have experienced. In short, familiarity with his habitat facilitates a better comprehension of how and why he spent his energies as he did. Crucial, too, were the people he knew and resisted. Each and every person's identity without exception is directly moulded by other people encountered in the course of a life. A familiarity with the people, or the kinds of individuals Jesus met, loved, confronted and disputed with, helps to illuminate his identity. The only politically powerful person he ever encountered in his life, Pontius Pilate, killed him. The clash between the two sheds light on both.

It is always a bafflement why people today say they love, follow and believe in Jesus, while simultaneously showing not the slightest acquaintance with the localities and customs in and with which he lived. This deficit of historical detail breeds unbridled anachronistic speech about him. Even to speak of Jesus' 'ministry' is an anachronism, because the concept and practice of what Christians now call ministry incubated in the Church during the centuries after Jesus' death.

Galilee: The Land of Jesus

Jesus lived between the undulating hills of Galilee. In Hebrew, Galilee means 'the circle', which since antiquity has also been described as 'the circle of the nations' (Isa 9: 1).[45] Either local clans, or tribes surrounding Galilee, constitute 'the nations' thus designated.

The Jewish historian Josephus provides a vivid description of Galilee when he was writing around 70 CE. He informs his readers that 'There are two Galilees, known as Upper and Lower, shut in by Phoenicia and Syria' (*JW* 3: 41). Indeed there are, and Josephus goes on to observe of Galilee that 'The whole area is excellent for crops or cattle and rich in forests of every kind, so that by its adaptability it invites even those least inclined to work on the land. Consequently every inch has been cultivated by the inhabitants and not a corner goes to waste' (*JW* 3: 42–43).

The Imperial Archives of pharaonic Egypt discovered at Amana contain references to Galilee in the fourteenth century BCE.

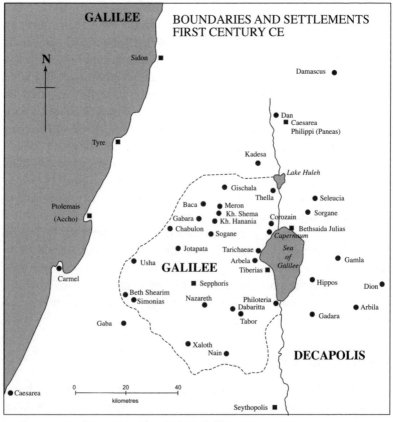

Map 4: Galilee

Intriguingly, correspondence from local Palestinian leaders to Egypt's pharaoh complain of a group of people from Egypt called the *hapiru* who were raiding their region.[46]

The entire area of Galilee in Jesus' time had Samaria to its south and Phoenicia to its north and northwest. It extended to the Sea of Galilee and the Jordan River on its east. The north of Galilee is more mountainous and less accessible than the south. Lower Galilee consists of a series of undulating valleys and ridges in them. In the first century it was exceptionally fertile and produced the most important staple food of its inhabitants – grain. Wine and olives were cultivated in the hillier regions of Galilee, while Lower Galilee produced enough grain to supply (often under compulsion) other segments of the Empire.[47] A major trade route stemming from the city of Ceasarea Maritima, in the south of Palestine, connected with the capital of Galilee, the fortress town of Sepphoris. This town is not mentioned in the New Testament, but archaeological excavations have established that it was very close to the village where Jesus lived. Caesarea Maritima, a port city, was the political seat of the Roman prefects of Judaea who, contrary to a common misperception, did not reside permanently in Jerusalem.

Galilee was not a cocooned backwater. Even before Rome invaded Palestine in 63 BCE, the people of Galilee were greatly experienced in coping with foreign domination. They had endured a century of Greek-speaking rulers (the Seleucids) before their Jewish Hasmonean leaders, and another century of the Hellenistic Ptolemies before Seleucid domination began.[48] Greek had long been spoken in Galilee, along with Aramaic, well before Jesus was born.

Sepphoris

The citadel of Sepphoris was a major influence on the life of Jesus, although it is normally ignored in theological textbooks discussing Jesus' identity and significance. Josephus describes it as 'the strongest city of Galilee' (*JW* 2: 510–11). It served as the residence of the tetrarch of Galilee, Herod Antipas, until 19–20 CE when he moved to Tiberias, a city he built in eastern Galilee in honour of the emperor Tiberius. Sepphoris was burned to the ground by General Varus' legionaries when King Herod died and its inhabitants rebelled. It fell to Herod's son, Antipas, to rebuild the place.[49] The client ruler of Rome in Galilee thereby lived only a few miles from where Jesus was a boy and young man.

In reconstructing Sepphoris, Antipas had grand plans. He had studied in Rome as a young boy and had seen its more elegant buildings. He envisaged a city of 25,000 people in Sepphoris.[50] Such a large building programme involved not only the collection of sizable taxes to pay for it, but the engagement of tradespeople to complete the work. These would have included architects together with stonemasons, bricklayers and carpenters. The Gospels describe Jesus as such a person with the Greek word *tekton*, which designates a manual worker like a stonemason or carpenter.

The Birth of Jesus

It is not known assuredly when or where Jesus was born. The calendar which dates his birth in the year 1 was calculated by Dionysius Exiguus, a sixth-century monk living in Rome, who did not know the date of King Herod's death (4 BCE). It is likely that Jesus was born right towards the end of Herod's reign, between 7 and 4 BCE.

The Bible contains two traditions regarding the whereabouts of Jesus' birth. One assumes he was born in Bethlehem and was therefore a Judaean. Another presupposes that he was born in Nazareth and hence was a Galilean. It may be the case that the tradition of his origin in Bethlehem is a fictional creation driven to link him to the lineage of King David. Whatever the case, it is safe to assume that Jesus was raised in Nazareth, where he spent by far the majority of his life (Mk 6: 1; Lk 4: 16).

The question as to where Jesus was born was rendered all the more intriguing by a nineteenth-century archaeological discovery in Galilee: a village called Bethlehem was discovered and excavated only 7 miles (11 kilometres) from Nazareth.[51] The baffling query arises as to whether Jesus was born in Bethlehem of Judaea, as Matthew's Gospel states (Mt 2: 1), or Galilee's Bethlehem. Nobody knows with certainty. He was in any case, by his upbringing, a Galilean.

Nazareth

From additional archaeological excavations, it has been discovered that the small Galilean village of Nazareth was built in lower Galilee on a rock promontory in a fertile high plain at an altitude of about 1300 feet (400 metres). It lies roughly 20 miles (32 kilometres) from the Mediterranean Sea, and 15 miles (24 kilometres) from Lake Gennesaret, also called the Sea of Galilee.[52] It is not mentioned in the Hebrew Bible (Old Testament). Caves have been found at the village site, but these were for storing wine and housing animals, and were not human residences.

Nazareth lies only 3.5 miles (5 kilometres) to the southeast of Sepphoris, which was visible from the village across a valley. An adolescent could walk from Nazareth to Sepphoris in about an hour. It is barely conceivable that Jesus never went there as a boy. The discovery of Jewish ritual baths (*miqvaoth*) and images of the menorah (candelabra with seven branches) signify that a sizable Jewish population was housed at Sepphoris, and Jesus need not have feared them.[53] As he grew older, he may have become wary of being in the vicinity of the tetrarch. It was Herod Antipas who beheaded a man known to Jesus – John the Baptizer.

Jesus and his people of Nazareth lived in an advanced agrarian society. This means firstly that agriculture was the primary activity in their society. Most people were rural farmers: free or tenant farmers, day workers, and extended families. Roughly 90 per cent of the people in Palestine during the first century were peasants; that is, a stratum of society that worked the land at or just above a subsistence level.[54] Agrarian societies (as distinct from previous horticultural and later industrial societies) first evolved in the Near East about 5000 or 6000 years ago.[55]

Jesus and other Nazarenes did not enjoy an existence of bucolic bliss. Agrarian societies in first-century Galilee were theatres of political subjugation and financial extortion. Galilee was monarchically governed, and once Antipas became tetrarch Galileans came directly under his rule and indirectly under the religious sovereignty of the Temple. Galileans were compelled to pay taxes to both. Those who ruled in Palestine and elsewhere in the Roman Empire constituted only about 2 per cent of the overall population of the first-century lands bordering the Mediterranean Sea.[56]

Nazarenes and other Galileans had at least three levels of rulers making demands for taxes and tribute: the emperor, the tetrarch and the High Priest of Jerusalem. They frequently fell into debt if they borrowed money to pay taxes, tithes and tribute.[57]

A Portrait of Jesus

All that has been said thus far in this chapter is intended to shed light
on the life of Jesus under the premise that attempts to portray him
will inevitably be misguided and misleading if they do not scrutinize
the long history of his people, and the social circumstances he then
endured in Lower Galilee.

He was most likely born in Nazareth after 7 BCE and before 4
BCE. His original Aramaic name was *Yēshûa'*. It is an abbreviated
version of the Hebrew word for 'Joshua', which is *Yĕhôshûa'*. His
parents were known as Miryam (or Miriam), the equivalent of
'Mary', and Yôsēf or 'Joseph'. Many ancient texts speak of Jesus' siblings, including the Gospels, Paul, the Acts of the Apostles and
Josephus. The Gospels of Mark and Matthew mention four brothers:
Jacob (James), Joseph, Judah (Judas or Jude) and Simon (Simeon).
They speak of sisters but do not name them or say how many they
were. Minimally, Jesus grew up in a household of seven children (five
sons and at least two daughters).[58] In the centuries after Jesus' death a
tradition developed, based on the Gospels of Luke and Matthew, that
Mary did not conceive with the agency of a man, and was hence a
virgin mother. Christian art often portrays Joseph as a man much
older than Mary, to inhibit any suggestion that they were sexual partners. Joseph is not mentioned after Jesus' infancy in the Gospels. He
may have died while Jesus was an adolescent.[59]

The names of Jesus' family members are highly significant and
help explain the religious intensity of his adult life. The names of
each member of his immediate family echo the origins of Israel's history. His brother James refers to the patriarch Jacob, who was given
the new name of Israel; Judah, Joseph and Simeon refer to three of
the sons (tribes) of Israel; Miriam was Moses' sister; and the very
name of Jesus or Joshua recalls the Israelite leader who took over
Moses' mantle and led the Israelites into the promised land of
Canaan.[60]

It was noted in a previous paragraph that Jesus grew up in 'a
household' (rather than a 'home'). The idea of a closely knit family of
two parents and their children united in a home does not apply to
Galilee of the first century. The basic unit of villages in Galilee,
including Nazareth, was a household directed by a patriarch (authoritative father), together with his wife and children. Yet it could also

be transgenerational, including the patriarch's parents, the families of his brothers, and enslaved people who were required to meet his needs, including sexual. People behaving in a modern individualistic, self-promoting way was inconceivable. Everybody cooperated according to kinship bonds as a matter of survival to produce their own food and make their own clothes. Nearly all adults married: women normally by their upper teens, and men a little later. Patriarchs decided who would marry whom.[61]

Nothing is known of the precise details of Jesus' boyhood and adolescence, and anything concluded is done so obliquely from what can be ascertained of the agrarian societies of Galilee and Nazareth. Once he grew to manhood, there is more direct indication of how he lived, what he did, and the matters of which he spoke.

As a young adult of around the age of 30, Jesus left home and began to move around Galilee. It is noteworthy that he did not launch out as a solitary figure: he joined a group. In his travels, he encountered a religious firebrand widely known in Palestine as John the Baptizer, or Baptist. John was a Jewish ascetic and a preacher, inviting people to repent of their sins so as to be forgiven (Mk 1: 14). Matthew, Mark and Luke introduce him as calling for his contemporary Palestinians to change their ways. He practised a ritual of cleansing in water to symbolize a washing away of people's sins. 'In those days', says Mark's Gospel, 'Jesus came from Nazareth of Galilee and was baptized by John in the Jordan' (Mk 1: 9). This ritual of immersing penitents in water passed into subsequent Christianity as the primary form of initiating individuals into the Church. Baptism begins a Christian's career.

The Gospels record that Antipas arrested and later beheaded John for objecting to his marriage to Herodias, his second wife. After John's arrest, Mark states that Jesus returned to Galilee from the Jordan River where he had encountered John and began proclaiming 'the good news of God' (Mk 1: 14a). The notion of 'good news' is the linguistic root of the terms 'gospel' and 'evangelical' ('relating to the good news'). These terms are omnipresent in subsequent Christian discourse. According to Mark, Jesus proclaimed the good news by saying: 'The time is fulfilled, and the kingdom of God has come near; repent and believe in the good news' (Mk 1: 15).

Mark's Gospel tells its readers that after Jesus was baptized by John they parted company. Jesus then set out on a new venture and began,

*Figure 4: Lake Gennesaret viewed from near Bethsaida, the type of terrain
Jesus liked to frequent*

as depicted by Mark, preaching and healing people of their illnesses around the northern shores of Lake Gennesaret (Sea of Galilee). Before Jesus' death, he spent most of his time in the area between three towns: Capernaum, Chorazin and Bethsaida. Lines drawn between these towns on a map reveal a triangle which envelopes the area where Jesus spent most of his time after he left Nazareth.[62] It was in this region that he first attracted followers.

After John's incarceration, Mark's Gospel makes no secret of the embarrassment (for later Christians) that Jesus fell out badly with his family (Mk 3: 21). By this stage, groups were showing interest in him. After visiting Capernaum, Mark records: 'Then he went home; and the crowd came together again, so that they could not even eat. When his family heard it, they went out to restrain him, for people were saying, "He has gone out of his mind"' (Mk 3: 19b–21). After this comment, Mark in his Gospel never mentions again by name any member of Jesus' family. Only in John's Gospel does Mary accompany Jesus to a marriage feast at Cana after he had left home, and later on was present for the crucifixion.

The length of time Jesus spent among the towns to the north of the Sea of Galilee could have been as brief as six months and as long as about three years. John's Gospel gives the impression that Jesus went to Jerusalem for several celebrations of Passover, whereas the Synoptics only mention one visit. In any case, Jesus' presence among the peasants of Galilee away from his home had a catalytic effect on those who heard him speak and watched the way he treated people, especially the downtrodden.

After Jesus' contact with John the Baptizer, he became emboldened to proclaim a message to anyone who would listen. It concerned God and an imminent social situation in which God would initiate a new reality. The main features of this new situation would be that God would finally save the Israelites from all that imperilled them and ensure that love and justice would overwhelm mundane human concerns and exploitations. This message was the historical core of Jesus' religious intensity. It proclaims what he called the kingdom of God. This expression dominates his speech and actions in the Synoptics (Lk 6: 20; 7: 28; 10: 9, 11; 11: 2, 20; 12: 31; 13: 18, 20, 29; 14: 16; 16: 16; Mt 22: 2).

Jesus never describes or defines the kingdom or rule of God in the Gospels directly. He regularly speaks about it in the literary form of parables: stories that proceed by way of comparing and contrasting dissimilar realities. God's kingdom is thus compared to a replete harvest or a mustard seed. The kingdom is a reality of fullness, peace, justice; an existence free of sickness, warfare and poverty; a time for the release of captives and the end of oppressive exploitation. The theme of God viewed as a king and God's kingdom were commonly discussed in texts dating from Second Temple Judaism.[63]

It is not at all surprising that Jesus pined for and announced the imminent arrival of God's ways among his people, precisely because of what has been said previously in this chapter about the long history of political subjugation of Israelites, and the entrenched form of monetary exchange in Palestine that saw a privileged and wealthy 2 per cent of society keep the rest of the populace in debt, burdened by taxes, and struggling to survive year by year.

The sociologist Gerhard Lenski has illustrated tellingly the structure of agrarian societies, such as those known to Jesus.[64] According to this framework, the majority of power, money and privilege rests with a ruler and the retainers who manage the ruler's affairs. Under the rulers are priests, merchants and governors. By far the majority of the population is constituted by peasants, and worse off than them were people regarded as unclean, degraded or expendable ('does not matter if they die'). Relationships of power and vulnerability in ancient agrarian societies are illustrated in Figure 5.

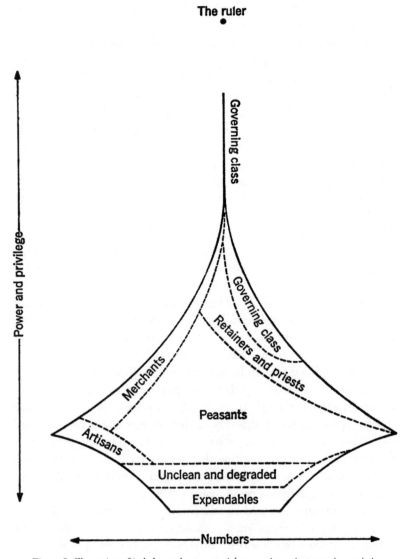

Figure 5: Illustration of imbalances between social groups in ancient agrarian societies

In such a setting, the announcement of the imminent arrival of an alternative situation – God's kingdom – must have had an enlivening effect among Galileans. In Jesus' vision of the kingdom, there would be no more poor people (Lk 6: 20; 12: 28, 29; Mt 6: 31); hunger would be unknown (Lk 6: 21; 10: 7; 11: 3, 11–12; 12: 24, 29; 13: 28–29); sickness and bodily disabilities would no longer afflict the masses (Lk 10: 9); exploitation would cease (Lk 6: 29–30); evil forces would be spent (Lk 4: 13; 11: 14, 20, 21–22); mentally unwell people would no longer be disturbed (Lk 11: 14).[65] The vanquishing of villainy, the obliteration of poverty, the suppression of oppression, the indictment of injustice – all these would be ushered in among people in the kingdom of God. What is more, the first privilege of enjoying the kingdom belongs to the poor: 'It is easier for a camel to go through the eye of a needle than for someone who is rich to enter the kingdom of God' (Mk 10: 25; Mt 19: 24; Lk 18: 25).

The Synoptics illustrate that Jesus not only proclaimed the imminent arrival of God's kingdom; he also regarded it as the basic reality of his life and lived accordingly in the hopeful expectation of its realization (Lk 6: 43–49).[66] Luke is particularly memorable in his account of Jesus' activities. When Jesus travelled in Galilee he did not carry any money (Lk 10: 4), a change of clothes or provisions of food (Lk 10: 4). He was not armed in any way, was prepared to turn the other cheek if struck on one side of his face (Lk 6: 29a), and was willing to give to another the shirt off his back (Lk 6: 29b).[67]

The Gospels are suffused with stories of Jesus working wonders: healing sick people, giving sight to those without it, restoring dead people to life, feeding multitudes of people with limited resources, and exorcising individuals of their torments. Whether or not these actions are understood actually to have happened, later Christians interpreted them as miracles. Their primary significance in the Gospels is to illustrate that the new reality of God's kingdom announced *verbally* by Jesus was made *visibly* manifest in his actions in an anticipatory fashion. The summation of what he was doing was soon to be seen. Israel would be saved.

Enthralled listeners found Jesus so riveting that they banded around him. He is remembered in the Gospels as attracting followers. These were of three principal types: crowds who wanted to see and hear him; disciples who decided to follow him around; and among disciples an inner circle of apostles. From the first two groups he chose a select group known as the Twelve. These 12 apostles became his primary collaborators in preaching his message. The number twelve operates symbolically in Jesus' life to recall the 12 patriarchs of Israel, and triggers even more a heightened expectation that the tribes of Israel will once more be restored in God's kingdom.

While alive, Jesus confined his activities to Israel. There are texts in the Gospels referring to him commanding apostles to 'Go into all the world and proclaim the good news to the whole creation' (Mk 16: 15), and to 'make disciples of all nations' (Mt 28: 19), but these jar with another tradition indicating that his activities were for the exclusive benefit of Israel: 'These twelve Jesus sent out with the following instructions: "Go nowhere among the Gentiles, and enter no town of the Samaritans, but go rather to the lost sheep of the house of Israel"' (Mt 10: 5–6). Both situations cannot have been the case: either Jesus wanted his activity and that of his apostles to be confined 'to the lost sheep of the house of Israel' or not. It is likely that after his death, when people who were not Jews wanted to join assemblies celebrating his memory, some of the evangelists lessened the embarrassment of Jesus' attention to Israel by creating a tradition of him looking outward to the world.

There is much more recorded in the Gospels about Jesus' words and deeds. His proclamation and behaviour centred around six major preoccupations: the faithful observation and interpretation of Torah; the announcement of God's kingdom; an understanding of God as a loving parent; the insistence that his followers should pray or talk to God; the denigration of wealth and siding with poor people; and care of the sick.

In the past, it has frequently been argued that Jesus dismissed the Jewish law and wanted to found a new religion. This case is illustrated, for example, by the charge that Jesus broke the Jewish stricture not to work on the Sabbath, thereby showing for all to see his insouciant disregard for the law. Such a view collapses once it is known that the Torah explains that God created the world in six days, and continued on a seventh: 'And on the seventh day God finished the work that he had done, and he *rested on the seventh day from all the work that he had done*' (Gen 2: 2). So God *worked and rested* on the seventh day. In John's Gospel Jesus is accused of infidelity to the Torah by healing on the seventh day of the week a man who had been ill for 38 years. When Jesus was confronted by Judaean Jewish leaders about this action, John reports that in his defence, Jesus said: 'My Father is still working and I also am working' (Jn 5: 17). In this text, Jesus successfully defends himself by alluding to a teaching in the Torah itself, which speaks of God 'finishing the work he had done' on 'the seventh day'.[68] He was not a saboteur of Torah, but one of its rival interpreters in first-century Palestine. He remained faithful to the challenges and strictures of the Mosaic Law, including fidelity to one God; devotion to Israel as God's People; male circumcision; observance of the Sabbath and dietary limitations; and, fatefully for Jesus, pilgrimage to the Temple if at all possible.

The Death of Jesus

In the week before Jesus died, he travelled to Jerusalem for the great festival of Passover. Because this feast celebrated the Israelites' escape from slavery, it could be an explosively tense time in Jerusalem whenever it was held. In Jesus' last week there, the Prefect Pontius Pilate was in residence at the Antonia fortress, having travelled from Caesarea Maritima no doubt to keep the peace. Pilate was the Prefect of Judaea from 26 to 36 CE.

Jesus and other pilgrims to Jerusalem needed to arrive days before Passover for ritual purification, which involved washing in ceremonial pools. Ritual purity is largely an alien concept for contemporary Westerners. It was not a matter of sin, but was still an impediment to worshipping in the Temple. Elements of daily life in Palestine that rendered people ritually impure were normally linked to processes of life and death. The Jewish contemporaries of Jesus in Palestine were rendered ritually impure if they touched a corpse, or because of the issue of bodily fluid such as semen or menstrual blood (Lev 12: 15; Num 19). A person could be rendered impure just by inadvertently touching someone else who had been become impure. Ritual cleansing in pools was a necessary requirement for returning to a pure state, and hence to be able to worship in the Temple.[69]

When Jesus entered Jerusalem with friends and followers, the city was governed cooperatively by the High Priest, Caiaphas and the Prefect. Both became aware of Jesus' presence. His following may have unwittingly drawn attention to him. He is thought to have created an affray in the Temple precincts by challenging the practices of selling animals for Temple sacrifice. Any political leader of ancient Palestine knew full well that the best way to avoid trouble in extremely tense situations is to isolate and eradicate potential trouble-making leaders without delay. The message of Jesus – the imminent arrival of God's kingdom – may have been an affront to Pilate. Any mention of a kingdom to unseat the emperor's ways could have sounded alarm bells. The High Priest and his cohort consorted with Pilate to deal with Jesus. Pilate obliged, and had Jesus crucified during the reign of Tiberius.

After the crucifixion, Jesus' closest followers and friends fled back to Galilee. The prophet of God's kingdom seemed himself to have been squashed, but his end was not the end. From it, the shoots of what later became Christianity began to sprout.

Who was Jesus?

Josephus instructs that Palestine in the first century was home to four main groups of Jews: Pharisees, Sadducees (*Ant.* 13.10 6), Essenes (*Ant.* 13.5.9) and Zealots (*JW* 4.3.9). Pharisees lived among Palestinians and interpreted the Mosaic Law. Jesus was not among them, but wandered as a rival, independent interpreter. Sadducees belonged to priestly lineages and did not include Jesus, nor did the ascetic Essenes of whom the New Testament never speaks. Jesus could not possibly have been a political Zealot because they were only formed as a movement of resistance to Rome in 66 CE. Collectively, all of these groups represented only a very small proportion of Palestinian Jews during the first century.

Since Jesus' death, he has been called by many honorific designations: 'The Christ', 'Son of God', 'Son of Man', 'Teacher', 'Lord' and 'Master'. One of the first designations used to pinpoint his distinctiveness was the title 'prophet' and historically, it is an apt tag. As a Galilean, Jesus enacted in his own life the preoccupations of the northern prophets Elijah and Elisha. Echoing Elijah, Jesus galvanized a group of 12 primary disciples to join him in preaching to Israel an urgent message of repentance. Why change one's life and repent of one's wrongdoing? Because finally and unequivocally, after centuries of imperial domination over Israel, God is coming in triumph to establish a kingdom among Israelites in which they will be healed, saved from perdition, and re-gathered into their Twelve Tribes. Whatever else the conceptual symbol of the kingdom of God signifies, it at least announces God's imminent arrival among the people of Israel for the purposes of saving them from peril and regathering their tribes. Finally and climactically, after humiliation in Babylon, following conquests by Assyrians, Chaldeans, Persians, Macedonians, Ptolemies and Seleucids, in the wake of King Herod's mischief, and in the midst of the kingdom of the Julio–Claudian emperors, God's kingdom was about to overturn all human iniquity and establish the Israelites, the People of God, in a commonwealth of equity, justice and love. Jesus was thus a prophet of apocalyptic ('revealing God') eschatology ('at the end of time'). Mark's Gospel, as previously indicated, captures his historical priorities in a nutshell: 'The time is fulfilled, and the kingdom of God has come near; repent and believe in the good news' (Mk 1: 15).

Yet Jesus the eschatological prophet was done in. He was destroyed on a Roman crossbeam of torture. The significance of his life has been ceaselessly interpreted and reinterpreted ever since. The story of Christianity is embedded in these interpretations, and begins to be unravelled in the next chapter.

Chapter II
Ancient Christianity

'The next day Jesus decided to go to Galilee.
He found Philip and said to him, "Follow me."'
John 1: 43

With Jesus dead, his friends must have been acutely dispirited and disorientated. Their state of mind can only be conjectured. What is certain is that they were bereft of their leader and teacher. What now? He had told them confidently in pithy parables that God's rule would dissipate the tyranny of imperious overlords and bullies, so as to inaugurate a divinely controlled and blissful social co-existence of peace, love, mercy and justice. His utopian vision was a flop. His announcement of an impending situation in which people would enjoy God's benevolence in a loving society has still not been realized among humans. However Jesus understood it, God's kingdom stands in abeyance. That does not mean he was deluded. The love, sacrifice, sharing and peace-making he countenanced were observable in his own life and remembered, indeed celebrated, by his friends. These gathered together frequently after his death in Galilee and Jerusalem to dwell on what he had told them. It is because of Jesus' immediate associates that he can be discussed by anyone today. They provide the channel of historical access to him for all subsequent generations. Had they not kept a reminiscence of him vibrant, and passed it on to their offspring, Christianity would never have evolved. He would thereby have been one more anonymous and forgotten carcass tossed aside on a pile of nobodies in the long tale of the triumph of executing empires.

This chapter charts the origins of Christianity in its ancient forms before the beginning of the Middle Ages. For most of the first century CE in Galilee and Judaea, people devoted to Jesus continued to worship as Jews. From roughly the middle of the century onwards, their ranks were swelled by Greek-speaking devotees who came from, or lived in, the Diaspora. As more Gentiles joined Jews who followed Jesus, dissimilarities and divisions soon arose between the two groups. Male Gentiles often saw no reason to be circumcised or to observe food purity laws. Those Jews who aligned themselves with the figure of Jesus confessed as Christ increasingly became regarded as deviants by other Jews. The gradual growth of discord between Torah-observant and Gentile enthusiasts of Jesus was the principal historical catalyst for the emergence of Christianity in contradistinction to Judaism.

The Destruction of the Temple

Another impulse was the destruction of the Temple in 70 CE. Judaeans began violently to resist their Roman overlords in 66 CE. The result of their uprising in the year 70 was that General Vespasian, under orders from Titus, lay siege to Jerusalem and razed its Temple. Judaism has never been the same since. The enormous variety of competing religious groups among Jews – including the Jesus enthusiasts – did not survive in the same way. The priestly cult of the Temple disappeared, and the principal groups to survive Rome's wrath were Pharisees and teachers of the Torah. These began to insist that their interpretations of the Torah were normative. Not everyone agreed. Around the year 90, synagogues directed by Pharisaic rabbis began expelling Jews who placed the religious vision of Jesus at the heart of their understanding of Judaism.[1] Once expelled, the enthusiasts of Jesus needed to form themselves into a cohesive group so as to keep alive and celebrate the memory of Jesus.

They were a messianic group. That is, they confessed that Jesus was a Christ, or messiah, sent by God to call humanity to change its ways. They reflected his intense apocalyptic anticipation of God's imminent judgement of the world, and expected the one they called 'Christ' to return gloriously to decide the fate of humankind (Mt 25: 31–46). Christians today still refer to the Second Coming of Christ when human history reaches its end.

The destruction of the Temple reconstructed by King Herod was a major event in the history of the world's religions. In its aftermath, two religious traditions evolved that have survived until now. These were Rabbinic Judaism and Christianity. Priestly sacrifice of animals among Jews disappeared with the obliteration of the Temple, as did cenobitic styles of Judaism typified by a community centred around caves in Qumran. Writings of these Jews, discovered in the twentieth century, were a major archaeological discovery because they include texts coeval with the life of Jesus and his devotees.

What is a Christian?

There are clear indications in the Bible that the word 'Christian' was coined during the first century CE. It appears in Acts 11: 26, which states that followers of Jesus were first called Christians in Antioch; in Acts 26: 28; and in 1 Pet 4: 14–16. The followers of Jesus initially designated themselves as disciples, saints or 'the Way'. People who were not among them were probably the first to designate them as Christians. The original meaning of 'Christian' is 'a follower of the Messiah'.[2] It later came to designate anyone who believed that Jesus was divine and human, and that God is triune. The latter kind of Christian arose in the fourth and fifth centuries CE. To call someone a Christian in the first century usually referred to a Jew in a small circle of Jews who all regarded themselves as disciples of the Messiah Jesus, and who struggled to make their voices heard in a rich variety of rival Jewish interpretations of the Torah.

Genetic Fallacies

Two historical fallacies regarding the genesis of Christianity are best avoided in any attempt to understand its origins. One is the idea that, like a tree sprouting from a mustard seed, Christianity's growth was inevitable and unimpeded. The other is the notion that Christianity originated in a pure, undifferentiated state without major discrepancies and disagreements among its followers. Both fallacies can commonly be found among the assumptions of contemporary Christians and in historical reconstructions of Christianity's origins.

The mustard-seed fallacy takes its name from a parable in Mark's Gospel, in which Jesus likens the kingdom of God to a seed:

> With what can we compare the kingdom of God, or what parable will we use for it? It is like a mustard seed, which, when sown upon

the ground, is the smallest of all the seeds on earth; yet when it is sown it grows up and becomes the greatest of all shrubs, and puts forth large branches, so that the birds of the air can make nests in the shade (Mk 4: 30–32).

In the hands of later Christian theologians and preachers the simile of a mustard seed was used to equate the kingdom of God with the Church. The birds of the air became Gentiles who would nest in the Church, and the growth of the Church was envisaged as an inevitable, unstoppable progress. What did transpire in the first and second centuries is that localized assemblies of Christians in the sense of followers of the Messiah developed their own, often starkly different, styles of worship, ways of living, and forms of theology.

The idea that Christianity since its origins has been a blissfully cohesive, uniform, monochromatic entity is dispelled by documents in the Bible. Paul could be a caustic, divisive person, as witnessed in a rebarbative comment he hurled at his opponents who, like him, were enthused by Jesus Christ. To those who insisted they were justified before God by observance of the Law rather than by their faith, Paul expressed the wish that they would castrate themselves (Gal 5: 12). In speaking of self-mutilation, Paul was building on an earlier allusion to cutting: 'You who want to be justified by the law have cut yourselves off from Christ; you have fallen away from grace' (Gal 5: 4). Diversity among those who responded favourably to the life of Jesus is also evident in the portraits of him provided by the Gospels.

Dispersal in the Diaspora

The Christ-confessors who had finally been expelled from synagogues during the late first century dispersed throughout the Roman Empire. By around 125 CE, their presence had been clearly noticed by Rome. During the early years of the second century, the Roman historian Tacitus referred to Jesus as 'Christus', and described him as the founder of 'a pernicious superstition' that originated in Judaea (*Annals* 15: 44). Again in the early second century, Pliny the Younger, the Roman governor of Bithynia, sent a letter to the emperor Trajan, explaining that followers of Jesus sang an antiphonal hymn 'to Christus as to a god' (*Epistles*, 10: 96). Seutonius, a contemporary Roman historian of Tacitus, noted that the emperor Claudius expelled Jews from Rome because, instigated by 'Chrestus', 'they continually caused unrest' (*De Vita Caesarum, Divus Claudius*, 25: 4). Christ-confessors, or Christians, persisted in drawing attention to themselves in the Roman Empire, and were a noted and watched presence in the cities of the Empire by the middle of the third century.[3]

These Christians formed clusters of domestic communities. By the early decades of the second century CE, they numbered about 100,000.[4] Statistically, they were a very minor presence in an empire of about 60–65 million people.[5] Recalling that there was no such reality as a middle class in the Roman Empire, the urban Christians of antiquity were mostly gathered in households of labourers and impoverished families. Their relationships were dyadic, not individualistic, and they were compelled by the fraught drama of staying alive to help each other find food and ward off diseases.

The Resurrection

The gradual emergence of Christianity in counterpoint to Judaism was further fanned by a strong belief concerning the final fate of Jesus. The recollection of him kept alive by those who met him was not merely a matter of fond reminiscence of a life once lived and then snuffed out. It also came to be sustained by an ardent belief that once killed by Romans, he was soon restored to a new life by God. No one saw this reported restoration to life, and the New Testament never and nowhere attempts to describe it. What survived were two types of stories consequent upon it: one recounting followers discovering that his body was no longer in the place in which it had been anointed and entombed after his crucifixion; another describing encounters between Jesus alive once more and his baffled followers. Stories of an empty tomb and appearances of Jesus to his friends after his death do not depict his actual return to life, but follow it chronologically, and struggle to account for the situation that his followers became convinced that he had not passed into oblivion. Their conviction came to be known as belief in Jesus' resurrection – a tenet according to which God raised his dead body to a new, transformed and glorified mode of existence. Belief in his resurrection is not faith in the resuscitation of a cadaver; it involves the conviction that Jesus' renewed mode of living was a transfigured, more glorified or divinely altered

state of existence. Strictly speaking, belief in resurrection is an eschatological (characteristic of the end times) tenet, and hence cannot be
adequately imagined in a mundane time–space continuum. Christians
today profess a hope that they will enter a similar divinely wrought
sphere of existence after their deaths, when God will resurrect their
bodies to a new remodelled life.

In the first century, no clear and final separation was obtained
between a Christian Church and synagogues. While the resurrection
became important for the followers of Jesus after his death, the genesis
of what became Christianity cannot be explained solely with reference
to belief in resurrection. This is so, firstly, because stories about people
appearing to others after their deaths in visions and dreams were
commonplace in ancient Hellenized cultures; and, secondly, there
were people who believed in and followed Jesus in his way of living
and believing before he was killed.[6] An example of an ancient cultural
readiness to believe in stories of killed people appearing to the living is
found in Book 2 of Virgil's *Aeneid*, which tells the story of the dead
Trojan prince Hector appearing in a dream to Aeneas.

The historical catalyst for the genesis of what grew into
Christianity was a two-fold historical link: first, between Jesus and
groups that banded around him; and second, between these groups
and later assemblies which survived them and initiated a long
historical chain of interpretations of Jesus' identity and worth. While
Jesus was not the founder of Christianity, it would never have
emerged had it not been for his ability humanly and religiously to
enthrall the friends and followers who enjoyed his company and
were transfixed by his words and deeds in Galilee.

Disciples and Apostles

Jesus was fond of inviting select individuals to join him in his
wanderings and way of living. A person who responded to him by
abandoning family ties and adopting an itinerant lifestyle was called a
disciple. The Greek word for 'disciples' is *mathētēs*, a masculine noun.
The disciples of Jesus included men as well as women from the very
beginning. The Gospels designate 12 men as an inner circle of primary apostles of Jesus. This circle is often simply called 'the Twelve'.
An apostle is a person sent forth to preach. The Synoptic Gospels
testify that the first apostles invited by Jesus to follow him were two

brothers, James and John, the sons of Zebedee. The James involved is not to be confused with Jesus' brother of the same name. Others invited by Jesus to join the Twelve were Andrew (originally a follower of John the Baptist) and Simon Peter. The eight additional members were Philip, Bartholomew, Matthew, Thomas, James the son of Alphaeus, Thaddaeus, Simon the Cananaean, and Judas Iscariot (Mk 3: 16–19). No one from Jesus' immediate family or any of his other relatives was among his circle of Twelve.

Not everyone Jesus called to be a disciple responded positively. Mark's Gospel recounts that an unnamed man 'who had many possessions' floundered when asked by Jesus to sell what he had, give the proceeds to the poor, and then follow Jesus (Mk 10: 17–22). The challenge issued by Jesus to sell possessions and give the profit to the poor has been the most widely ignored recorded instruction of Jesus by most Christians throughout the history of the Church.

Two groups of women are noted as following Jesus. Mark's Gospel names Mary Magdalene, Mary the mother of James the younger and Josus, and Salome (Mk 15: 40–41). Luke's Gospel speaks of Susanna, Mary Magdalene and Joanna, who was married to an Herodian steward called Chuza (Lk 8: 2–3).

After the death of Jesus, his disciples banded around a few authoritative leaders based in Jerusalem. Paramount among these were James, the brother of Jesus, and John, the son of Zebedee. John's Gospel highlights the significance of a disciple in the Jerusalem community with the description 'the one whom Jesus loved' (Jn 13: 23; 19: 26). Bands of followers gathered wherever Jesus and his primary apostles camped and spoke. Those who first knew him after he had left home were, like himself, Galilean Jews. They remained as such even after his death. They came primarily from regions to the north of the Lake of Gennesaret. Other followers had their base in Jerusalem. After his death, many of his followers returned from the celebration of Passover in Jerusalem, to take up once more in Galilee the families and trades they left behind to follow Jesus in his quest to convince Israel of God's impending rule.

Within five years of Jesus' execution, groups of his followers had regrouped in Jerusalem. They shared four principal features. They were all fervent Jewish monotheists; they continued to live under Roman and Herodian rule; they recounted the sayings and stories of Jesus as they ate together; and they interpreted him as a messiah who would return to their midst to inaugurate the end of time and a passage to paradise. The Greek word for an assembly of Jesus' followers in Jerusalem is *ekklēsia*, translated in English as an assembly or church. The word 'synagogue' also means 'assembly'. It is important not to regard anachronistically the assemblies of the people who first believed that Jesus had been resurrected as if they resembled communities of Christians today. The primary difference between contemporary churches and the first Jesus-assemblies in Palestine is that the former do not profess the sum total of Jewish beliefs of either the latter or of Jesus. There were no clearly recognizable Christians split irrevocably from Judaism in Palestine for most of the first century after the beginning of the reckoning of time.

Assembles grouped around James, Peter and John began to mark their identity by practising baptism for newcomers, and by gathering to enjoy meals commemorating Jesus' final supper before he died. These groupings were eventually designated with names like 'the saints' (Rom 15: 26; 2 Cor 8: 4; 9: 1, 12; Acts 9: 13, 32, 41; 26: 10) or 'the assembly (or church) of God' (*ekklēsia tou theou*; 1 Thess 2: 14; 1 Cor 15: 19; Gal 1: 13; Phil 3: 6).[7]

Paul

A contemporary of Jesus, living in the city of Tarsus in Cilicia (to the north of Syria, now in Turkey), became one of Jesus' greatest champions. His Hebrew name was Saul. He became known as Paul in Hellenized settings. Unusually for a Jew of his time, Paul was a Roman citizen. Tarsus was a major ancient city. Mark Antony and Cleopatra of Egypt met there. As a Jew of the Diaspora, Paul was raised in a Greek-speaking environment and received a good education in his local synagogue. As an adult he travelled to Jerusalem where he studied the Torah. When he heard of the activities of Jesus' followers he became antagonistic to the point of hounding them.[8]

Paul was not a Christian, but a Jew who became convinced that Jesus was God's anointed one. This led to him having to explain and balance a relation between his faith in Jesus the Messiah and the Law. This balance is seen in his Letter to the Galatians, wherein he can say: 'in Christ Jesus neither circumcision nor uncircumcision counts for anything' (Gal 5: 6); and a few verses later: 'why am I still being persecuted if I am still preaching circumcision?' (Gal 5: 11).

While travelling to Damascus in Syria, Paul recounted that he became intensely aware of Jesus Christ's presence to him, and he likened his unusual experience, which came to be called his Damascene conversion, to the experiences of disciples who attested that they had seen the Risen Jesus. It is disputed whether their 'seeing' involved ocular perception, or was more akin to a new awareness in their thinking, as in 'now I see what it meant', or 'now I grasp his worth'.

After Paul's change of heart on the way to Damascus he spent the rest of his life travelling in Asia Minor, visiting communities of other Jews who interpreted their faith along lines sketched by Jesus. His letters were occasional documents written to specific assemblies of Christ-confessors in the Roman Empire with problems that had arisen in their communities. A tradition survives that he was beheaded in Rome in the mid-60s CE during the reign of Nero.

Paul never met Jesus, or at least no historical record of a meeting between the two survives. He still remains a primary historical witness to Jesus' life for the simple reason that he came to know very well both Peter, who had accompanied Jesus in his travels, and James, Jesus' brother.

Paul is occasionally described as the founder of Christianity, but this is attributing too much to him for two reasons. First, there were Jews prepared to spend their lives preaching about Jesus, and to instruct their children in things he had said, before Paul's Damascene transformation. And second, Paul's own writings indicate that he expected an immanent end to the world. For him, the resurrection of Jesus was the first stage of a general resurrection of all the dead that would clearly signal the world's end.

The earliest document bearing witness to Jesus is Paul's First Letter to the Thessalonians. Paul's letters are strikingly different from the Gospels. They show little interest in details of Jesus' life, and talk more about him than what he talked about, especially God's kingdom. Paul's primary ambition was to preach and instruct that Jesus the Christ died to reconcile a sinful humanity with God, and that God subsequently raised him to a new life.

Paul regarded his credentials as a Jew as faultless: 'If anyone else has reason to be confident in the flesh, I have more: circumcised on the eighth day, a member of the people of Israel, of the tribe of Benjamin, a Hebrew born of Hebrews; a Pharisee; as to zeal, a persecutor of the church; as to righteousness under the law, blameless' (Phil 3: 4b–6). Paul did not reject the Law, but downplayed its significance in his life compared with his faith in Christ. He became eager to allow Gentiles to regard themselves as saved from God's wrathful judgement if they professed faith in the Risen Christ. 'Yet whatever gains I had', he says, 'these I have come to regard as loss because of the surpassing value of knowing Christ Jesus my Lord' (Phil 3: 7–8). For such a stance, Paul has often been labelled as the founder of Christianity. That once more is claiming too much for him because he wrote to and for the benefit of specific communities in Asia Minor. His writings were not intended as a blueprint for a world religion.[9]

Jesus As Sent By God

By the final third of the first century, Christ-confessors had attracted devotees around the Roman Empire who were neither Judaean nor Aramaic-speakers. In the decades immediately following Jesus' death, nothing has survived that was written about him. Stories about his life and deeds circulated among the largely illiterate peasants of Palestine. Orally transmitted narratives concerning Jesus were transformed over time so that particular audiences could respond better to them. Then they were recorded in written form.

A clear indicator that by the 50s CE, and decades immediately following, Christ-confessors who were not Galilean or Judaean had joined Jesus assemblies, especially in the Diaspora, lies with the writings in Greek that form the 27 texts of the New Testament. These texts were not originally composed as chapters in a book, but as documents circulated among communities.

None of them was penned in the language spoken by Jesus. All of them are interpretations of his life and legacy cast in the verbal and conceptual categories of the Hellenized Roman Empire. They are replete with theologies that strive to explain Jesus' identity, significance and teachings in relation to God.

The theologies mix Hebraic and Greek concepts in their attempts to interpret the significance and superlative worth of Jesus pondered in relation to God. A golden thread unifying the texts of the New Testament is the idea that Jesus was sent by God among people to save them from eternal damnation. This theme unifies honorific titles predicated of Jesus. He is called *Kyrios*, Lord (as the emperor was); Master; Teacher; Prophet; Christ (or Messiah); Son of God; and Son of Man.

One of the more remarkable titles accorded Jesus is that of *logos* ('word' or 'reason'), a concept borrowed by early proto-Christian writers from ancient Stoic philosophy. For Stoics, the *logos* was 'the universal rational principle permeating and organizing the material world'.[10] John's Gospel begins in the same way as the Book of Genesis: 'In the beginning ...' (Gen 1: 1; Jn 1: 1). In the opening poetic lines of the Gospel, Jesus is identified as the eternal Logos who pitched a tent among human beings. The notion became one of the more prominent Christian teachings: Jesus was an historical embodiment of an eternal Godhead, otherwise labelled as the incarnation. The Latin word for flesh is *carnis*: in Jesus, so the doctrine asserts, God was enfleshed.

John's theology of Jesus, interpreted as the incarnate Logos, came to dominate later Christian theology more than any other notion in the New Testament. It also led to major splits between Christian groups. Identifying Jesus with divinity is problematical. To say that in the beginning was the Logos, and the Logos was with God, and the Logos was God generates further questions. In the Greek original of the first verse of John, the text states that the *logos* was with 'the God' and the Logos was God. It is unclear whether the phrase 'with God' might mean that the Logos, Jesus, shared the same status as God, or if it signifies in the mind of John's author(s) that there was a High God and a lesser God, the Logos.

The text is ambiguous. So too are other passages in the New Testament that appear to identify Jesus as a divinity. None of them is unambiguous.[11] Take the vignette of the Apostle Thomas, recognizing the identity of the Risen Jesus and saying to him: 'My Lord, and my God.' While that may appear as a straightforward declaration that Jesus was or is God, it need only be recalled that 'My Lord and my God' was also a form of address for the emperor, and no Christian would regard the emperor as God.

The Apostolic Writings

As embryonic Christianity spread throughout the Mediterranean heartlands during the second and third centuries, it often attracted scornful and aggressive comment from pagan writers. These challenged Christians to give an intellectually intelligible account of their beliefs and patterns of living. The pagans' challenges produced a body of Christian apostolic and apologetic writings. 'Apostolic' refers to writings thought by Christians after the second century to date from a time when the last of the Twelve Apostles was still alive. 'Apologetic' refers to authors bent on providing a defence or apology for Christian life. Well-known apologists were Justin Martyr (c. 100–c. 165) and Athenagoras (late second century). Another body of extra-biblical writings devoted to Jesus was also penned in the last stages of the first century and during the second. These are known as the texts of the Apostolic Fathers. These include two letters bearing the name of Clement (a leader in Rome); seven letters by Ignatius; a letter by Polycarp, coupled with a depiction of his martyrdom; a brief text called the Didache (Teaching); a letter to Dionetus with an unnamed author; and a lengthy text called the *Shepherd of Hermas*. Collectively these documents are called 'Apostolic' writings because later Christians believed they were composed before the death of the last member of the Twelve Apostles. A later authoritative creed known as the Apostles' Creed does not date from the first century or from the Twelve, but was composed as a testament of Christian faith. It appears mentioned among Christians around 390 CE.

Syria

After the Jewish revolt against Rome between 66 and 70 CE, a group of Judaean Christ-confessors left Jerusalem to live in Pella in the Decapolis. There they came into greater contact with Gentiles and began to attract pagan converts. Other communities settled in Syria, 'the cradle of early Christianity'.[12] By the third century CE, Christians had become an important part of Syria's population. Antioch and Damascus became the bases for Christian communities. The Roman Legate was stationed in Antioch, which was thus a major Syrian hub of military administration.

Matthew's Gospel may well have been composed for the benefit of Antioch's Christ-confessors. It is directed at an audience that existed under difficult economic constraints. In the contemporary West, wherein large segments of society enjoy health and financial prosperity, it is easy massively to underestimate the vicissitudes endured by 97–98 per cent of the populace of the Roman Empire, including the people of Syria:

> Most inhabitants of Antioch lived in atrocious and cramped conditions marked by noise, filth, squalor, garbage, human excrement, animals, disease, fire risk, crime, social and ethnic conflicts, malnutrition, natural disasters (especially flooding), and unstable dwellings (Seneca, *Ep.* 56; Martial, *Epig.* 12.57).

Fear and despair were pervasive. The life expectancy of most people was low: for men, 25–40 years; less for women. Infant mortality was high: about 28 per cent born alive in Rome died within a year; 50 per cent did not survive a decade. The poor comprised Matthew's people.[13]

To take stock, the first major grouping of Jesus' devotees after his death was centred in Jerusalem. After its destruction, the most important base for devotees was Syria, especially the cities of Antioch, Damascus and Caesarea.[14]

The Growth of Structure

With the beginning of the second century, Christianity in forms still recognizable today began to take shape. In this century, the legacy of the deviant first-century Jews who styled themselves as followers of a Messiah called Jesus began to crystallize into a new religion. By the end of the century, it is possible to speak of Christianity that was directed by leaders who assumed specific functions within communities. Prominent among these were overseers, or bishops, who were the principal leaders and teachers in local areas called dioceses (a Roman term). The bishops were helped by deacons and presbyters. This three-fold pattern of leadership and community service still obtains in many Churches at present. The bishops of the second century were not monarchical in the way bishops can be today. They knew the people they served and taught, and could not be appointed to oversee the welfare of an assembly without the people's consent.[15]

At this stage of Christianity's evolution, women were active in teaching, preaching, leading communities, prophesying and caring for the poor. Members of communities participated in its life by using particular skills and gifts they enjoyed. Some worked with the infirm.

Others taught children. All gathered regularly to share their religious interests.[16]

All was not unencumbered serenity among Christians of the second century. Their number grew throughout the second century, and by its end there were Christians in Spain.[17] These and others were keen to disseminate their faith in Jesus Christ, but were not always able to agree on the pivot of their faith. As soon as there are interpretations of Jesus' significance, there are also conflicts of interpretations. During and after the second century, clear disparities between religious dispositions emerged among Christians, as did a tendency for groups to slight their opponents. The second to the fifth centuries constituted a period of intense disputation among Christians about what ought to be the nature and content of their beliefs.

Gnosticism

One understanding of nascent Christianity that proved contentious has been given the modern label of Gnosticism, which refers to a world-view prevalent in antiquity announcing that human beings are saved by an esoteric knowledge (from Greek, *gnosis*, 'knowledge'). Gnostics tended to believe that creation is the accomplishment of a demiurge, or lesser deity, together with his minions, called *archons*. Humans are trapped in matter, but they can escape their condition and find God if a redeemer reveals knowledge to them. Gnosticism predates Christianity, but when the knowledge-revealing redeemer at its core is identified with Jesus, Christian Gnosticism prevails.[18]

The study of Gnosticism in North Africa was impelled considerably by the discovery in 1945 of a small library of gnostic texts in Upper Egypt. They are now known as the Nag Hammadi manuscripts. Valentinus (c. 100–c. 153) was a gnostic who came to prominence in the second century. He was based in Alexandria and taught that Jesus did not rise bodily from the dead. The core belief unifying gnostics was a conviction that matter and physicality are evil, a belief over which they fell out with other Christians. Eventually, they were condemned as heretics by Church councils because the belief that matter is evil jars with the more common belief among Christians that creation is good, as well as being good enough for God to become active in it in human form.[19]

Trouble With Emperors: Christianity as a Persecuted Underling

Even though Christians of antiquity were a tiny minority in the Roman Empire, they were sizeable enough to elicit the ire of emperors. In 250 CE, the emperor Decius started to persecute Christians. His hounding of them did not last long, but constituted the first notable imperial persecution of Christians. Nero had been nasty to Christ-followers in the first century. Decius' successor, Valerian, continued to persecute between 257 and 260 CE.

The fourth century began with a determined imperial effort to obliterate Christians: in 303 CE, the emperor Diocletian ordered another persecution of Christians.[20]

A by-product of imperial killing of Christians was the burgeoning of a cult of Christian saints and martyrs. Originally, a saint was a baptized person. The community of saints was the sum total of baptized people. A martyr was a witness: a person who would endure death rather than renounce faith in Jesus the Messiah. Not all saints became martyrs. One who did was a Roman soldier called Sebastian. His cult is still popular in Mediterranean lands today. He is normally depicted in art – paintings, reliefs and statues – as a dying, nearly naked young man, tied to a stake, and whose body is riddled with arrows.

Cults of saints and martyrs nourished the lives of believers around the Empire. Pilgrimages and trade in relics thrived in late antiquity. A pilgrimage involved a journey, often long and precarious, to visit the burial site of a saint or martyr. People throughout the Empire bought relics of saints to keep on their bodies or in their homes. A relic was frequently a tiny part of a dead saint's remains, like a chip of bone or a lock of hair.

The practice of treasuring relics may seem repulsive and ghoulish to many today, but it is perfectly understandable anthropologically and religiously. Venerating relics is a standard practice in nearly all of the world's ancient religions. To be near a portion of a person who was recognized as holy, or close to God, or to be at the burial site of such a person, was to be brought into closer physical contact with an unseen God. Relics were popular ciphers between the divine and the human. And they were hugely profitable for those who traded in them. Their sale generated notorious instances of fraud.

East and Greek, West and Latin

The development of Christianity in the third century was directly affected by major political instability in the Roman Empire. Gothic and Germanic armies made frequent incursions into Roman territory from the North, while the Sassanian Persians in the East posed an additional threat.[21]

Christianity nowadays is often labelled or lamented as a Western phenomenon, but up until and including the seventh century, its heartlands lay in Asia and Africa, not Europe. The Asia intended here is not the Far East, but ancient Asia Minor (contemporary Syria/Turkey). Contemporary Christianity is also correctly observed to include thousands of distinct Churches, often aligned on national grounds, and speaking an array of diverse languages. The divisions – regional, territorial, cultural and linguistic – that obtain among Christians now stem in large part from corporate separations that unfolded in the Late Roman Empire.

The reign of the emperor Diocletian (284–305) is often associated with the beginning of the Empire's late phase. During this period, rule of the Empire was not exclusively autocratic. Power could be shared by a number of dominant emperors, who enjoyed the title of 'Augustus', supported by subservient emperors called 'Caesars'.[22] Such a sharing of jurisdiction was balanced by a period in which a single emperor governed. For much of the fourth century, 'Romans' (inhabitants of the Empire) were ruled by three principal emperors – Constantine (306–37), Constantius II (337–61) and Theodosius I (379–95).

Upon Theodosius' death in 395, the Empire was split into two major regions – East and West. Theodosius was the last emperor to rule both. After him, each part was governed by a separate imperial ruler. Greek was the dominant language of the Eastern Empire, while Latin was the regnant tongue in the West. Constantinople (modern Istanbul) served as the administrative centre of the Eastern Empire, while Africa was directed from Alexandria. The Western Empire continued to be governed from Rome. The Churches of principal regions were overseen by senior clerics called patriarchs. Rome, Constantinople and Alexandria were all patriarchates.

With linguistic division arose distinct though related bodies of religious and theological literature. While Latin was the exclusive

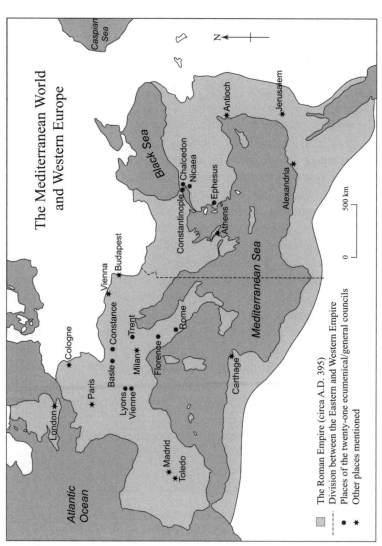

The Mediterranean World
and Western Europe

Caspian Sea

Atlantic Ocean

London
Cologne
Paris
Basle ● Constance
Lyons ●
Vienne ●
Milan ●
Madrid ★
Toledo ★
Florence ●
Trent ●
Rome ●
Carthage ★
Vienna ★
Budapest ★
Black Sea
Constantinople ● Chalcedon
Nicaea ●
Ephesus ●
Athens ★
Antioch ★
Jerusalem ★
Alexandria ★
Mediterranean Sea

N

0   500 km

The Roman Empire (circa A.D. 395)
Division between the Eastern and Western Empire
Places of the twenty-one ecumenical/general councils
Other places mentioned
■

●
★

Map 5: The divided Roman Empire

official language in the West, Semitic languages, especially Syriac, were used apart from Greek in the East.

As Eastern forms of Christianity grew in Africa, they encouraged the use of languages apart from Greek. In the patriarchate of Alexandria, Coptic religious literature evolved in association with Greek and Latin. Coptic Christians started Churches in Ethiopia and the Sudan. The Ethiopian Church became well established between the fourth and the sixth centuries. It generated its own literature in Ge'ez, or Ethiopic.[23]

The West dominated Christian life and thought during the Middle Ages and the modern period, so much so that it is easy to forget that Christianity in its origins and growth was initially Eastern. Even great currents of Latin theology were generated in the East. Africa alone produced great Latin-speaking theologians, one of the earliest of whom was the bishop Tertullian (c. 160–c. 225) in Carthage. Another and later Latin-speaking theologian in North Africa was Augustine (354–430), the bishop of Hippo. If Tertullian was the North African father of all later Latin theology, another North African, called Origen (185–c. 254), may be regarded as the parent of later Greek Christian theology.[24]

The political and geographical changes of the late fourth-century Empire were not mere historical curiosities. They directly affected the lives of all Christians who lived in the ensuing 16 centuries, until now. The most basic of all Christian doctrines, those concerning God and Jesus Christ, and the fate of human beings, were all formulated officially in the East during the first seven centuries. Divisions between Churches arose constantly because of disagreements on these doctrines and how to formulate them. Discord over doctrines was not prevalent simply among emperors and bishops. It unsettled all varieties of members in churches throughout the Empire. When Christians gathered to meet in councils or synods in the third century to discuss what was appropriate for them to believe and to do, their numbers included linen-workers, actors and athletes.[25]

Households, Locality and Variety

During the first three centuries of the Common Era, both Jewish Christ-confessors and Christians endured difficult, poor lives. Throughout this time, there was no universal authority governing all those devoted to Jesus Christ. In the second and third centuries, more than 95 per cent of Christians were labourers – in households, fields, vineyards and workhouses for making crafts. They decided what to believe and how to live religiously on a local basis. Very few Christians were people of means, and fewer still were highly educated. Most were illiterate and so locally bound that they rarely travelled long distances. Life for all was precarious. The majority of Christians were preoccupied with running households and raising households. Women who became pregnant endangered themselves. If they survived childbirth, they began a daily struggle to keep their offspring alive until and beyond the age of five. By the time a child in the Early and Late Roman Empire reached the age of ten, 50 per cent of his or her birth cohort were dead.[26]

In view of the large, centrally controlled and international nature of many Christian Churches today, it is easy to overlook that Christians of antiquity managed activities in churches consensually and locally. Where bishops and presbyters served communities, they were held accountable to the people to whom they preached. In the fourth century, a bishop in Alexandria was lynched for irritating his people.[27] Most presbyters, deacons and bishops were married, and most worked to earn money to support themselves.

Because churches of late antiquity were locally autonomous, yet related with other churches in their wider region, an enormous variety obtained among them with regard to the languages they used, the beliefs they preferred, and the forms of liturgy they developed.

It is potentially startling for contemporary Christians, who normally worship in specially constructed buildings for the exclusive use of worship, that Christians before the fourth century met to worship in households. The early Church was thus thoroughly domestically based.

Theologians as Local Leaders

While this book is primarily focused on Christianity concretized in people's lives and not on theology, the historical unfolding of Christianity during its nascent centuries was moulded by adroit Christian thinkers, as well as by hordes of nameless peasants and artisans. These thinkers were educated enough to be able to write so that their observations could be disseminated. They were not, of course, university professors, but themselves struggling Christians trying to work out the implications of their faith in the Late Roman Empire. Many of them combined their scholarly work with responsibilities as leaders in local Christian assemblies. Augustine functioned as both a bishop and magistrate in Hippo. Origen was an intellectual giant of the third century. Educated in Alexandria, he excelled at writing hundreds of treatises and sermons, and enjoyed an intimate acquaintance with Hebrew and Greek biblical texts. He was martyred in 254.[28]

The writing of theologies from roughly the second to the sixth centuries (or eighth at a stretch) is remembered as an era of theological 'Masters' or 'Fathers' – the patristic age for short. The thought of the Fathers gained wide acceptance among Christians in the East and West. Their ideas informed several councils of bishops that promulgated doctrines seeking to specify the features of Christian faith. The patristic age produced the doctrines of the Trinity (there is One God in Three Persons) and the full divinity (as well as the true humanity) of Jesus Christ.

Patristics

The Fathers of the Church were theologians of the early post-biblical age who wrote in Greek, Latin, Armenian or Syric. Prominent among them were Irenaeus (c. 130–c. 200); Gregory of Nyssa (c. 330–c. 395); John Chrysostom (c. 347–407); Gregory of Nazianzus (329/30–389/90); Ambrose (c. 339–97); Augustine of Hippo (354–430); Leo the Great (d. 461); and Gregory the Great (c. 540–604). The study of their *theological* thought is designated as **patristics** (from the Latin, *pater*, meaning 'father'). By contrast, **patrology** is the study of the *historical* context and *literary* styles of the Fathers' writings. Notice the complete absence of women from the gallery of the early Church's theological lodestars.

A colourful example of a Christian, who served his community as a bishop, theologian and politician, was Ambrose of Milan (c. 339–97). Together with Saints Jerome (c. 345–420), a biblical scholar, Augustine and Gregory the Great, Saint Ambrose is revered as one of the four great Doctors ('Teachers') of the Latin Church. He was born into a Roman senatorial family, and subsequently appointed to the imperial government of Milan in northern Italy. For a century after 305, Milan, not Rome, was the seat of imperial jurisdiction. It was from Milan that the Emperor Constantine ended persecutions of Christians. In 374, Ambrose was chosen by popular consent to be Milan's bishop. In that role he exerted far more influence over Milan than he could have as an administrative functionary.[29]

Is God One or Three?

The Jewish followers of Jesus, like Jesus himself, were monotheists. They believed that there is only one God who is the living Creator of the world, present to Israel and active in its history, smiting its adversaries and punishing its sinners. Belief in the oneness of God continued to be asserted by the Apostolic Fathers (mentioned above) and Christian followers. They needed to attest that there is only one God in counterpoint to contemporaneous paganism, or polytheism. Christians of antiquity normally baptized initiates with a formula invoking the Father (Creator), the Son (Jesus), and the Holy Spirit (of the Risen Jesus). What baptismal formulas did not specify in the second century were the precise relationships obtaining between Father, Son, and Spirit. Are the three all part of God? Are there three Gods? Or might there be a three-fold dynamism within God? The third century was a time when such relationships were ardently thrashed out by communities and their theologians. How could the oneness of God be maintained, if Christians kept referring to God as Father, Son, and Holy Spirit?

The answer to that question was one of the most famous and debated of all Christian dogmas – the Trinity. This doctrine asserts that there is indeed one God who is Triune. The Latin word for Trinity or Triune is 'trinitas', and it was coined by Tertullian. John McGuckin, an historian of the Church, explains how the teaching of God as Triune can be understood, and he does so by relying on the Eastern theologian, Gregory of Nazianzus. God, according to Gregory,

> is to be acknowledged as being one in nature, and three in hypostasis. The three hypostases (persons, or subsistent entities), are each possessed of the same nature (or being). The diversity appears in the manner in which the contingent world experiences the unapproachable God. God is unapproachable in his essence, but reaches out to the created world by means of his hypostases. Thus, the Father who 'begets' the Logos, and 'sends out' the Holy Spirit is the solitary cause

of the Trinity. This justifies Christians claiming to believe in only one God. The Father's hypostatic existence is explained as the sole cause of the other two, and as such he is the ground of unity of the divine being. … The Trinity is fundamentally the outreach of its cause: that is the Father's dynamic concern to draw all creatures back to himself, through the Son, in the Spirit.[30]

What the doctrine of the Trinity might mean involves the crucial issue of Jesus' identity in relation to the Father God in whom he believed. Disputes over that issue came to a head in the fourth century, and now need to be unravelled a little.

Constantine and Theodosius I

Before the fourth century, Christian communities around the Empire needed to be wary when meeting together or while travelling. They could still be unpopular enough to be hounded by imperial policies. Their lot was made easy when Constantine became emperor. In 313 he decreed that Christianity was to be tolerated in the Empire. He moved the seat of the Empire from Rome to Byzantium in 333. Churches of the East are often called 'Byzantine', after the city of Byzantium. Its name was changed to Constantinople in 333. It was seized by Muslim Turks in 1453 and is now called Istanbul.

Constantine's toleration of Christianity was only an initial impulse to impel it into transforming from a minor persecuted web of local communities to a religion of confidence. A second impulse came with Theodosius I. He went further than Constantine by taking the hitherto unthinkable step of outlawing pagan worship in the Empire. More than that, after Theodosius, Christian emperors strengthened the hand of bishops, priests and deacons by creating an *ordo clericorum* – order of clerics.[31] While Roman aristocrats could enjoy the privilege of belonging to either the Senatorial or Equestrian orders, now it was possible to speak of a third hierarchical group, the clergy.

'Hierarchy' technically means 'rule by priests'. It is not a recognizably ancient Greek or modern Western form of government. With and after Constantine and Theodosius, Christianity was not merely saved from extinction. It also became imperial itself. Much of it remained so, as Christendom, for the next 1500 years. Christendom is a socio-cultural manifestation of Christianity that has two primordial features. First, in a society marked by Christendom, all people almost without exception assent intellectually to tenets of Christian faith; and second, such a society enjoys the legal, political and military might of a state or ruling power.

An Antidote to Imperialism – Martin of Tours

The history of Christianity in the Late Roman Empire is more than a tale of the emergence of a Christian Empire. It also involves refreshing instances of individuals who were determined to live in the same way Jesus had spent his life, demonstrating love for the poor. One of these people was Martin of Tours (316–97). Such was his eventual popularity among later Christians that he was one of the very few Christians of antiquity to be declared a saint without martyrdom. As a child, Martin lived in Italy where his father served in the imperial army. Following his father, Martin became a soldier. During his time in the army he converted to Christianity. He was baptized in 354 and thereafter sought to live as a hermit. He attracted too much local attention for that and moved to Milan. He was then ordained a bishop in Gaul in 371 and appointed to the See of Tours.[32]

Martin showed not the slightest interest in the regalia of an imperially sanctioned bishopric and instead dressed as peasants did. Rather than residing in a house reserved for the Bishop of Tours, he went to live in a monastery that he established outside the city. From his base he worked tirelessly to help his people and to combat paganism. After his death, several miracles were attributed him and his fame spread throughout Europe. A cult of Martin soon became international. In the mid-sixth century, Agnellus, the Archbishop of Ravenna (556–69), dedicated to Martin a palace church that had been built by the Ostrogothic monarch Theodoric (493–526). The church, which is now called S. Appollinare Nuovo, contains a large mosaic depicting a procession of crowned saints headed by Martin. When Martin died, he was entombed in Tours' western suburbs, but several decades later Perpetuus, one of his episcopal successors in Tours, built a church over the tomb.[33]

Crises Over Christ

With Constantine as emperor, Christian leaders could meet with much greater ease. They needed to by 325 CE. By then a dispute had arisen in the Eastern Church, concerning the identity of Jesus Christ in relation to God the Father. It constituted a major crisis among Christians of the period. So grave was this turmoil that Constantine invited bishops to attend a meeting in Nicaea, to see if a solution could be found. The crisis was precipitated by the ideas of a clever and popular presbyter or priest called Arius. He was based in Alexandria of North Africa, in the parish of Baucalis. A parish among Christians was then and remains now a local region with its own church building and clergy. A city could have several parishes.

Arius began to draw attention to himself with his preaching around 319. His central idea which sparked controversy was his conclusion that there must have been a time when there was no Logos (Christ). Jesus had been identified with the Logos at the outset of John's Gospel. Arius suggested that Christ the Logos had a beginning: only God the Father Creator could be worshipped as eternal and unoriginated (devoid of origin). He concluded that Christ was pre-eminent among humans, but like them must have been created. He could not as a consequence be identified unequivocally with God.[34] By this stage, other Christians in the Empire had begun to accept that Jesus could be identified with God the Father Creator as God the Son.

Constantine saw that the crisis of faith sparked by Arius needed to be calmed. To enter a crisis is to stand at a crossroads. A crisis is an impasse. Facing it, a decision needs to be made about the best direction in which to go. Crises of faith have bedevilled Christians throughout their history. Of the multiple crises until now, four stand out as more severe and debilitating than others. The first continued from the first until the fifth century, and focused on the question of Jesus' identity in relation to God. The second occurred in the eleventh century when the Eastern and Western Churches split. This schism (formal separation) was followed by another crisis and schism within the Western Church with the Protestant Reformation of the sixteenth century. The fourth severe crisis marks a return to the question impelling the first – Jesus' identity. It started in the seventeenth century when Jesus began to be investigated with historical rather than theological methods, and it continues unabated today.

Creeds and Councils

Faced with crises, followers of Jesus since the first century have met in assemblies to thrash out their differences. The New Testament mentions one of the first and calls it the Council of Jerusalem. It was attended by Paul and Peter and members of the Jerusalem assembly of Jesus-enthusiasts, to decide whether they should follow a path of allowing people who had not been circumcised to join them, or to demand that they be circumcised as a condition for entering their community. Paul and Peter agreed to allow the non-circumcised to join their circle.

Throughout the history of the Church, major gatherings of Christians, especially of their leaders, meeting to resolve disputes, have been called either councils or synods. The two words are largely synonymous, but derive from different languages. 'Synod' stems from Greek (σύνοδος; transliterated as *synodus*), and 'council' from Latin (*concilium*). Both terms mean 'assembly'. And they both connote journeys or following a path, as would be needed by a group when coming upon a crossroads. 'Synod' in Greek is a compound of two words: σύν, 'together'; and ὁδός, 'journey' or 'way'. In the words of the historian Norman Tanner, 'the sense is that of an assembly of travelling companions, people meeting for a purpose, with a partly unknown future before them, in hope and expectation: a beautiful image of the pilgrim church'.[35]

There have been at least 21 major councils in Christianity's life, and a host of lesser ones. Councils that involved participants from the East and West were called 'ecumenical', 'involving the whole inhabited world'. Those attended solely by Westerners could be termed 'general', 'involving participates from a part of the world, and not universally inclusive'.

The Councils of the Church – General and Ecumenical

Councils take their name from the location in which they convened. The first eight were ecumenical (involving delegates from 'the inhabited world' (Greek: *oikoumene*). While they were conducted in Greek and included Eastern bishops, their authority was later recognized by the Western Church. The medieval and modern councils, although often styled as 'ecumenical', may also be regarded as general though not all-inclusive, because of their insufficient representation by bishops not in communion with the Bishop of Rome.[36] Eighteen councils were held before the advent of Protestantism (see Chapter VI), and no Protestant has ever been able to vote in either an ecumenical or general council. Vatican I was the first council to address at length the theme of divine revelation. It was the first episcopal assembly to be convened after the French Revolution and the Enlightenment, during which the bases of the Church's authority, including deference to revelation, were increasingly dismissed.

Greek and Early	Latin and Medieval	Latin, Baroque and Modern
Nicaea I (325)	Lateran I (1123)	Trent (1545–63)
Constantinople I (381)	Lateran II (1139)	Vatican I (1869–70)
Ephesus (431)	Lateran III (1179)	Vatican II (1962–65)
Chalcedon (451)	Lateran IV (1215)	
Constantinople II (553)	Lyons I (1245)	
Constantinople III (680–81)	Lyons II (1274)	
Nicaea II (787)	Vienne (1311–12)	
Constantinople IV (869–70)	Constance (1414–18)	
	Basil–Florence (1431–45)	
	Lateran V (1512–17)	

Good Christians

To the question 'What is entailed in living as a good Christian?', no unrivalled answer has ever been given. By the fourth century, a large spectrum of responses vied for credibility. For some, a good Christian forsakes marriage and family ties. For others, giving possessions to the poor is the criterion that marks an estimable Christian. Thinking in a particular way was nominated by others. The more distant in time people became from the era when Jesus was alive, the more difficult it was for them to be sure of what he was like. For the first few centuries of Christianity's childhood, a wide range of interpretations of Jesus co-existed and competed among Christians. These included Gnosticism, Arianism, Montanism, Manachaeism and Pelagianism.

Montanism stemmed from three people from Phrygia (present-day Turkey) around the 150s CE – Montanus, Maximilla and Priscilla –

who predicted an imminent end of the world and regarded themselves as vehicles of the Holy Spirit. Manichaeism, after Manes (216–74 or 77), a Persian, believed that matter is evil and goodness is found in spiritual reality. Pelagianism is named after the monk, Pelagius, who lived around the time of the transition from the fourth to the fifth centuries. The thrust of his thought was a theory of salvation: human beings can be saved *by their own efforts*. Pelagianism was condemned by the Council of Ephesus in 431.[37]

Toleration of differing views did not last indefinitely. Constantine decided to call a halt to doctrinal bickering about Jesus that he fretted was unduly dividing Christians. He decided to intervene to settle disputes about Arius' view that Jesus was subordinate to God in virtue of his creatureliness. In 325, he invited bishops to meet to determine what Christians in general ought to believe about the identity of Jesus.

From Nicaea to Chalcedon

Constantine even offered to pay for the expenses bishops would incur by travelling. He presided over an assembly of them in Nicaea in 325. Contemporary Catholic, Orthodox and Anglican Churches acknowledge this assembly as the first ecumenical council. Church councils are like punctuation marks in the life of Christians. They attempt to control or end chaotic conversations. Their decisions effectively declare: 'Here the conversation ends; this is what is to be believed henceforth. Full stop.' Against Arius, the assembled leaders at the First Council of Nicaea taught that Jesus was and is of the same essence, substance or being as the Father Creator of the world. With this teaching, there was a shift among Christians from individually or in small local groups deciding what could be believed, to acknowledging that in order to be a good Christian it is necessary to subscribe to doctrines formulated by bishops in synods. The term normally used to designate episcopally prescribed beliefs is orthodoxy – correct teaching. With Nicaea I, conciliar orthodoxy was born: Jesus is of the same essence as God.

Yet orthodoxy did not kill off either Arius or the views of his allies (Arianism). Christological disputes only became more intense. The Council of Ephesus (431) tried to punctuate disputes by teaching that Mary, Jesus' mother, could be called a bearer of God because she had been pregnant with a divine son. The First Council of Constantinople (381) insisted that Jesus 'came down from the heavens and became incarnate from the holy Spirit and the virgin Mary'. It does not speak of a 'God-bearer', although the Council of Chalcedon did.

The participants at Constantinople I revised the statements of Christian faith promulgated at the Council of Nicaea to produce a creed that remains in widespread use today among Christian Churches. It is called either the Nicene Creed (in a revised form) or the Nicene–Constantinopolitan Creed. The word 'creed' comes from the Latin term, *credimus* ('we believe'). For anyone wanting to know what Christians have believed over the past 16 centuries, this creed of 381 serves as a sure guide.

The Nicene–Constantinopolitan Creed (381)

We believe in one God the Father all-powerful, maker of heaven and earth, and of all things both seen and unseen. And in one Lord Jesus Christ, the only-begotten Son of God, begotten from the Father before all ages, light from light, true God from true God, begotten not made, consubstantial with the Father, through whom all things came to be; for us humans and for our salvation he came down from the heavens and became incarnate from the holy Spirit and the virgin Mary, became human and was crucified on our behalf under Pontius Pilate; he suffered and was buried and rose up on the third day in accordance with the scriptures; and he went up into the heavens and is seated at the Father's right hand; he is coming again with glory to judge the living and the dead; his kingdom will have no end. And in the Spirit, the holy, the lordly and life-giving one, proceeding forth from the Father, co-worshipped and co-glorified with Father and Son, the one who spoke through the prophets; in one, holy, catholic and apostolic church. We confess one baptism for the forgiveness of sins. We look forward to a resurrection of the dead and life in the age to come. Amen.[38]

The Nicene–Constantinopolitan Creed contains a doctrine that Jesus Christ is 'consubstantial with the Father'. Briefly put, it means by this that Jesus is divine. It also espouses a clear Trinitarian understanding of God as Father, Son and Spirit. But where is Jesus' humanity in this doctrinal grid? Once it began to be taught that Jesus is divine, thought needed to be given to his humanity. He was, after all, a male human being. How could a man be God? Two bishops argued over this bitterly in the fifth century. Nestorius, the Bishop of Constantinople, insisted that Jesus Christ has a human and divine nature that are separate. His nemesis, Cyril, Bishop of Alexandria, agreed about there being a human and divine nature, but insisted that they are indivisibly unified in Jesus Christ.

Nestorius would not agree, so yet another synod needed to be convened. This met in 451 at Chalcedon (in present-day Turkey), and is the most famous of all councils. Chiming with Nestorius, it concluded that there are indeed two natures in Christ, but siding with Cyril, it insisted that the natures are indivisible.

Chalcedon identified Jesus with the Logos who existed before the creation of the world. It referred to the person of the Logos as being 'truly God' and 'truly a human being'. The one person of the Logos for this council has a divine and human nature that is indivisible and immutable. The council did not explain how two natures could be united in a single person, but declared that this is the case.

Council of Chalcedon (451)

So, following the saintly fathers, we all with one voice teach the confession of one and the same Son, our Lord Jesus Christ: the same perfect in divinity and perfect in humanity, the same truly God and truly man, of a rational soul and a body; consubstantial with the Father as regards his divinity, and the same consubstantial with us as regards his humanity; like us in all respects except for sin; begotten before the ages from the Father as regards his divinity, and in the last days the same for us and for our salvation from Mary, the virgin God-bearer, as regards his humanity; one and the same Christ, Son, Lord, only begotten, acknowledged in two natures which undergo no confusion, no change, no division, no separation; at no point was the difference between the natures taken away through the union, but rather the property of both natures is preserved and comes together into a single person and a single subsistent being; he is not parted or divided into two persons, but is one and the same only-begotten Son, God, Word, Lord Jesus Christ, just as the prophets taught from the beginning about him, and as the Lord Jesus Christ himself instructed us, and as the creed of the fathers handed it down to us.[39]

The paradoxical two-nature teaching of Chalcedon is the most famous of all *Christian* doctrines. Without it, a doctrine of a Triune God collapses. Without it, too, falls any attempt to say that the Church is divinely instituted by the divine–human Jesus. There would be no point to Christians worshipping Jesus were this doctrine false. Martyrdom and missionary endeavours would similarly be rendered futile if the Christians assembled at Chalcedon were deluded. The teaching of Chalcedon is still regarded by many Christians as the primary measuring rod for deciding what is or is not Christian belief. From the eighteenth century till now, it has been subjected to withering intellectual critique, as later chapters will illustrate. No matter how frequently it has been derided, it remains remarkably resilient among Christians.

Churches East and West

At the time of Chalcedon, not everyone was pleased by its para-doxical formulation. Far from it. Disputes in its aftermath fanned a division between Eastern and Western Christians. The fifth century witnessed a gradual bifurcation between Christians. In Syria in par-ticular, the teaching of Chalcedon proved unpopular. Yet Christian unity had begun to teeter in significant ways a little earlier in the century. The Council of Ephesus in 431 spoke of Jesus' mother as the Virgin Mary and called her, in Greek, *Theotokos*; that is, 'God-Birthgiver' or 'Mother of God'.[40] This formulation bred disputes and divisions between later Christians.

Varieties of beliefs were held by Eastern and Western Christians throughout the Early Middle Ages, but despite views held in com-mon, Christians after the Fall of Rome began to diversify markedly in what they believed and the ways they worshipped. This diversifi-cation can be traced to doctrinal disputes during the fifth century following the declarations of two Church assembles – the Councils of Ephesus and Chalcedon. It is important to consider briefly the aftermath of these councils because, in their wake, two major families of Christians developed that are still prominent today. One family is represented by the Western, Catholic and officially Latin-speaking Christians, who were normally led from Rome in the Middle Ages by the bishop of Rome, who bore the title of 'Pope'. The other fam-ily was and is Eastern. It included a cluster of Churches variously called Byzantine, Eastern, or Orthodox.

To recall, the divisions between Eastern and Western Churches stem directly from the differentiations between the East and West Roman Empire. Greek was the dominant language in the Byzantine (after Byzantium) or East Roman Empire. Churches in this area, including those in Egypt, Syria and Jerusalem, enjoyed good relations with each other and with Churches beyond the Empire in Persia, Ethiopia, India, Georgia and Armenia. No single bishop exercised jurisdiction over all these Churches.

Beginning in the fifth century and continuing well into the Early Middle Ages, these Churches began to separate from each other, largely because of doctrinal disputes. The Council of Ephesus in 431 CE was an initial catalyst for such a fragmentation. The principal decision of the Council was to declare that Mary, because she was the mother of Jesus, could rightly be venerated as the Mother of God (Greek: *Theotokos*). A Syrian theologian, Theodore of Mopsuestia (c. 350–428), who was based at Antioch, recoiled at the idea of calling Mary a 'God-Birthgiver' because he feared Jesus could not be regarded seriously as a human being were his mother unlike other mothers. Theodore died before the Council of Ephesus took place, but his disinclination to speak of a *Theotokos* was sustained by Nestorius, who was Patriarch of Constantinople between 428 and 431. He was opposed by another patriarch, that of Alexandria in Egypt, called Cyril. The followers of Theodore would not accept the teachings of Cyril of Alexandria and so formed a largely Syriac-speaking Church called the Church of the East. Christianity in the East was thus divided. The principal Church in Syria today is known as the Syrian Orthodox Church. Its members speak and worship in Aramaic, a dialect of Syriac.

Division did not stop there. Further fragmentation between Churches in the East continued after Chalcedon when opponents refused to accept its teaching that Jesus Christ is one person (*hypostasis*) in two natures (*physeis*), divine and human. Those Christians who could not accept Chalcedon preferred to say Christ is one person '*from* two natures', not '*in* two natures'. Those who could not accept the preposition 'in' were never reconciled with Chalcedonian communities because they feared speaking of Christ in two natures implied that he was a hybrid rather than a unified entity.

Lest it be thought that such disputes were arcane and irrelevant, they effected the way Eastern Churches organize themselves to this day. Christians who rejected Chalcedon are found today in six different independent Churches, known as Oriental Orthodox Churches. They include: (a) the Syrian Orthodox Church; (b) the Orthodox Church of India, founded from Syria; (c) the Egyptian Coptic Orthodox Church; (d) the Orthodox Church of Ethiopia; (e) the Orthodox Church of Eritrea, which became independent of the Ethiopian Orthodox Church in 1994; and (f) the Armenian Orthodox Church.[41]

Because of doctrinal disputes that festered throughout the Early Middle Ages, especially from the fifth to the seventh centuries, Eastern Christianity as it is recognized today includes three major and distinct groups: (a) the Churches of the East (mainly in Syria); (b) the six Oriental Orthodox Churches listed above; and (c) the Byzantine Orthodox Church, which embraced Romanians and Slavs.[42]

Asceticism and Monasticism

It was common for Christians of antiquity to meditate on the Gospels, especially after they had been sung or read in liturgical assemblies. Their ruminations produced starkly divergent results. The more astringent teachings of Jesus were ignored by some and taken to heart by others, with life-changing consequences. Some of the hardest teachings of Jesus for people to mimic in their lives deal with money and possessions. How ought a person aspiring to live as a Christian respond to blunt observations and commands: 'It is easier for a camel to go through the eye of an needle than for someone who is rich to enter the kingdom of heaven' (Mk 10: 25; Mt 19: 24; Lk 18: 25); or 'go, sell what you own, and give the money to the poor, and you will have treasure in heaven; then come, follow me' (Mk 10: 21; Mt 19: 21)? While adherence to orthodox teachings marked a good Christian for many, others became insistent that the body and the world need to be subjugated for anyone wishing to be a latter-day disciple of Jesus. Especially in the fourth century, ways of living evolved among groups of Christians in the Middle East that entitled the abandonment of riches, the renunciation of family links, the abjuring of marriage and sexual relations, fasting, and praying. Such types included asceticism, hermeticism, anchoritism, stylitism and coenobitism, or monasticism. The impulse driving them all is the same: since Jesus lived a property-less life focused on God, so too ought a good Christian.

Christians have often been divided, especially since the fourth century between clerics (of the *ordo clericorum*) and laity (from the Greek, *laos*, people). Monasticism first grew as essentially a Christianity of and for the people. Monks were not normally clerics. Their impact on Christianity's historical unravelling is beyond measure. Some of their traditions will be discussed in subsequent chapters.

Conclusion

What is particularly striking about ancient Christianity is the difference between the ways its adherents lived then compared with now. Up until the dawn of the Middle Ages, Christians could elect their own presbyters and bishops; their beliefs were starkly divergent and varied; their clergy were free to marry; women could often speak freely in, or lead, assemblies; bishops were responsible for their own people and were not papal pawns; and there was no unchallenged superintending monarchical papacy. Popes ruled in concert with emperors. There were no pews in churches. Christians could celebrate the Lord's Supper in their homes. Children were not educated in schools, but taught and led in their faith in households. Before the mid-fifth century, many Christians did not believe that Jesus had a divine and a human nature unified in the Logos. The extensive majority of Christians during this era could not read or write, spent most of their time cultivating food in rural areas, and could not expect to live long. Today, there are large numbers of Christians continuing to show allegiance to hierarchically governed Churches in which they do not enjoy freedoms previously enjoyed by members of ancient forms of the same People of God. The largest growing body of Christians today, Pentecostals and Charismatics, are reclaiming many of the freedoms and customs of ancient generations. They will be discussed in the final chapter.

The form of Christianity forged in the waning years of the Roman Empire was severely tested during the fourth and fifth centuries by marauding Vandals (from North Africa) and Visigoths (from Spain). By the end of the fifth century, both Rome and Byzantium had been overtaken by Vandals and Visigoths. This time was a period of both the collapse of the Empire and a transition to the Middle Ages.

Part 2
Medieval Christianity

Chapter III

The Early Middle Ages, 500–1000

'*So Jesus called them and said to them, "You know that among the Gentiles those whom they recognize as their rulers lord it over them, and their great ones are tyrants over them. But it is not so among you; but whoever wishes to be great among you must be your servant, and whoever wishes to be first among you must be slave of all".*'
Mark 10: 42–44

Jesus was not remembered by those who knew him as being preoccupied with making money, sustaining a family, owning a home or hoarding profit. All signs indicate that he was a wanderer. He moved from place to place, through valleys and fields, up and down hills, talking to anyone who would listen about God's kingdom. No matter how much he liked to help the lame, mad, lonely, poor and frightened people he encountered, his obsession remained God's rule over and among them, rather than Roman law. One of the strongest injunctions ascribed to him was his instruction for his devotees not to behave like overlords. They were to be servants and slaves. As Christianity grew older, exerting authority collectively over people, often coercively, is precisely what it did. Medieval Christianity, which endured for roughly a thousand years, was aligned with kings, emperors and princes. The Middle Ages (between antiquity and modernity) spawned Christendom: a society whose members almost universally lived according to Christian beliefs, and which enjoyed the patronage of monarchs. The purpose of this chapter is to chart the evolution and diversification of Christianity during the Early Middle Ages; that is, from roughly 500 to 1000 CE. This period was preceded by the Fall of ancient Rome.

Empires always peter out: no matter how fiercely militaristic they may be; no matter how much land they conquer and how many people they subdue; and despite their spectacular artistic and engineering achievements, they always and everywhere die out. Such

was the fate of Rome. Its empire began to teeter rapidly in the fifth
century through a combination of military defeats, and a failing ability to administer its territories firmly and efficiently. It has already
received a good deal of attention in these pages because Jesus lived in
one of its provinces, and Christianity was forged under its reach
while it was strong. The beginning of its end seemed symbolically
clear once Goths attacked and sacked Rome in 410. For those keen
on the Gods of Rome, it would have been only to be expected that
they lamented the disaster that befell their beloved city as a punishment for abandoning the Gods and turning to Christianity. To refute
such a charge, Augustine of Hippo wrote a huge treatise called the
City of God Against the Pagans.[1] This book defends Christianity ener-
getically, and was used by generations following him to negotiate a
manageable working relation with powerful rulers.

The Middle Ages lasted from roughly the end of the Roman
Empire in the fifth century to the discovery of lands and peoples
unknown to the Bible in the late fifteenth century. For the purposes
of coming to grips with such a large span of time, the period as a
whole can be divided between the Early and Later Middle Ages. The
pontificate of Gregory VII (1073–85) serves as a landmark to distinguish the two periods, whose differentiation really applies mainly to
Europe. What was happening in China, Japan and Australia during
the same years is another story altogether. Gregory engineered a far-
reaching reform of the papacy and the way Western Christianity was
governed from Rome.[2]

By the end of the fourth century, proto-Christian assemblies had
laid their roots in Palestine, Syria and Asia Minor. Major Christian
centres developed thereafter in Africa, notably so in Alexandria and
Carthage. For the thousand years following the fall of Rome,
Christianity gradually spread through the entirety of Europe. As it
did, its leaders were by necessity preoccupied by three major tasks.
First, they had to ensure that the story concerning Jesus' life, death
and resurrection were announced to a variety of Europeans. Second,
they needed to devise administrative structures to give order and
structures to Churches that were established. Finally, they needed to
articulate creeds tabulating the various tenets of their belief.[3] All
three tasks were accomplished by missionary monks, kings who converted to Christianity by the efforts of missionaries, popes and gifted
individuals revered as Christian saints.

Like Christians of antiquity, it is not really possible to understand the beliefs and behaviour of medieval Christians by transposing contemporary assumptions and convictions into their time. Far more so than is frequently the case now in the West, inhabitants of the Middle Ages lived with an intense awareness that they populated the earth along with devils, angels, demons and saints. Theirs was a world of belief in devil-possession, superstition, magic and miracles. It was very widely believed during the Middle Ages that praying to saints could move them to intercede with God to extract divine favours for the people praying. It was common for people in this period to embark on long and arduous pilgrimages to visit the burial sites of saints and to buy relics of saints' bodies. To enter the medieval mind is to take for granted that the world is a stable and static three-tiered structure with God, angels, archangels, and saints in heaven above with God, people tempted by devils on earth below, and souls of dead people tormented by hell fire below heaven and within the earth. An almost universally held belief was that the way one lived determined one's everlasting fate. To sin seriously or to break a law of the Church could mean consignment to hell forever, or a sentence in purgatory – a celestial waiting room where sins would be purified before a soul could enter heaven. People often went to great expense to pay for Masses (ritual re-enactments of Jesus' Last Supper) to be said for the souls of deceased relatives, so that the relatives' time in purgatory would be decreased.

The millennium that encompassed the Middle Ages heralded far-reaching social, political, cultural, economic and religious changes for the people of Europe. These transformations were reflected regionally in the disparate ways Christians lived. Despite constant change and clear diversity, medieval Christianity was marked by a cluster of regionally pervasive and abiding features. Most of its adherents in Europe lived in rural regions and were uneducated and illiterate. Even priests were often barely able to write. In rural areas, priests shared the beliefs and ways of living of their parishioners. Before the eleventh century, they could live legally with wives and work alongside other married people in peasant societies: 'Minimally literate, they often had only a rote mastery of the liturgy it was their responsibility to celebrate. That sacred function aside, they were relatively well-to-do peasants, village big shots, who worked their lands, drank their beer or wine, and gambled and swore like any other peasant.'[4]

Bishops and abbots during the Middle Ages could become extremely powerful local rulers. They often shared the same pastimes as the local lords with whom they associated: feasting, drinking, hunting and fighting. Records from the eighth, ninth and tenth centuries chronicle the behaviour of warrior bishops, who were 'every bit as rough and rude (and, needless to add, illiterate) as their secular counterparts'.[5]

At the same time, learning was preserved among a small and highly educated minority of clerics who could read and write in Latin. Their number was greatly increased during the Later or High Middle Ages. The privileged education of such clerics easily marked them off from other Christians and from clerics who had not been well educated. An increasingly clear division came to obtain among medieval Christians between the clergy – bishops, abbots, priests and deacons – and the laity. The division between the two groups concerned the professional role the clergy assumed to mediate divinely offered salvation to the laity by conducting liturgies observed *by* the people and by administering sacraments *to* the people.

Until the eleventh century, lay and secular rulers enjoyed the privilege of appointing clerics to high ecclesiastical office in the functions of bishops or abbots. The collaboration between secular rules and ecclesiastical leaders in the Early Middle Ages explain the key mechanism in which Christianity was able to spread throughout Europe during the Middle Ages. When local rulers converted to Christianity under the influence of monastic missionaries, they frequently built churches on their estates. They insisted on being able to appoint priests in their village churches. As these propriety churches spread, Christianity was able to disperse from city centres to rural regions, where most medieval people lived and laboured.[6]

Once villages, towns and valleys were converted to Christianity during the Early Middle Ages, the lives of local peoples frequently mixed attachment to pre-Christian pagan rituals with the celebration of Christian sacraments – rituals initiating and sustaining people in churches.[7] Three sacraments dominated the lives of medieval Christians: baptism, by which they became Christians; confirmation, through which they sought to strengthen the life they adopted at baptism; and the Lord's Supper, commonly called Mass.

While baptism and confirmation were sacraments that were not repeated in an individual's life, the Mass was the central and frequently enacted ritual of Christians during the Middle Ages. It was a ritual charged with religious meaning because, first, it refers to the last meal of Jesus before he was killed, and second, it re-enacts what the Gospels describe as Jesus sharing blessed bread and wine with his disciples. Medieval Christians normally believed that when their priests prayed over bread and wine at Mass, the bread became the body of Christ, and the wine was transformed into his blood. The doctrine of the change from bread and wine to body and blood was regarded so literally that people were often reluctant to eat and drink these religious symbols for fear of committing sacrilege. Priests often became reluctant to offer the sacramental wine to communicants because of the risk they would spill it and defile the blood of the Lord.[8]

Monasticism

The late Roman Empire bequeathed both to Christianity and to its larger world two institutions that have survived until the present day: monasticism and the culture of ancient Rome, the most prominent legacy of which among Christians was the papacy.

Monastic communities began to flourish in the Near East in the third century. A particularly Western form of monasticism was conceived by Benedict of Nursia (c. 480–550). Details of his life are scarce. He was an Italian who spent his entire life in Italy. After being educated in Rome, he became disenthralled with the society in which he lived. His strategy for coping was to withdraw to live as a hermit in a cave at Subiaco. In c. 529, he moved to Monte Cassino where he lived with a small community of monks until his death. He does not appear to have intended to create an institution or establish a religious order. Instead, he composed a guidebook for his companions on how they should live, the majority of whom were laymen. Originally, monasticism was decidedly lay, not clerical.

Benedict's directory for the life of his monks came to be called the *Rule of Saint Benedict*. Until recently, the Rule was thought to have been composed in its entirety by Benedict. Modern historical scholarship has uncovered that although Benedict contributed chapters to the texts and made several editorial adjustments, it was almost certainly based on an earlier work called the *Rule of the Master*.[9] In its final form, the *Rule of Saint Benedict* envisages a monastic community that is directed by an abbot – a patriarchal figure of authority who is responsible for the welfare of the monks, whose chief responsibility is to follow a regimen of regular prayer. This the monks called the *Opus Dei* ('work of God'), not to be confused with a twentieth-century religious institute of the same name, notoriously discussed in Dan Brown's novel, *The Da Vinci Code*. The monks filled their days with liturgical and private prayer, manual labour and spiritual reading. They did not intend to shun humanity by escaping to a cloister, as it is often thought monks do, but to create a radically egalitarian community wherein monks are treated as brothers, all striving in concert to be faithful disciples of Jesus Christ by renouncing possessions, eschewing marriage and family ties, and relinquishing the privilege of directing their own lives. Benedict's monks were coenobites, not hermits. That is, they always lived in communities. They vowed to stay in one location for their lives and to observe periods of silent meditation throughout the day. Importantly, they laboured to support themselves and thereby contributed to the well-being of local financial arrangements. Originally, monasteries needed to rely on the patronage of kings and lords to survive, but by the tenth century, many of them in Europe were financially independent and self-supporting.

It was inevitable that renunciations distinguished monks and nuns from the majority of their surrounding populace. By seeking to create an ideal community, monks simultaneously distanced themselves from people who married and raised families. Like the people, they were lay, not priestly, but unlike the populace, they devoted the majority of their time to the practice of liturgical rites. Their communities often contained priests, though most of their number were not members of a hierarchy.

Benedict's *Rule* was eventually followed in monasteries apart from Monte Cassino. By the seventh and eighth centuries it was followed in parts of Germany, Gaul and England. Communities of nuns also adopted it. By the ninth century there was a sizable family of religious communities of monks and nuns following Benedict's example, and thus it became possible to speak of the Benedictine order. Its members, Benedictines, were a major civilizing force in Europe during the Middle Ages.

Contrary to what might be expected, medieval monasteries impinged directly on the lives of peasants, families and children. By far the majority of Christians in the early medieval period were rural people. They were locally bounded and could not afford the luxury of regular extended travel. Their days were filled by a regular routine of toil to harvest crops and care for livestock, all undertaken in the cause of trying to stay alive. Monasteries in the midst of such people provided work for peasants, encouraged trade, held fairs for the sale of local produce, provided hospitality to travellers and infirm people, and educated the young. Poor farmers frequently sent their children to live in monasteries so that they could be fed and educated. The seventh-century monk Benedict Biscop brought stonemasons to England to build a church. He sought to instruct illiterate people by filling his church with paintings depicting scenes from the Bible.[10]

Apart from encouraging local farms and craftspeople, monks also undertook to pray for them and with them. Rural peasants were normally free to enter monastic churches during the day to watch as monks and nuns performed increasingly more solemn and prolonged liturgical acts of worship.

More learned and literate monks devoted their lives to maintaining libraries and illustrating artistically ritual prayer books and bibles. Their monasteries were the precursors of Western universities which first developed in the Later Middle Ages. Contemporary academic dress that includes black gowns is an offshoot of medieval monastic clothing, which by necessity was voluminous so as to protect monks and nuns from the cold.

The daily routine of worship was undertaken by monks as a *social duty*. In return for monies received from patrons, the monks would pray for their supporters and their wider community. They rose at about 2.00 a.m. in winter before finishing the day at 6.30 p.m. During winter and Lent (40 days preparing for Easter), they ate once a day, otherwise twice. Most of them normally observed a mainly vegetarian diet. They gathered in the middle of the night for prayers known as Matins. A few hours later they met for the prayers called Lauds, at dawn for Prime, two hours after that for Terce, followed by Sext at noon, None in the afternoon, Vespers at the end of the afternoon, and Compline before going to bed.[11]

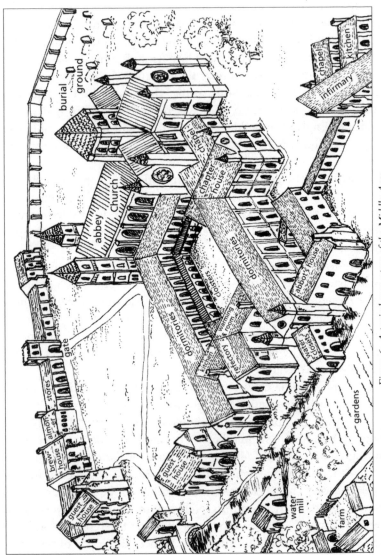

Figure 6: A typical monastery of the Middle Ages

The Papacy

If monasticism is one major bequest of late antiquity to the Middle Ages, another is the classical political culture of Imperial Rome that became incarnated in Rome's bishops, the popes. Rome has long been esteemed by Christians as the place where they believe Jesus' disciple Peter was martyred and buried. Matthew's Gospel records an encounter between Jesus and Peter during which Jesus declares: 'And I tell you, you are Peter, and on this rock I will build my church, and the gates of Hades will not prevail against it' (Mt 16: 18). The linguistic root of Peter's name in Greek is *petra*, meaning 'rock'. Among Christians, Rome thus came to be revered as the Apostolic See, the site from which the successors of Jesus' primary apostle Peter, the popes, were to direct the affairs of the Church. If this is what Jesus wanted, who could quibble with the authority of popes?

It is historically unlikely that Peter was a pope. According to the earliest available historical records, the first person named as a bishop of Rome was Linus, about whom virtually nothing is known except that he lived after Peter and Paul and is linked to Rome. He is identified as the Bishop of Rome by Irenaeus (c. 130–c. 200), Bishop of Lyons, and Eusebius (c. 260–c. 340), Bishop of Caesarea.[12]

In the Early Middle Ages, the primacy of Rome's emperor was transferred to the papacy. Popes dressed in imperial regalia, and their throne rooms, basilicas, mimicked the architectural style of imperial galleries. The title of 'pope', meaning 'father', became common in the latter half of the fourth century. Pope Leo the Great (reigned from 440 to 461) played a prominent part at the Council of Chalcedon.

Leo's later successor, Pope Gregory the Great (590–604), proved to be a strong catalyst for missionary expeditions. He was the first monk to become a pope. In 597, he dispatched a Roman monk, Augustine, together with a band of 40 other monks, to convert the English. Augustine and his brothers arrived and settled in Canterbury, of which he became its first archbishop. England had formed out of a cluster of seven localized kingdoms: Sussex, Kent, Essex, Wessex, Northumbria, Mercia and East Anglia. These were established by immigrants from the mainland of Europe, including Angles, Saxons and Jutes (all pagans in Christian eyes). They eventually converted to Christianity at different stages.

Irish monks had been at work earlier in the sixth century, establishing churches in Northern England, Scotland, Wales, Brittany and Iona (an Island near Scotland) before Augustine arrived in Kent. An Irish shepherd, Patrick (d. 493), had previously established Christian monasteries in Ireland. He is still widely venerated as a saint today. His work paid fruit in Columba (521–97), an Irish prince, who introduced Christianity to Iona. Three Irish monks introduced Christianity to Wales by founding monasteries: David (c. 545), Deiniol (514) and Kentigern (c. 555).[13] The peoples converted to Christianity by these monks were Celts, and they were established as Christians before Augustine began to convert the Angles, who became 'the English'. When Augustine made overtures to the Celts they turned their backs on him as an upstart. The two parties were reconciled at a synod held at Whitby during 664.[14]

Christians as the New Israel

The Early Middle Ages was a time of widespread religious conversion. In the West, Christianity evolved according to where it was implanted. A highly distinctive feature of Western Christianity in the Early Middle Ages was that its development was very closely tied to its adoption in Germanic lands. The Frankish King, Clovis (466–511), was the first Germanic monarch to adopt Christianity as his religion, and he did so around 497.[15] Clovis initiated the Merovingian dynasty of kings, who controlled Gaul and Germany from roughly the sixth to the eighth centuries. One of his successors, Pippin III (d. 768), became King of the Franks in 751. He followed his Merovingian predecessors in promoting the idea that Franks, led by their king, constituted the Chosen People or New Israel lionized in the Bible.[16]

The missionary who prepared for the conversions of the Franks was the Irish monk Columbanus (d. 615). He worked in Gaul (contemporary France) for many years, establishing churches and monasteries. He and his successors converted previously pagan Germanic peoples. Willibrord preached among the Friesians on the coast of the North Sea, and Boniface (680–754) brought Christianity to Hessians, who worshipped the God Thor, whence the word 'Thursday' derives. A sacred oak served as the central site of Thor's cult, so Boniface cut it down. He was eventually murdered by pagans when he was 80 years old.[17]

Charlemagne

Themes broached thus far in this chapter, such as the imperial bequest to the papacy, the rise of Christendom and the rule of Christian monarchs, are all enshrined in the figure of Clovis' son, Charlemagne, or Charles the Great. Charlemagne became the greatest of all medieval monarchs, not because of his prowess at soldiery, but because of his encouragement of learning and cultivation of monarchical humility.[18] He ruled the Franks from 768 to 814. In Rome on Christmas Day 800, Pope Leo III crowned him as the Roman Emperor, thereby launching under German leadership a medieval empire that was called the Holy Roman Empire three and a half centuries later. For the last 28 years of his life he was primarily engrossed in extending the territories of his Frankish kingdom through a series of military expeditions. To begin with, he conquered Lombardy, Saxony, Bavaria and Pannonia, and was eventually successful in Spain after an initial defeat.

Charlemagne was based in Aachen. He invited scholars from throughout the West to visit his court and began to collect Christian writings for his library. Despite his power and influence, he shared one frustration with peasants of his time: he could not read. He learned about the scholarship that was popular among his associates by having the contents of books read aloud to him. He tried to learn to write, but failed. With the ambition of one day being able to write, 'he used to keep writing-tablets and notebooks under the pillow on his bed, so that he could try his hand at forming letters during his leisure moments; but, although he tried very hard, he had begun late in life and made little progress'.[19]

Charlemagne ordered that all monasteries in his territories were to adopt the *Rule of Saint Benedict*, thus ensuring that by far the most common form of monasticism during the Middle Ages in the West was Benedictinism.

The People's Christianity

From its inception, Christianity was a domestic religion. Christians gathered for prayer and liturgy in their own households. When imperial persecutions of Christians petered out during the fourth century, Christianity could assume a much more public profile. Its

Figure 7: Seventh-century Visigothic church, Spain

newly found, imperially sanctioned, situation was visibly embodied in communally owned buildings – churches – for common worship. After the fourth century, a 'church' could be either an assembly of believers or a building housing believers.

Throughout late antiquity and the Early Middle Ages, the construction of churches proliferated in the East and the West. Churches served multiple purposes: they were foci for public meetings, sacred spaces for liturgical rites, and local landmarks architecturally expressing Christian cohesion and purpose. Consecrated hosts (breads) from Eucharistic celebrations were kept in churches, to be offered to sick or dying people who were unable to attend public gatherings. Churches were often constructed over the graves of saints, investing in them a holy awe. People venerated relics at churches and set out on arduous pilgrimages to visit churches serving as reliquaries. Incubation was widely practised in the Middle Ages. It was a custom whereby Christians spent the night sleeping in a church near a saint's remains in the hope of being cured by proximity to the saint.[20]

In the Middle Ages, people at worship were not mewed in pews. Parallel rows of pews only appeared in late medieval buildings. The principal rituals performed in medieval churches were the Mass and baptism. Unlike today, when Mass is normally presided over by a priest in a church's sanctuary, in the Middle Ages a priest might preside at Mass in a building's nave, aisle, side chapel, gallery, tower, under an arch or at a high altar.[21]

The counties of England preserve a rich heritage of early medieval churches. In county Durham, a church built at Enscomb in the

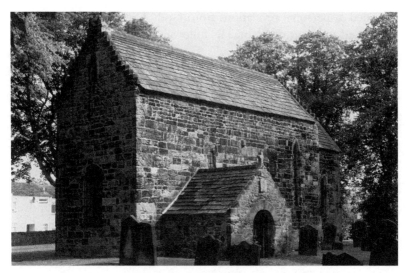

Figure 8: The seventh-century Enscomb church

seventh century still stands: 'The nave is long, high, and narrow. A tall arch connects the nave with a small chancel. While the south side has been much altered, the north side with its small, high windows gives a reasonably good sense of what such a church might have looked like in the early Saxon era.'[22]

Local lords often constructed churches or chapels on their land. The peasantry, rather than travelling afar to a more public church, were normally welcome to worship in a manor's private church.[23]

Muhammad and the Rise of Islam

In the seventh century, the course of Christianity's growth was shaken by the religious enthusiasm of an Arab, Muhammad ibn Abdullah. He was born in the Arabian desert town of Mecca in 570. He first married when he was about 25. Mecca of his time boasted the Ka'bah, the pagan shrine of the Black Stone. As an adult, Muhammad began to question the integrity of the shrine, thereby incurring the wrath of his neighbours. He fled Mecca and settled 290 kilometres away (180 miles) in Medina. Here he attracted like-minded friends and followers who, with him, founded the first known Muslim state. Around 622, he began recording what he regarded as personal revelations from God. These form the Qur'an, the sacred writings of Islam. His followers revered him as a prophet of God.

Muhammad's understanding of God, whom he worshipped as Allah, was powerfully simple: there is but one God for all peoples. God is not Triune, but one. A person can relate to Allah without priests, saints and elaborate rituals. Muslims venerate Jesus as a prophet, like Muhammad, but they do not worship him as an incarnate deity.

Muhammad was a warrior. Once settled in Medina, he gathered an army and attacked Mecca. His soldiers destroyed the idols in the Ka'bah, but retained the site of the Black Stone itself as the principal terminus for visiting pilgrims who had heard of the religious movement he had initiated.[24] Muhammad devoted the energies of his later life to conquering all Arabia by military force and converting its inhabitants to Islam, a word which means 'submission' (to Allah).

He died in 632, but his followers set about spreading Islam to as much of the world as they could conquer. They were spectacularly successful. They conquered Spain in the eighth century. Charlemagne managed to take back Barcelona in 801, but it would be several centuries before the Iberian Peninsula would be ruled by Christian monarchs.

Byzantine Christianity

The Eastern Empire evolved differently after the fall of Rome. Constantinople (formally Byzantium, hence Byzantine Empire) was founded in 324 and thereafter remained an epicentre for Eastern Christianity for the next 11 centuries until it was vanquished by Ottoman Turks in 1453. In the Early Middle Ages, Byzantine Christianity flourished, especially under the reign of the Emperor Justinian, who ruled from 527 to 565. His territories encompassed the eastern Mediterranean, southern Spain, the Italian peninsula and North Africa. His empire boasted the cities of Constantinople and Alexandria, both of which at the time had populations as large as 500,000 inhabitants.

Justinian made Ravenna on the north-east coast of the Italian peninsula his imperial seat. He was clear that his authority was supreme over the Church of the East. His achievements were manifold. He routed Persians, Goths and Vandals who had seized lands in Africa, Spain and Italy during the fifth century. He proved to be a master builder, financing the construction of churches in Ravenna, the reconstruction of the major church Hagia Sophia in Constantinople, as well as St Catherine's monastery on Mt Sinai. He also promulgated a code of imperial laws (the Codex Justinian) in 529.[25]

During the sixth century, Byzantine Christians were exceptionally tolerant of people who wished to remain polytheists (also called pagans). Christianity of the East can boast a long history of religious tolerance because, compared with the West, Jews always found a home among them.[26]

The Byzantine Empire was marked by another distinctive trait: an imperial Christianity that was governed principally by the emperor, who appointed patriarchs and bishops and convened synods. In the West, the emperor needed normally to cooperate with the pope.

The growth and dissemination of Byzantine Christianity was extraordinary. The number of churches painted with vivid images grew in Greece between the seventh and the fifteenth centuries to a total of at least 2000; 900 medieval churches are still standing on the island of Crete alone.[27]

The Christianity of the East entered dark times in the latter half of the sixth century and these lasted until around 843. Thereafter, it revived and flourished until the fifteenth century, when Constantinople was overtaken by Turks. In the sixth, seventh and eighth centuries, it was blighted by war with Persia, plagues, earthquakes, and the growth of Islam. Arabs conquered much of the southern Mediterranean in the first half of the seventh century.

Icons

Not all was bleak. The cardinal distinguishing feature of Byzantine Christianity is the veneration of icons. This practice seems to have emerged during the troubled years of Byzantium (in the sense of Byzantine culture) before 843, the year in which an acrimonious dispute over icons was resolved.

An icon is an image of a person revered by others as holy or saintly. It can be painted on a wall or wood panel. It could also be created in enamel, ivory or steatite. Its primary purpose is easy to state, but difficult to appreciate fulsomely. An icon is rendered so as

Figure 9: Miniature icon (enkolpion) *depicting three soldier saints,*
late thirteenth–fourteenth centuries

to mediate to anyone observing or kissing it the holiness of the like-
ness depicted. The mediation of the saint is meant to operate on
more than a visual level. It is meant to engage all senses apart from
sight. Gazing at an icon of a saint, for instance, could act as a stimulus to imagine hearing that saint's voice. Icons were not merely
visual, but tactile. They could be touched, smelt or kissed. Pious
Christians could even carry icons around with them in the form of
an *enkolpion* (Greek: 'on the breast') – a pendant containing relics and
adorned with an image.

Images represented by icons were distorted by design. Instead of depicting an image realistically, icons skewed specific figures to point to a spiritual meaning underlying mere appearance. Such pointing is known as *anagogic* representation. Enlarged iconic eyes, for instance, could signify that eyes provide access to a person's soul or real identity. Reality for an icon is its *spiritual* meaning. In icons depicting the crucifixion, the body of Christ is not usually depicted as a corpse, but alive as the vanquisher of death and redeemer of humanity.[28]

In medieval Byzantine churches, such prominence was accorded to icons that a screen, an iconostasis, was erected between the nave and sanctuary so that icons could be displayed in full view of the people.

The Iconoclastic Controversy

The Byzantine Empire was beset by a bitter and very violent controversy over icons from the 720s to 843. The controversy began on the basis of complaints that people were worshipping iconic images themselves, rather than the identities of those to whom they refer. It would be a sin of idolatry for a Christian to worship an image of Christ in place of Christ himself. In 754, the Emperor Constantine V convened a council that agreed to destroy religious images in churches. Monks who were iconophiles (or iconodules, 'lovers of icons') duly resisted the emperor and were slaughtered in their thousands. John of Damascus (d. 749), Theodore of Studios (759–826) and Nicephorus (758–929) were iconophiles, who argued that to reject icons was to denigrate matter as being incapable of representing divine power.[29] The controversy appeared to end in 787 when the Second Council of Nicaea allowed icons to be displayed in churches. The Emperor Michael II (820–29) enflamed the controversy again by decrying icons. This second wave of controversy lasted from 815 to 843. It began to end in 842 with the death of the Emperor Theophilius. The following year his wife, Theodora, convoked a council which chimed with Nicaea II in allowing the veneration of icons.

Trouble in the West

After the reign of Charlemagne, social organization in the West began to deteriorate badly in the late ninth century, and continued during the tenth. The territories of Charlemagne were distributed among his sons, who fell into conflict with each other. This period is often referred to as the 'Dark Ages'. Problems for Christianity in the West were compounded by invasions by Vikings (from the north), Magyars (from the east), and Saracens, who from Spain set out to command regions stretching from the Mediterranean to Ireland.[30]

Trouble in the West was compounded by trouble with the East. The Western or Catholic Church began to conflict with the Byzantine Church, principally over two issues: the jurisdiction of the papacy; and the form of the Nicene Creed. Patriarchs of Constantinople, while willing to defer to the Bishop of Rome as a brother patriarch, were completely disinclined to regard him as a sovereign over the entire Church. The pope in the eyes of Byzantine patriarchs may well be the 'first among equals' because of Peter's link to Rome, but his authority is certainly not above theirs.

When it is thought that theology is a social irrelevance, or that intellectual theological disputes have no practical consequence, a Trinitarian dispute that intensified in the tenth and eleventh centuries suggests otherwise. The dispute in question revolved around a single Latin term, *filioque*, which is a compound of two smaller terms, *filius*/'son'/*filio*/'from the son', as well as *que*, meaning 'and'. *Filioque* simply means 'and from the son'. Transferred to a Trinitarian controversy, the 'son' in question is the divine Son, the Second Person of the Trinity.

Filioque does not appear in the earliest Latin version of the Nicene Creed. It was interpolated in the text of the Creed at various times and places in the West. It was sanctioned by the Third Council of Toledo in 589, and was in use among the Franks in the ninth century.

Byzantine Christians objected to the Latin Church making an addition to the Creed on its own behalf. They had had no part in its inclusion. Creeds are formal, solemnly declared articulations of Christian beliefs. The fateful terminological dispute that emerged between Catholic and Byzantine Christians was at root a disagreement about the interpretation of John's Gospel. There are many verses in John indicating that God sent Jesus into the world (Jn 3: 17, 34; 4: 34; 5: 30; 8: 18). In Trinitarian theology, this sending was referred to as the first divine procession: the Son proceeds from the Father. John's Gospel also declares that the Father will send an Advocate, the Holy Spirit in the name of Jesus (14: 26). The question then presents itself: does the Spirit proceed from the Father alone, or from the Father *and the Son*? Byzantine Christians insisted that it is the Father alone who sent the Spirit.

One word, *filioque*, thereby came to symbolize and encapsulate Latin arrogance in the East, as if Catholics could determine the content of Christian faith without regard for other Christians. Disaccord over papal jurisdiction and Trinitarian belief fermented gradually. Finally, in the eleventh century, to be considered in the next chapter, the Churches of East and West, represented by their representative patriarchs, anathematized each other. Thus began a schism within Christianity that has never been breached.

Tribal Incursions and Migrations

The evolvement of Christianity during the Early Middle Ages was markedly shaped by four factors: the institutional strengthening of the papacy; the continuing birfurcation between Eastern and Western Churches; tribal migrations and resettlements; and the enormous growth of monasticism. The efflorescence of monasticism during the Middle Ages was a massive salve to heal the wounds inflicted on the culture built by Charlemagne by tribal invaders.

As mentioned above, Charlemagne's empire began to deteriorate badly after his death in 814. No one proved strong or wise enough to take his place. Throughout the ninth and early tenth centuries, migrating invaders made incursions in Western Europe from its north, south and east. The entire period spanning the fifth to the tenth centuries constitutes what has been deprecatingly called the age of Barbarian invasions. The migrating invaders of this time included Huns, Vikings, Magyars, Saracens, Visigoths, Vandals, Ostrogoths and Scandinavians. Their influence in Western Europe was both positive and negative. Their diversity enhanced the cultural diversity of the region, but traces of their militaristic aggression passed into Christian customs and is 'reflected in the new regalia worn by bishops (mitres, crosiers, rings), in hymns celebrating Christians as "soldiers of Christ", and in the development of a clerical caste system in the Church'.[31]

In the ninth and early tenth centuries, the Saracens, Huns, Vikings and Magyars in particular were bent on rapine in the successive waves of pillaging they launched in the heartlands of Europe: 'Whatever else we choose to call the ninth and tenth centuries, they were characterized by lawlessness. Warfare was constant in an almost capricious struggle for mastery in which bravery and brawn, charisma and cunning, all counted for more than either right or legitimacy.'[32] The populace of early medieval Europe lived with a pervasive social fear of murderous plunder. Its fear was compounded by a profound religious fretfulness about the prospects of being condemned to hell: 'The early medieval church taught remorselessly that the human race lived under the stern judgement of God, and that His punishment was imminent. The end of the world was nigh, and everywhere you looked offered the first clear signs of it. Every flash of lightning, every eclipse, every flood or famine was a forewarning.'[33]

Cluny

One of the greatest institutions Christianity ever spawned was the abbey of Cluny, in the countryside of the French region of Burgundy. It is now almost entirely forgotten, and only the derelict shell of a former architectural wonder remains. It began in the tenth century as a hunting lodge, given by a local duke to a Benedictine monk. From that it grew to the largest building in Christendom, and remained so for 500 years before St Peter's Basilica was completed in Rome during the sixteenth century. From the site of the monastery of Cluny grew a family of at least 1500 related Cluniac monasteries in Europe. By any standard, this was an enormous flourishing of monasticism. Always to be remembered is that medieval monasteries were hubs of religious and financial support for hard-pressed rural Christians. They were invaluable sources of commerce, reservoirs of learning, education and sacred music and, above all, places of worship that inspired and led local peoples. It is rare today to hear contemporary Christians being enthralled by the importance and legacy of Cluny. Even those who visit Paris' Musée de Cluny could be easily forgiven for underestimating the cultural impact of Cluny in Europe:

> A thousand years ago, this now-shattered place in southern Burgundy made an impact on the Christian world more profound and more enduring than that of any pope or emperor, or any ruling monarch of the day including the kings of France and England. Cluny's abbots

were as influential as any president, statesman or business leader in our own times. Wielding immense political power, backed by unmatched moral stature, they were men who saw their star, and followed it wherever in might lead. They inherited a Europe that lay in ruins and proceeded to rebuild it, laying many of the foundations of Christian culture and civilization. For more than two centuries Cluny was the spiritual heart of Christianity.[34]

The birth of Cluniac monasticism can be dated to 910, when two men were riding together through a valley in the County of Burgundy. The valley was heavily wooded, included the Grosne River, and was near the town of Mâcon. Both men were in their 60s. One was William I, Duke of Aquitaine, Duke of Mâcon, and Count of Auvergne. The other was a Benedictine abbot called Berno. He was responsible for the monastery of Baume-les-Messieurs to the north of the valley in which the two men were riding. William wanted Berno to establish a monastery in his territories. His motive was prudential care for his eternal fate. He was entering advanced age and did not enjoy good health. Both his wife and only son were dead.[35] Playing on his conscience was a murder he had perpetrated. He needed to take steps to ensure that on a cataclysmic day of divinely enacted Final Judgement he was not consigned to the sempiternal horrors of hell. A monastery on his lands in which monks could pray for him would be an ideal guarantee against damnation.

The valley William and Berno were traversing contained a hamlet that had been known to the Romans. It housed a lodge called *Cluniacum*. Berno chose this hamlet and its cluster of buildings as the site for his new monastery. William agreed, even though it was his favourite hunting lodge. Berno's choice was judicious because the area was rich in water, fauna and flora. It also enjoyed natural protection from marauding invaders because it lay between the Duchy of Burgundy to its west, which was loyal to France, and to its east the County of Burgundy with its Saône River. In a wider setting, the geographical zone in which Berno decided to establish a monastery lay within the Holy Roman Empire.[36]

William provided for the stability of a monastery by signing a charter on 11 September 910. He undertook to furnish the expenses needed to establish a monastic community. Shrewdly, William also took steps to ensure that the foundation of *Cluniacum* was to be unimpeded by him and his family, and to be protected from the meddling of either ecclesiastical or lay grandees. In a clever stroke, which he was able to sustain because he was a powerful duke, he shielded the fledgling Cluny from diocesan bishops and local lords by placing it under the direct jurisdiction of the papacy. The patronage and protection of popes helped to impel the growth of Cluniac monasticism.[37]

The original ninth-century church of Cluny was small. Berno built and consecrated a new church, Cluny I, around 916. He died a decade later (926/7) and was succeeded by Abbot Odo, a monk in his 40s. Odo, a gifted poet and musician, died in 942. Abbot Aymard took his place in 954, and was himself followed by Mayeul in 963. Abbot Mayeul promoted the construction of a new abbey church, Cluny II, which was not completed until well into the tenth century. The following century it was pulled down and replaced by a gigantic building, Cluny III, the shell of which remains today.

From the secluded hamlet of Cluny and Cluny III, Burgundian Benedictinism spread throughout Europe. Cluniac monks disseminated Romanesque architecture when they built new abbey churches. The distinctiveness of this style, stemming from ancient Roman architecture, involved large open naves, rounded at their eastern ends beyond their altars, curved arches and windows, with ceilings supported by sturdy classical columns.[38]

By the early 1100s, there were around 1500 depended monasteries of Cluny populated by an international confraternity of monks dispersed throughout France, Germany, Italy, Spain and Britain.[39] The cultural achievements of Cluniac monasticism were colossal:

> The Cluniacs were among the most lavish and enlightened builders Europe had ever known, and the landscape of Western Europe remains richly decorated with their achievements. They may have built for God, but the beneficiary has been humanity. In stone-carving and wall painting, metalwork and book illumination, they were pioneers responsible for some of the most beautiful art of the Middle Ages. In music the Cluniac psalmody remains the finest example of Gregorian chant ever composed: it can hardly be an accident that the tunnel-vaulting, which Cluny's stone-masons perfected for their churches, produces an acoustic that is ideally suited to the resonant

chanting of a monastic choir. To listen to these psalms sung in one of
the Romanesque churches of Burgundy raised by Cluniac Masons is
enough to dispel any thoughts of hellfire and damnation.[40]

Figure 10: The surviving rump of the south transept of Cluny III. Most of its outlying
buildings were destroyed during the French Revolution

Figure 11: The Romanesque architecture of the Cluniac Abbey of Paray-le-Monial,
France, early twelfth century

Today, glimpses of the sublimity of Cluniac art can be caught in the
Musée de Cluny of Paris' Latin Quarter. Yet the legacy of Cluny was
not confined to gemstones, Romanesque buildings, melismatic
chants or artful paintings. Its primary benefit for Christianity and
Europe was that after the waves of pillaging invasions and throughout
the Middle Ages, it provided moral leadership, economic security,
educative instruction, and religious inspiration in the valleys, towns
and regions of Europe.

Conclusion

By 1000 CE, Christians were flourishing in Greenland and Iceland.[41]
The primary mechanism by which most of Europe was converted to

Christianity by missionaries, monks and nuns during the Early Middle Ages was, first, to be successful in converting Frankish rulers, and thereafter to prove equally able in convincing a string of powerful kings, dukes, barons and princes to live as Christians. Once the rulers were won over, it was only to be expected that they would require their peasant peoples to follow them in shedding magic and superstition, and in beginning to live according to an annual calendar celebrating the life and achievements of Jesus.

By the end of the Later Middle Ages, the religious customs of European Christians differed markedly from those of Eastern and Western Christians during the first few centuries of Christianity's growth. In place of the ancient practice of baptizing adults by emerging them fully in water, medieval Christians widely practised the baptism of unaware infants. Instead of Christians celebrating the Lord's Supper in their own homes, medieval Christians were required to attend liturgies in public buildings conducted in Latin and led by clerics. While medieval monasticism was a culturally and religiously impressive achievement, it often amounted to a story of men told by men for men, and the active responsibilities undertaken by women in ancient Christian communities were frequently denied to women in the Early Middle Ages, or were simply never recorded. Throughout the Middle Ages, as in every other historical period in which Christianity has spread, women were just as vital as men to the prospects of Christianity's social impact, but their abilities were often confined to their families and homes because they were not permitted to lead local Christian communities outside nunneries. By the twentieth century that situation had decidedly changed.

Chapter IV

The Later Middle Ages, 1000–1500

'You cannot serve God and wealth.'
Matthew 6: 34

All human beings, of whatever historical period, think they are contemporary. It is only later generations that label earlier ones as prehistoric, unsophisticated, pre-modern or ancient. So too with the Later Middle Ages, which lasted from around 1000 to 1500 CE. The designation 'Middle Ages' (*Medium aevum*) is not in itself an expression belonging to the period so classified. It was coined at a later juncture during the Renaissance as a way of styling that epoch as an age of rebirth and new knowledge, in contradistinction to ancient and superseded periods, as well as the ages in between. It is only to be expected that people living in the days marked 'Middle Ages' would normally not have viewed themselves as situated in a spent era. They are more likely to have been inclined to sense themselves as having reached an advanced stage of human development because of the art, architecture, churches and monarchies they had formed.

The periods of the Renaissance and the Reformation (to be considered in subsequent chapters) could not have unfolded as they did were it not for the religious, cultural, and political achievements of the Later Middle Ages – a time of massive population growth in Europe, dazzlingly fertile artistic creativity, and religious enthusiasm.

People who are now called 'medievals' would have had every reason to suppose that they lived at a high point of history, general and Christian, and not during an interim period. The era of the Later Middle Ages was the high watermark of Latin Christendom. It represented the second major period of the conversion of Europe (after initial missionary work among the Franks). Christianity's strengths and successes multiplied throughout the medieval period, and especially from 1000 to 1500 CE. During the Later Middle Ages, the population of Europe, and hence of Christianity, doubled in size. As a consequence, cities similarly grew to become thriving centres of commerce, political influence and cultural expression.

If ever there was a Golden Age of Christianity, medieval people could be forgiven for surmising it was theirs. In the eleventh century, the papacy was reformed to become stronger, more influential and monarchical than it had ever been. New religious orders were founded during the eleventh and twelfth century, and they still operate today. They were complemented by an untold number of individuals who cultivated intense lives of prayer and meditation in their own homes. The financial and economic vitality of cities, monasteries and local churches promoted Gothic architecture, one of the artistic glories of the Middle Ages. The High (or Later) Middle Ages also witnessed the regaining of lands lost during earlier Islamic invasions; the establishment of universities with theology as their paramount discipline; the creation of a body of celibate clergy regarded as sacred and utterly independent of secular political control (some regard this as a loss for Christianity); the creation of the musical styles of organum and polyphony; and the regular organization of religious revivals among lay Christians throughout Europe. By the end of the Middle Ages, each and every Western European, almost without exception, lived from childhood to old age according to the beliefs and laws of the Catholic Church.

The triumphs of Christianity during the last five centuries of the Middle Ages were discoloured by practices which seem clearly opposed to the gospel of Jesus Christ. Theologies of war were devised during this period. As Catholic Orthodoxy became more confident that it articulated absolute truth, its proponents became more intolerant, not only of Jews and Muslims, but of Christians it slighted as heretics or false teachers. Triumph was thereby accompanied by crusades against Muslims styled as infidels, military campaigns against heretics, the Inquisition (founded in the thirteenth century to interrogate suspected heretics), and the burning alive of people accused of witchcraft.

Throughout late medieval Christendom, the religious expression of lay and clerical Christians was in the first place public, communal, visual, liturgical and oral. Worship was conducted in buildings publicly accessible to all people. Churches were art galleries. They hosed statues, tombs, and reliquaries of saints and martyrs. In the second place, prayer and meditation were fervidly practised in households during quieter moments throughout the day.

Theologians laboured to produce intricate theologies of sacraments – liturgical rituals marking stages in a person's life during which God is symbolized in a vivid way. Sacraments marked the major stages in life from birth to death. By the later medieval period, all Latin or Catholic Christians believed that their eternal destiny was determined by their participation in sacraments, paramount among which at this time were baptism and the Mass. Without baptism one would suffer the fires of hell for ever. Without Mass, no one could really and tangibly commune with God. By the High Middle Ages, the principle was established among Europeans that 'only by being in a legally correct relationship with the administrative hierarchy of the Catholic Church in the West could one's soul achieve eternal salvation'.[1]

The Gregorian Papacy

It is instructive to realize that the way the papacy functions in the early twenty-first century is without historical precedent. Now the pope is a sovereign head of state. The Vatican is a politically independent territory, with its own international diplomatic corps. Never before has a pope been able to appoint all bishops around the world, independently of the wishes of local churches. Even in the early twentieth century, the papacy was constrained in its appointment of bishops by concordats which allowed local cathedrals to elect their bishops. The Second Vatican Council in the 1960s tried to balance papal monarchical rule of the Catholic Church with collegial government by bishops. It failed. The pope now governs without the constraint of a council. The lunge towards an absolute monarchical exercise of papal office began clearly in the eleventh century.

At the beginning of the eleventh century, popes cooperated with emperors of the Latin West in the exercise of political and religious authority in Europe. In the second half of the century, the pope and emperor of the time clashed, with the eventual submission of the emperor to the jurisdiction of the pope. The pope was Gregory VII, who remained in office from 1073 to 1085. The emperor with whom he jousted was a young man of 26: Henry IV, the emperor-elect, King of Germany, Burgundy and Italy, and the most powerful political ruler of Latin Christendom.

The seeds of the conflict had been budding since the beginning of the century. The primary issue in dispute was the legal autonomy of bishops with their clergy. The centre of the disagreement was Germany, the kings of which exercised dominion over a vast territory which later became known as the Holy Roman Empire. It included much of Germany, Austria, Switzerland, what is now called the Czech Republic, most of Italy, and from south-east France extending to Slovenia. Its bishops also operated as local princes. Lay princes argued for the right and privilege of installing bishops in office. Clerics in Rome protested, insisting that the Church, especially its clerics, should be independent of lay rule.[2]

The crisis came to a head when Gregory VII excommunicated Henry IV in 1076. No pope had ever before dared to place an emperor under such a severe penalty, which bore the consequence of eternal damnation in hell. Henry had not yet been crowned as emperor at the time of his excommunication. In decreeing his punishment, Gregory pronounced that he could not participate in sacraments, and that his vassals were relinquished from their oaths of fealty to their king. Many of the princes of Germany sided with the pope and gave Henry a year in which to seek reconciliation by having the excommunication rescinded. If he did not, he was to be deposed.

Fearing the worst, Henry travelled to Italy to meet the pope at the beginning of 1077. At the time, Gregory was staying at the castle of the Countess Matilda of Tuscany. Henry reached the castle on 25 January. For three days, the pope refused to meet the king. During all this time, Henry waited and fasted in bitterly cold winter weather at the gatehouse of the castle, dressed as a penitent without headdress or footwear. Inside the castle, 'Gregory VII, armed only with a great religious idea, finally relented, and at the end of the third day formally re-admitted Henry to the communion of the Church'.[3]

The idea arming Gregory was that of the Petrine ('of Peter') office: the belief that Jesus invested Peter with supreme authority in the Church, an office that was bequeathed to all popes regarded as Peter's successor. For this way of thinking, the pope rules by the express intent of Jesus Christ. The biblical text used to buttress the notion of a Petrine office is Mt 16: 13–20: Peter is the rock on which the Church is built. Exactly the same idea that inspired Gregory VII is used to legitimize the current papacy.

Henry's submission to Gregory was not a relinquishment of political power. It signalled a new arrangement of power. Thereafter, the pope alone (in theory) would exercise authority over the clergy, but papal power was to be balanced by clerics' recognition of the political authority of secular rulers. Later history proved to be a struggle to maintain a balance when an ambitious pope or aggressive kings sought to gain an upper hand.[4]

Clerical Celibacy

Priests in the Catholic Church could be married until the eleventh century. Therein, and thereafter, it became increasingly difficult for Latin clerics to live with a wife. Still, by the middle of the eleventh century there were large numbers of married clerics living, for instance, in Milan. Countervailing forces accumulated elsewhere to forbid clerics from marrying. In 1050 an episcopal synod in Rome decreed that priests were to live in sexually continent ways by dissociating themselves from their wives. This meant they were constrained to expel their wives from their homes. Even before 1050, bishops had been decreeing punitive measures against married priests. A council of bishops meeting in Pavia (Lombardy), in 1022, ordered that the children of priests were to be enslaved to the local churches where the priests lived, with no ability to inherit goods from their fathers. A similar decree was promulgated in Bourges during 1031.

Under Pope Leo IX (1048–54), strictures against the marriage of clergy proliferated. These were amplified by Pope Nicholas II (in office from 1058 to 1061), who ordered that lay Christians were not to participate in Masses led by priests with wives or concubines. These two popes paved the way for Gregory VII, who instructed that priests who did not banish and abandon their female partners were to be dismissed from office. He commanded bishops throughout Christendom to enforce his laws vigorously and without delay.[5] He was frequently ignored. Those bishops who obeyed him often met the fury of their clergy. Both the Archbishop Jean of Rouen and, in Bavaria, Bishop Altmann of Passau narrowly escaped being stoned by their subordinate clerics when they tried to implement the Gregorian celibacy reform.[6]

Compulsory clerical celibacy was not concocted during a dream overnight. It had a theological motivation with a long history, and a

Figure 12: Monk and woman being punished in a stock with an accusing onlooker,
c. 1300–25

practical, financial impulse. The theological stimulus stemmed from the idea that since God is a Spirit, flesh is antithetical to God and spiritual life. The practical thrust derived from fear among bishops that the sons of priests who owned property would inherit the homes and holdings of their fathers, thereby depriving the Church of financially lucrative assets.[7]

From ancient Rome and Greece, Christianity inherited a dualism that conceived of the human being as a composite of body and soul. The body was both venerated and disparaged among Christians. The human soul or spirit was consistently regarded as reflecting the Spirit which is God. Christians since the imperial Roman period had professed that God became incarnate in the body of Jesus, that Jesus was raised bodily from death, and that they could eat his body and drink his blood when they commemorated the Last Supper. Theirs was a bodily religion. At the same time, Christians were also inclined to be fearful and demeaning of the body. Pope Siricius (in office from 384 to 399 CE) taught that sexual coupling was inimical to God. He did so by drawing attention to Paul's Letter to the Romans:

> For those who live according to the flesh set their minds on the things of the flesh, but those who live according to the Spirit set their minds on the things of the Spirit. To set the mind on flesh is death, but to set the mind on the Spirit is life and peace. For this reason the mind that is set on the flesh is hostile to God; it does not submit to God's law – indeed it cannot, and those who are in the flesh cannot please God (8: 5–8).

Fathers of the Latin Church, such as Jerome and Augustine, taught that sexual relations were impure, with Jerome bluntly observing that *omnis coitis immundus* ('all sexual relations are dirty'; *Against Jovinian* [1.20]).[8]

Priests of the Early Middle Ages could not only marry like anyone else, but also live, drink, gamble and labour like other peasants. Their specific duty was to preside at sacraments. Apart from that, they helped their wives to sustain families and support children. Canon laws of the Later Middle Ages, beginning in the eleventh century, signalled the demise of a widespread symbiosis between the daily lives of priests and all other Christians in feudal Europe. The creation of laws applying only to clerics established them as a privileged class above and apart from other Christians. A privileged group by definition has laws peculiar to itself. 'Privilege' literally means 'private law'.[9] From the eleventh century onwards, priests could more easily be regarded as sacred persons who were immune from the strictures of secular laws because they could be thought to differ from the laity not only in essence (they are different kinds of humans), but also in degree (they are superior instances of humanity because they are closer to God).

Pondering medieval Christianity helps enormously to illuminate crises among contemporary Christians concerning sexuality. An acute turmoil that has bedevilled Catholic Christians especially over the past three decades has not only been priestly sexual molestation of minors, but the wanton haughtiness of bishops who have tried to protect sexually predatory priests from criminal prosecution. Once it is known that canon law of the eleventh century enshrined clerical privilege as a legal principal, and separated clerical from lay classes, it becomes more comprehensible, though not pardonable, why bishops during recent decades thought they were justified in obscuring the crimes of their priests.

Feudalism and the People's Christianity

To appreciate the ways most people lived and thought as Christians during the medieval period, it is revealing to consider the structure of the societies in which they lived. Feudalism was the social situation in which most medieval people lived. It forms one of the distinguishing features of the Middle Ages, along with monasticism, a strengthened papacy and Christian territorial growth. Ancient Roman societies were not feudal. Everybody in them was subservient to the emperor and laboured for the structures that supported the emperor's interests. The empire of Rome depended on enslaved labour, a vast intercontinental system of roads, armies made up of legions, and provincial governors who enacted locally the decrees of the emperor.

In the immediate aftermath of the collapse of the Roman Empire, local communities that lay within the former territories of the Romans attained more self-sufficiency. They were still agrarian social arrangements, but were able to improve their production of goods by using technologies developed since the sixth century. Fewer horses were able to plough fields more efficiently once they were harnessed in breast-collars. Their efficaciousness was enhanced by the more extensive use of wheeled ploughs, and water mills (not used during antiquity).

A more efficient cultivation of land stands at the root of feudalism, a form of local government that developed in the ninth century and characterized the High Middle Ages. The end of the Early Middle Ages were troubled times for Christians in Europe, principally because they were ceaselessly vulnerable to attack from invaders. Feudalism emerged as a way of strengthening local Christian regions and as an antidote to chaos stemming from constant warfare.

The word 'feudalism' stems from a medieval Latin word for a plot of land – *feud*. It designates a local arrangement between a king or lord and his vassals or serfs. The former owned land but engaged vassals to farm it. In return for the property on which serfs were allowed to live, they pledged allegiance to their local lord. A primary purpose of feudalism was to raise armies. A lord's grant of land (feudum or fief) to a vassal often entailed a promise from the vassal to enter into military service for the lord.

The social pivot of a feudal system was a manorial house supported by a village or cluster of villages. Cumulatively, the villages farmed enough land to feed the serfs, but especially soldiers and their lords. The serfs were not enslaved because their families could live off the land and embark on journeys, yet they were still obliged to work by manual labour several days a week. Their freedom was limited.[10]

The social revolution represented by feudalism developed most extensively in France, which, by 1000 CE, 'had been subdivided into fifty-five separate territories whose ties with the monarchy were limited, conditional, and contractual'.[11] The Christianity practised in these and other feudal countries by lords and their vassals was public and communal, centred either on a village church or manorial chapel. Weddings and funerals were normally celebrated in homes. Relics, shrines, sacraments and indulgences, mixed with vestiges of local pagan customs, formed the staple ingredients of religious lives.

Redemption by Satisfaction

A medieval theologian of the medieval Latin West, Anselm (1033–1109), devised an account of the drama of human salvation that is based on a feudal understanding of human relations. Anselm was a monk in the Norman town of Bec. An Italian by birth, he travelled to Bec as a young man to study with Lanfranc, a monk of the town's abbey. Anselm became a monk himself and later in his life succeeded Lanfranc as the Archbishop of Canterbury.

Anselm was a philosopher as well as a theologian. Shortly before 1100, he wrote a treatise called *Cur Deus Homo?* ('Why did God become a human?'). It was a Christian treatise on salvation that concentrated on Christ's death. The Greek theologian, Origen, had argued in the third century that Jesus, known by later Christians as Christ, died on a cross to make amends to God for the offence rendered to God by human sin. According to Origen, Jesus willingly sacrificed himself on a cross to pay a ransom to the Devil, and so rescue humanity from the consequences of God's wrath. Christians in their long history have never pronounced in favour of one theory of salvation over another, as they did in the field of Christology. There has never been a dogma of salvation shared by all Christians. Origen's was one of the earliest soteriologies (theologies of salvation), but many others vied in later centuries for the allegiance of theologians.

Anselm's soteriology was among them. He regarded all humans as serfs, living under an obligation to serve and obey God. In the Middle Ages, if a serf wronged a lord of a manor, the serf needed to satisfy the lord's right of redress by making reparation for the wrongdoing. The key term in Anselm's account of the drama of human sin and redemption is 'satisfaction'. Something needed to be done by someone to repair damage between God and humans engineered by the latter's sins, as well as to satisfy God's right to be placated. In *Cur Deus Homo?*, Anselm concluded that 'Every sin must be followed either by satisfaction or by punishment' (1.15). In his view, in order to escape punishment, humans needed not only to stop sinning, but also to undertake an act of supererogation; that is, an activity that will make amends for the offence caused by sin. The problem for humans in Anselm's terms is that they have nothing extra to offer God, since they already owe everything they have to their Creator. The solution Anselm proposed to this dilemma is the unavoidability of the Incarnation. Only Christ, recognized as a God–man, could offer himself on the cross as a substitute for humanity and thus make satisfaction for all human beings.[12]

Anselm is still studied by students of philosophy around the world for his ontological arguments that there is a God. An ontological argument is an a priori process that does not observe human experience, but draws a conclusion from a premise or premises concerning God's nature or being (hence 'ontological', from the Greek, *ontos*, 'being'). For Anselm, God is that which nothing greater can be thought. Since there is an idea of God that is not excelled by any other thought, Anselm concluded that there must be a reality of God that corresponds to the idea of God. Philosophers have argued ever since about whether his argument is true or false. For Christians of the Later Middle Ages, Anselm was revered neither because of his soteriology nor because of his ontological arguments, but for the devotional books of prayers and meditations he produced. Even his ontological arguments were not addressed to infidels, but to believing monks in his monastery, for whom he wished to articulate reasons why they were justified in their beliefs.

Crusades

The feudal system of local government worked effectively to sustain Christian warrior knights in the twelfth century who embarked on long military expeditions to subdue Muslims in the East, and especially in Jerusalem. Muslim soldiers seized Jerusalem in 637, but for centuries after allowed Christians to visit there on religious pilgrimages. Throughout the Middle Ages, Christians regarded Jerusalem as the centre of the world. Western cartographers depicted Palestine and Jerusalem in their maps as the pivot of the world, with Western territories drawn on its periphery. The reason Jerusalem was so venerated by medieval Christians is that they believed it was the originating site of the drama of human salvation: Jesus Christ lived and died there, consecrated its soil by shedding his blood, and, by sacrificing himself on a cross, reconciled sinful humanity with a gracious God.[13]

All was relatively well as long as medieval Christians could visit Jerusalem. Such a situation changed forebodingly in 1071, when Turkish Muslims took over control of Jerusalem. They refused to allow Christians, even those who had travelled long distances from Europe, to visit the sacred city. Papal reaction was swift. In 1095, Pope Urban II, at the Council of Clermont, demanded that an army be formed to win back control of Jerusalem. He and other popes of his age did not think of Europe as a hybrid entity ruled by religious and political leaders. Rather, it was a single society governed by the pope, whose authority stemmed directly from Jesus Christ.

The result of Urban's determination that Jerusalem should be controlled by Christians was the creation of a new kind of Christian knight – the *crucesignatus*, or crusader. At the Council of Clermont, Urban had declared it was God's will that Jerusalem be seized by Christians. Robert of Rheims, a monastic chronicler of the events at Clermont, records the overriding sentiment of those who were there: 'When [at Clermont] Pope Urban … said these things … everyone, moved by the same feeling, shouted in unison, "God wills it", "God wills it!"'[14]

A crusader and the expeditions upon which they embarked – crusades – both take their name from the Latin word for cross, *crux*. The crusade launched by Urban II involved 40,000 warriors, 10,000 of whom were mounted on horseback.[15] The symbol of a cross, representing the Roman cross on which Jesus died, was the emblem of their army. Their shields bore crosses and they marched under banners with crosses.

Not all of the soldiers who embarked on the first crusade to capture Jerusalem were knights. Most were serfs who accompanied and supported their masters. The first wave of them left Europe during the summer there in 1096. Urban II had been busy writing letters to rulers throughout the Christian West calling for a crusade. Local lords responded by raising armies which gathered in Constantinople during a period of seven months. Once assembled, the crusaders left for Asia Minor, which was controlled by Turkish Muslims. They laid siege to Antioch, which fell to them in 1098. They gained control of Jerusalem later in the same year. Once in command, they massacred the Muslim inhabitants of the city and burned the synagogue in which Jews had taken refuge from the marauding crusaders.[16] Such behaviour sent shockwaves of terrified horror throughout the Islamic world.

To launch a war in the name of Jesus Christ illustrates how easy it is for him and the tenor of his proclamations to be distorted for entirely different interests. Jesus was not a warrior and there is no textual evidence that he ever countenanced anything like a war. Many medieval Christians, in the East and West, had grown very far away from him, not only in their ready acceptance of social inequity among aristocrats and vassals and the nobles' accumulation of wealth, but also through acquiescence to theologies advocating death–dealing warfare.

There were four major crusades of the Later Middle Ages. The first one concentrated on Jerusalem. A second was called for by Pope Eugenius III. It involved attacks on Wends in Europe who worshipped Slavic deities, and aspired to take control of the Iberian Peninsula from Muslim rulers. While Saxon crusaders attacked Wends in northern Europe, other crusading armies marched for the Holy Land in 1147. When they reached Asia Minor, they were attacked and defeated by a Turkish army. They retreated after they failed to overcome the Muslim commander Nur ad–Din.

In 1187 another Muslim general, Salah ad–Din, also known as Saladin, conquered Jerusalem. With these two military commanders, Nur ad–Din and Salah ad–Din, a traditional concept of Islam – jihad, meaning 'struggle' – was invested with the new meaning of 'holy war'. The jihad was the Islamic equivalent of the Christian crusade.

Hearing of the fall of Jerusalem, Pope Gregory VIII called for a third crusade: 'As with previous crusades the pope promised indulgences (relief in the afterlife from penalties for sins) to any who took what was called a vow of the cross, that is, a vow to go on crusade. Once a vow was taken, of course, one had actually to go on crusade or face excommunication.'[17] The third crusade involved the forces of Emperor Frederick Barbarossa of Germany, King Philip of France, and King Richard of England (Richard the Lion-Heart). Frederick drowned while swimming in the Goeksu River and part of his army went home. For a year Philip and Richard did battle with Salah ad–Din and negotiated a truce with him in 1192. Salah ad–Din retained control of Jerusalem and allowed Christian pilgrims to visit the city, while the coastal regions of Palestine were maintained by Christians.

Schism between East and West

Yet another pope called for yet a further crusade in 1198. Its main protagonists were French and Venetian crusaders. Their crusade ended in a highly perplexing and morally ignoble and inhumane way. The climax of the fourth crusade was baffling because it involved an attack upon, and slaughter of, Christians by Christians. It was ignoble because it involved military slaughter and pillage. The crusaders attacked the capital of Byzantium, Constantinople, in 1203 and again in 1204. During the second attack they entered the city, sent its Christian emperor and patriarch into exile, plundered the city, and killed local inhabitants who were not soldiers. They installed a Latin Patriarch and imposed Latin liturgies on the populace.

The crusaders' attack on Constantinople became a symbol for Byzantine Christians of a growing animosity between Christian East and West that had been brewing at least from the ninth century. To this day the East and West are in schism; that is, canonically and institutionally separated because of mutual antipathy. A schism is a divorce between Churches. Another symbol of this painful parting, and for some its beginning, is the year 1054, when papal legates visiting Constantinople excommunicated its patriarch, while he in turn excommunicated them.

The *filioque* controversy was discussed above, but it was aggravated in 1014 when Pope Benedict VIII decreed that the Churches of Rome could add the expression of *filioque* to the creed professed at liturgies. Also in the first half of the eleventh century, Latin-rite Normans invaded Sicily and the south of Italy and forced Greek-speaking churches they encountered there to worship according to Latin rites. Michael Cerularius, the patriarch of Constantinople, decided to act against what he judged to be Western ecclesiastical abuses. He decreed that Latin-speaking churches in Constantinople were to adopt Greek customs. The Normans strengthened their hold on Italy and took Pope Leo IX into captivity. In response, he sent three legates to Constantinople to seek assistance from the Eastern emperor.

The envoys were led by Cardinal Humbert. Once they arrived in Constantinople they met the emperor, but patriarch Michael refused to see them. Humbert wanted to deliver a letter to the patriarch complaining of the way Latin churches there had had changes to their worship forced upon them. After several weeks of dispute between the Greeks and the Latins, Humbert launched a daring course of action. He did so on his own authority, not knowing that Pope Leo had died while Humbert was travelling, and had not yet been replaced. During the morning of 16 July 1054 the legates entered Hagia Sophia, the principal church of Constantinople, and left on the altar a bull (a document with a papal seal, composed by Humbert, not Leo), excommunicating the patriarch. Michael Cerularius responded in the same year by excommunicating the legates.[18]

1054 is frequently cited in text books as the decisive period for the schism between East and West. It is more accurate to regard it as a symbol of a separation along with several others, such as the crusades, that had been set in motion by disputes between Greek and Latin Christians following the Council of Nicaea, seven centuries before Humbert and Michael Cerularius excommunicated each other. The rift signalled by such symbols still obtains between Latin Rite and Orthodox Christians. Unity for and among Christians currently eludes them, as they are dispersed around the globe as atomized communities having little or nothing to do with each other.

Flagellants

The Later Middle Ages constituted a time among Christians of intense religious fervour, conversion and revivalism. The crusades were medieval expressions of religious earnestness, despite their ferocity and barbarity and the irreparable harm they caused among Muslims and Byzantine Christians. They were simultaneously military campaigns, religious pilgrimages, and a call to Christians to take seriously their religious obligations. They were but one expression of medieval religious ardour that was accompanied by the founding of new religious orders, papal reform of clerical life, and the growth of monasticism.

Religious enthusiasm among medieval Christians was not confined to monks, clerics and crusaders. It also found voice among a general Christian populace who, in the High Middle Ages, were keen to conform their lives to that of Jesus Christ to such an extent that they inflicted pain on their bodies in imitation of the flagellation the Gospels recount Jesus received at the hands of soldiers in Jerusalem. As odd as it may seem to contemporary Christians and other audiences, medieval confraternities for flagellants were formed in many sites in Europe during the thirteenth and fourteenth centuries. Like crusades, they involved violence, but unlike crusaders, the violence was self-inflicted, not other-directed.

Flagellants were also known as Brothers of the Cross and *disiplinati*. The whip they used on their naked backs was called a *disciplina*, 'discipline'. Bands of flagellants formed in Italy, including Rome, and also in Germany, the Netherlands and Poland. They undertook to scourge themselves publicly as they processed through towns of Europe. They did this as a mimetic exercise to experience for themselves the suffering of their Christ, and as an act of penance for their sins. Most public flagellants were men, but women could discipline themselves in the privacy of their homes. Their involvement in the religious revival of the flagellants intensified after 1260.

Figure 13: Flagellants around the time of the Black Death

That year was a milestone in the history of medieval *disciplinati* because it marks the year Joachites (disciples of the Calabrian charismatic prophet, Joachim of Fiore [d. 1202]) announced an impending calamity, during which an Antichrist would persecute Christians. If apocalyptic predictions sparked the formation of groups of flagellants, their movement was further strengthened in the fourteenth century in response to the Black Death of 1347–50, when bubonic plague ravaged Europe (Figure 14).[19]

Pilgrims

Those medieval Christians who were not given to drawing their own blood by whipping themselves found other intense ways of expressing their religious enthusiasms. One was to enter monasteries and nunneries – recalling that most monks were not clerics. Another was to undertake pilgrimages to sacred sites.

Embarking on a pilgrimage could be dangerous as well as adventurous. In the Middle Ages, the three most popular termini for pilgrimages were Rome, Jerusalem and the Cathedral of Saint James, in the city of Compostella of northern Spain. Church architecture in all three cities during the twelfth and thirteenth centuries reflected a growing need to accommodate large numbers of pilgrims. Churches were built with very large naves, often with five aisles, as well as chapels in ambulatories that could house relics for pilgrims to venerate. Churches were built on hills along pilgrimage routes so that they could be seem from afar by pilgrims.[20] Participants in pilgrimages often travelled with a distinctive uniform called a *habitus* – tunic or dress. Whereas crusaders marched under the emblem of a cross, pilgrims took staves and wallets as symbols of their distinctive status.[21] Those medieval Christians who set out on pilgrimages could do so once, several times, or spend an entire lifetime as pilgrims. They were not meant to take money with them, but to rely on the hospitality of Christian households throughout their travels.

The motives for pilgrims were as interesting as they were varied. Enthusiasts could embark on a pilgrimage as an act of penance for their sins, imposed either by themselves or a clerical confessor to whom they had declared their sins. Pilgrims could also be sent on their journeys by a civil judge as a punishment for major crimes. When in the eleventh century John of Arundel was on his way from

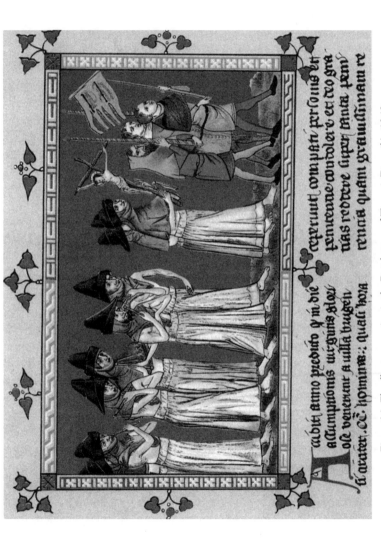

Figure 14: *Flagellants processing in the Dutch town of Tournai (Doornik), 1349*

England to engage in war in France, he kidnapped 60 women and girls from a convent near the port town of Southampton, and gave them to his soldiers for their pleasure. During a storm at sea on his way to France, it became necessary to lighten the load of his ship, so he had the women and girls tossed into the sea. He later went on a pilgrimage to Jerusalem in reparation for his crime. When he died, a further penance was imposed on him: he was buried without clothing and in chains.[22]

Pilgrimages could be perilous. Apart from poor diet and physical fatigue endured by unaccustomed travellers, pilgrims were vulnerable to attack by wild animals and brigands. A pilgrim recorded in the fourteenth century that during a pilgrimage to Rome in 1350, half of the pilgrims were killed or robbed before they reached their destination.[23]

New Religious Foundations

Crusades, confraternities of flagellants and pilgrimages were all public manifestations of what in the Middle Ages became known as *devotio* (heightened religious fervour). They all depended on revivalism – reawakening people's enthusiasm for Christianity – and conversion or the recruitment of devotees.

Devotio flourished throughout the entire Later Middle Ages. A further manifestation of its prevalence and intensity during the time was the foundation of new religious orders of monks, canons and friars. Whereas a monk lives in a cloistered community and follows a daily routine of liturgical prayer, manual labour and private contemplation, a canon is a cleric whose primary responsibility is the daily and public celebration of liturgy in a cathedral, basilica or major church. Friars are neither monks nor canons even though they place liturgical prayer at the centre of their lives. Friars (from the Latin, *frater*, brother) were mobile and mendicant. They were not vowed to live in one place for the entirety of their lives, but could be deployed to address specific needs wherever they arose. As they travelled, they were meant to beg (Latin: *mendicare*) for their daily sustenance.

At the beginning of the eleventh century the most significant monastic foundation was the Benedictine abbey of Cluny in Burgundy. It was founded in 910. It was a vast monastery, due in part to a papal decree allowing monks from other monasteries to be released from their vow of stability to enter Cluny. The abbots of Cluny were exempt from the control of bishops. Several churches were built at Cluny, but in 1130 Pope Innocent II consecrated an abbatial church there that was the largest anywhere in Christendom. It served as the principal site of worship for 300 monks, who spent up to eight hours involved in liturgical prayer. They were motivated by the belief that they were set apart from others to pray for sinful people. The more they prayed, the more they helped an unredeemed humanity. Unlike other Benedictine foundations, Cluniac monks were not devoted to manual labour.[24]

In this they strayed from the intentions of Benedict of Nursia. Late in the eleventh century, a new form of monasticism developed that was an attempt to revive the letter and the spirit of the *Rule of Saint Benedict*. Around 1098, a group of about 20 monks moved from the abbey of Moslesme to establish a new reforming monastery at Citeaux. The Latin name of this site is Cistercium. The reforming monks thus became known as Cistercians. They envisaged a simpler life than Cluniac monks, with a stricter observance of Benedict's monastic principals.

One of the most renowned Christian preachers of the twelfth century was the Cistercian, Bernard of Clairvaux (1090–1153). From his own monastery of Clairvaux he founded 68 subsidiary Cistercian houses. He travelled and preached extensively, and was responsible for a spectacular growth of the Cistercian Order in the twelfth and thirteenth centuries. Apart from his treatises, about 300 of his sermons and 500 of his letters are extant. He supported the second crusade with his preaching and he was so successful at promoting Cistercian ideals that by 1227 in Europe there were more than 130 Cistercian bishops and 19 cardinals. Pope Eugenius III (in office from 1145 to 1153) was also a Cistercian.[25]

Cistercians devoted themselves so much to manual labour that they were able to help surrounding local communities. In 1291, three Cistercian monasteries in Yorkshire became major producers of textiles: the abbey of Fountains kept 18,000 sheep for wool; Rievaulx, 1400; and Jervaulx, 12,000. By 1220, Burgundy was home to 200 Cistercian foundations with farms and vineyards.[26]

Medieval religious fervour manifested itself in the creation of several other religious orders throughout the High Middle Ages. St Bruno (c. 1032–1101) established one of the most exacting monastic foundations ever known and which continues today. It is known as the Carthusian Order. In 1084, Bruno founded a monastery called the Grande Chartreuse (hence 'Carthusian' from the Latin, *Cartusiae*), in the Chartreuse Mountains to the north of the French city of Grenoble. His monks led and lead a strictly contemplative life in virtually complete silence, apart from attending Mass on Sundays and solemn religious feast days. Each monk lived and worked in a cell, in isolation from others. Carthusians do not observe the same kind of daily liturgical timetable (*horarium*) as other monks.[27] A less rigorous form of vowed religious life was established by St Norbert of Xanten (c. 1080–1134) in Germany. He was a nobleman who decided to withdraw from society. He travelled to France and settled as a hermit in forests at Prémontré. Others joined him, and around 1120 they formed the Premonstratensian Order, thus named after Prémontré. Their abbeys spread throughout Europe. By the middle of the thirteenth century they had established around 500 houses of canons, in lands as diverse as Ireland and Palestine.

Premonstratensians were distinguished from monks in that they were an avowedly clerical order. As such, they were canons regular – that is, associated with a major church to celebrate liturgy (canons) – and vowed to follow a rule of life ('regular', from Latin, *regula*, 'rule'). Premonstratensians adopted the *Rule of Saint Augustine*.[28] To this day, Catholic clerics are divided canonically between regular and secular clergy. Secular clerics live alone amidst other people 'in the world' (*saeculum*, 'world'), while regular clerics live according to a rule in community. Premonstratensians are also called Norbertines (after their founder) and White Canons (because of their white habit).

The Friars

The thirteenth century gave rise to a new breed of Christian revivalists called friars. The Castilian canon, Dominic of Caleruega (c. 1174–1221), succeeded in 1216 in having constitutions for a new order of friars approved by Pope Honorius III. They were to be called the Order of Friars Preachers (*Ordo Praedicatorum*). Informally they were also called Dominicans and Blackfriars (because of a black mantle worn over an otherwise whitish habit). They were founded for the specific purpose of preaching wherever Christianity needed to be introduced or strengthened. Unlike monks and canons, they were mobile and could be moved from country to country. Most medieval Dominicans were priests. Their order was divided into three: a First Order included priests and brothers who helped clerics in work; a Second Order for cloistered nuns; and a Third Order including people who wished to adopt Dominican patterns of prayer in their homes. Since their inception, Dominicans replaced manual labour with study, regarded as a *religious* observance. They followed the Rule of Saint Augustine and their Constitutions modified those of the Premonstratensians. They reasoned that it is pointless to preach unless the content of preaching is intelligent, informed and reflective of the Gospel, so they liked to have their students study in the new universities that were growing in Bologna, Paris, Oxford and Cambridge. They arrived in Oxford in 1221, the year of Dominic's death. Dominic was canonized in 1234. Norbert was declared a saint by Pope Gregory XIII in 1582.

A younger contemporary of Dominic, Francis of Assisi (1181/2–1226), succeeded earlier than Dominic in securing papal approval for a *Regula Primitiva* ('Primitive Rule') for a band of like-minded friars who wanted to join him and practise a radical renunciation of property. Innocent III gave him the sanction he sought in 1209. Francis was the son of a merchant in Assisi, but renounced the commercial profession of his father radically to imitate the life of Jesus by not possessing property or means of income. Both Francis and Dominic wanted their friars to be wandering mendicants who would return to their bases for prayer, contemplation and study. While individual monks could lead extremely unencumbered lives, their orders and monasteries frequently became exceptionally wealthy with extensive ownership of land. After the deaths of Francis and Dominic, their followers soon lost the fire of their founders, and began to settle in large friaries (for Franciscans) and priories (for Dominicans). Both friaries and priories are convents. While convents are often thought to be homes of nuns, since the Middle Ages they have also been the religious houses of friars. The contemporary business 'convention' has the same Latin root as a convent (*conventus*, 'assembly' or 'meeting'). Dominic's convents were called priories because they were led by a friar who was regarded as a first among equals. Unlike monks and canons, Dominicans elect their priors, and were thus forerunners of modern democracy.

The other medieval friars that emerged were the Carmelites (The Order of the Brothers of Our Lady of Mount Carmel, founded in the late twelfth century), Servites (founded around 1233), Augustinians (or Friars Hermit, established in 1256) and Minims (founded in 1435). Servites, who still exist, take the name from their Latin title, *Ordo Servorum BVM* ('Order of the Servants of the Blessed Virgin Mary'), as do Minims (*Ordo Fratrum Minimorum*, the 'Order of Little (as in humble) Friars').

Devotion to Mary

The formal names of Carmelites, Servites and Minims reflect a piety that was common to medieval Christians – a pronounced devotion to Mary, Jesus' mother. Statues of her adorned convents, cathedrals and monasteries throughout the Middle Ages. Dominicans propagated throughout Europe a form of cyclical repetitive prayer called the rosary, which consisted of a string of beads forming a circle that was used to count the number of prayers. The recitation of the rosary became a standard domestic practice in Catholic homes from the High Middle Ages to the Second Vatican Council of the 1960s, and in many Catholic homes until the present. Three forms of prayer that constituted the rosary are among the most famous of all Christian prayers: the Lord's Prayer, or Our Father, the Hail Mary, and the Gloria (from its open phrases, 'Glory be to the Father and to the Son and to the Holy Spirit'). Most of the cathedrals in France, including Notre Dame ('Our Lady') in Paris and Chartres nearby, are dedicated to Mary. Of the 580 cathedrals built in Europe during the century spanning 1170 and 1270, by far the majority were dedicated to Mary. A study of 700 fourteenth-century religious paintings on panels discovered that 55 per cent of them depicted Mary, 35 per cent Jesus Christ, recognizable saints in 9 per cent, and unidentifiable saints in a further 15 per cent.[29]

Hounded Heretics

One of the more heart-rending stories of the High Middle Ages concerns attempts to exterminate movements of lay Christians who wished to follow teachings of Jesus in a literal way, especially his frequent counsels to avoid riches. Cluny, Cistercians, canons and friars all enjoyed papal support. Other zealous groups among Christians in the Later Middle Ages did not, and were hounded by papal crusades

Figure 15: Painting of Mary of Burgundy reading prayers before an image of the Virgin Mary, c. 1470s

and inquisitions. One such group were the Cathars (from Greek, *katharoi*, 'the pure ones'). They were also called Albigenses because the geographical centre of their attempt at renewing Christianity was the town of Albi, in the southern French region of Languedoc. Their religious world view was essentially Manichaean; that is, it posited the existence of two rival powers – evil and goodness. They regarded all manifestations of matter, including bodies, as evil. As a result, they taught that sexual relations, especially those that produced offspring, were to be avoided as evil activities. Of course, expecting human beings to renounce sexual encounters was expecting too much, so Cathars established two classes among themselves: the perfect (*perfecti*), who were celibate and sexually continent; and other believers who were not able to live without partners. Cathars lived extremely austere lives, renouncing dairy products and meat (evil matter). They did not believe in the doctrine of the Trinity because it maintained that the Second Person of the Trinity became incarnate, and they denounced sacraments, including the efficacy of the Mass, because

Figure 16: Cathars being expelled from Carcasonne in 1209 during the crusade against them

they linked God to material things. Their worship was centred on readings from the Bible.[30]

Pope Innocent III tried to persuade Cathars to relinquish their ways. He began by asking Cistercians to confront them, but this initiative failed. He then asked the French king to try to persuade them. The king responded by launching a wave of crusades against them.

The twelfth and thirteenth centuries represent a period of sustained religious creativity and earnestness among lay men and women. Apart from Cathars, other like-minded Christians banded together to imitate in their lives the unencumbered lives of Jesus and his disciples. These groups included Waldensians, the Poor Men of Lyons, Humiliati, the New Apostles and Dolcinians. What united them all was their admirable determination to live as poor people at exactly the same time as many monasteries and prelates had become exceptionally wealthy. All of these groups were eventually condemned as heterodox.

Valdès of Lyons, after whom Waldensians were named, converted in the mid-1170s from being a rich merchant to devote himself to preaching. He divested himself of his wealth and possessions. Other lay men and women joined him and undertook the task of preaching. The Waldensians spread from Lyons to Southern France and Lombardy. In Lombardy, a group of them fell out with each other, giving rise to yet another group of zealous preachers called the Poor Men of Lyons. Both groups sought to lead strict lives of evangelical poverty; that is, by conforming to the Gospels' warnings about wealth.

Concurrently with the rise of Waldensians, enthusiasm for evangelical poverty became intense among lay Christians in the Po Valley of Lombardy, and manifested itself in humbly clad men and women undertaking preaching. They were known as Humiliati (the Little Humble Ones), as an anonymous writer noted around 1200: 'They called themselves Humiliati because they did not use coloured cloth for clothing, but restricted themselves to plain dress.'[31]

By the early fourteenth century, lay reforming preachers who were determined to live according to the Gospels, had become widely distrusted by priests and bishops. The reason was not that the poor preachers were preaching nonsense, but that they dared to preach at all. Preaching for their clergy was their prerogative. None of the medieval lay preachers who sought to lead poor lives is as admirably notorious as Dolcino of Novara, whom Dante portrays in his *Inferno* (28: 55–60). Dolcino settled with a group of followers in the Sesia valley of Piedmont around 1304. This band, the Dolcinians, were distinguished from other lay movements by their intense apocalyptic predictions that they were living at the end of time before a calamitous apocalypse. Unfortunately for the group, Pope Clement V launched a crusade against them. The Dolcinians took up arms to protect themselves, but to no avail. They were captured and tried before an ecclesiastical court. Found guilty of heresy, they were put to death.[32]

The Inquisition

One of the most feared of all medieval institutions was the papal Inquisition. Dolcino met his fate because of it. By the fourth century, Christians could certainly be punished if their views differed from teachings defined by councils, but their punishments ranged from excommunication, the imposition of a penance or banishment.

In the early twelfth century, bishops were enjoined by Pope Lucius III to investigate accusations of heresy in their dioceses, and he prepared guidelines for the conduct of investigations. These episcopal inquiries, or inquisitions, were still not death-dealing. In the thirteenth century, episcopal inquisitions transmuted into a papal Inquisition, initiated by Pope Gregory IX in 1241. Whereas Pope Innocent III had tried to welcome and incorporate new religious initiatives, such as the Franciscans, into the Church, Gregory established a body of investigators to detect and root out heresy. These inquisitors were mostly Dominicans and Franciscans. The papal Inquisition occasionally dealt with heretics by handing them over to secular powers for execution.[33]

Sober reflection uncovers that Cathars, Waldensians, Humiliati and Dolcinians were just as devoted to the Gospel as any monk, friar, bishop or pope. Their virtual extinction in the fourteenth century ended a vibrant Christian culture that was devoted utterly to the Bible. With the often violent hounding of heretics, orthodoxy certainly triumphed: 'but in the process, a valuable religious force was lost'.[34]

A New Teaching: Transubstantiation

Amid papal concerns about heretics, a new Christian doctrine was formulated that remains one of the clear defining boundaries between Catholic and Protestants. It concerned the Mass, the central act of medieval worship. More particularly it focused on what transpired during Mass when a priest or bishop invoked the Holy Spirit over bread and wine, to transform them into the body and blood of Christ. Cathars had shunned the Mass and, in response, Innocent III convoked the Fourth Lateran Council in 1215. Its bishops produced 80 constitutions, of which the first three contain new Christian teachings. The first one is a profession of Catholic faith. It involves an account of what happens with the bread and wine when they are consecrated by a priest:

> There is indeed one universal church of the faithful, outside of which nobody at all is saved, in which Jesus Christ is both priest and sacrificed. His body and blood are truly contained in the sacrament of the altar under the forms of bread and wine, the bread and wine having been changed in substance, by God's power, into his body and blood, so that in order to achieve this mystery of unity we receive from God what he received from us. Nobody can effect this sacrament except a priest who has been properly ordained according to the church's keys, which Jesus Christ himself gave to the apostles and their successors.[35]

The new phrase that appears in this definition to define Catholic faith is 'changed in substance', which in the original Latin of Lateran IV is '*transsubstantiatis*'. This world became rendered in English in neo-Latin as 'transubstantiation'. From the Fourth Lateran Council until now, the doctrine of transubstantiation remains the preferred theory of the Catholic Church to explain what happens with the bread and wine at Mass. As a theory or doctrine, it relies on Aristotle's distinction between a substance and accidents. A substance is the underlying being of a reality that makes a thing what it is – that which renders bread to be bread and wine to be wine. An 'accident' is the aspect of a substance that is perceptible to human experience or sensation. The doctrine of transubstantiation asserts that by the power of the Holy Spirit the substance of bread is changed to the body of Christ and the substance of wine into his blood. The change involved is not perceptible to human senses or empirical observation, but only to the mind.

Mysticism

The doctrine of transubstantiation reflects an intense religious earnestness among medieval Christians. Another distinct symptom of religious creativity and intensity prevalent throughout the Later Middle Ages was mysticism. While the word 'mysticism' connotes for some cultish secrets or magic, it was and is essentially a particular form of human experience. Some people interpret intense experiences in their lives as involving a personal encounter with God that is mediated through human love, perception of beauty, or in moments of isolation. Mysticism is not a public, communal experience. A person cannot share a mystical moment with anyone else for the simple reason that each and every experience that is interpreted as mystical involves the interpretation of an individual interpreting *subject*. Medieval mystics included women as well as men, married as well as single, and regular Christians. Among them were Hildegard of Bingen (1098–1179), Meister Eckhart (c. 1260–1327), Catherine of Siena (d. 1380), who like Meister Eckhart was a Dominican, Bridget of Sweden (1303–73), Margery Kempe (b. c. 1373) and Thomas à Kempis (c. 1380–1471).

Scholasticism

Theologians of the Later Middle Ages were able to use the scholarship of earlier generations of Eastern and Western theologians, while benefiting from the universities of Europe that were created in the eleventh and twelfth century. They also benefited from Latin versions of Aristotle's works that had been preserved in Arabic by Muslims, and which were reintroduced into Europe in the twelfth century. The result was scholasticism: a systematic articulation of Christian beliefs based on Greek philosophy and Aristotelian logic. Great medieval theologians included Peter Abelard, Peter Damian, Duns Scotus, Albert the Great, Thomas Aquinas and Bonaventure. All of these theologians were adept at studying the Bible and they normally began their careers by studying to be masters of sacred scripture. Aquinas wrote scripture commentaries, as well as two large syntheses of theology: one intended for students of theology – the *Summa Theologiae* ('Summary of Theology'); and the other meant to be used to convert pagans, Jews and Muslims – the *Summa Contra Gentiles* ('Summary Against the Peoples').

Gothic Architecture

In the Later Middle Ages, Christian beliefs continued to be expressed with a striking creative fecundity in architecture, music and art. The Romanesque style of building churches, favoured by the Cluniacs, was less prevalent by the twelfth century because a new style of architecture labelled Gothic architecture emerged in the eleventh century, initially with one building – St-Denis, just to the north of Paris.

Gothic architectural style differed from Romanesque in that the walls of its churches were much taller, so tall that they needed to be supported by stone buttresses on the exterior of the walls. Taller walls allowed for larger windows, and hence far more light. Gothic cathedrals could be enormous, such as those in Rheims, Paris, Cologne and Salisbury. Their vaults and arches were often peaked rather than rounded.[36]

Each Gothic cathedral was a treasure trove of stained glass windows, murals, paintings, sculptures and statues. Art galleries for a general public were unknown in the Middle Ages. Works of art were housed in churches and the homes of people wealthy enough to afford their creation.

The acoustics of large Gothic cathedrals, with their rich harmonics and extensive reverberation times, facilitated the development of harmony in Western music, which is particularly notable in the medieval form of choral composition known as organum.[37] This form essentially involved tenors or baritones sustaining notes for a lengthy periods while more florid melodies were sung above them at a higher pitch, thus creating harmonic intervals between voices and in successions of simple chords. It was developed in large medieval cathedrals, notably so in Notre Dame de Paris.

Conclusion

At the beginning of the fourteenth century, the papacy was in acute trouble. A bitter row between the King of France and Pope Boniface

Figure 17: The Gothic Cathedral of Rheims, France, begun during the 1230s

VIII (1294–1303) ended in the Pope's death through excessive fretfulness. A succession of popes after him set up court in the French
city of Avignon. The papacy was transferred back to Rome in
1377/8, but a new pope, Urban VI (1378–89), proved to be a despot.

Cardinals disaffected with him left Rome and, returning to Avignon, elected a rival (Clement VII) whom others regarded as an antipope. The papacy was at any rate in schism, eventually producing three contenders for the papal throne. The schism ended in 1417 with a new election of a single pope.[38] After the fifteenth century, the papacy never again regained a hegemony over Western Christians. Its loss of power mirrors another: the Eastern Christian and Roman Empire died in 1453 when Ottoman Turks captured Constantinople and killed Constantine XI Palaeologus, the last of the Byzantine emperors.[39]

By the fifteenth century, Western Christians were largely united in believing the following 13 fundamental doctrines:

(a) God created the world in six days and rested on a seventh;
(b) God created archangels and angels;
(c) some angels became devils because they rebelled against God under their leader, Satan;
(d) God is a Trinity of Persons;
(e) the first parents, Adam and Eve, sinned against God in the Garden of Eden, bequeathing to all subsequent generations of humans their original sin;
(f) God sent the divine and human Christ into the world to save human beings by sacrificing himself on a cross to propitiate God and rescue them from the temptations of Satan;
(g) Christ founded the Church and its seven sacraments, which are Baptism, Confirmation, Eucharist (the Mass), Penance (going to confession), Matrimony, Holy Orders and Extreme Unction (an anointing at the time of death);
(h) those who commit mortal or deadly sins will go to hell along with all those who are not baptized into the Church so as to wash away original sin;
(i) the pope inherited the authority of Christ and shares it with bishops who are the successors to the Twelve Apostles;
(j) God works miracles in the world;
(k) Christians can pray to saints and martyrs in heaven asking them to intercede with God to procure help and favours;
(l) The human being is a composite of a body and soul. At the point of the body's death the soul will be judged immediately by God and will end up either in hell, purgatory or heaven. Those souls

who reach heaven will wait there until the last day of the world's history, when their Christ will triumphantly return to earth to judge all the remaining living and all the dead, raising the bodies of those pleasing to God to be reunited with their souls in heaven; and

(m) in heaven, resurrected Christians and they alone will join saints and martyrs, angels and archangels in seeing God.

To formulate this edifice of doctrine took 1500 years. In the fifteenth and sixteenth centuries, the subject of the next chapter, fissures began to appear in it as the Middle Ages came to a swift and unambiguous end.

Part 3
Discovery and Diversity

Chapter V
Renaissance and Discovery

'I came that they may have life, and have it abundantly.'
John 10: 10

Rebirth is an odd concept. No neonate or thing can be born twice. All human beings have one physical birth and a single death. A star is born in the sense of forming from gases only once before it dies out. Despite the strangeness of the term, rebirth was used by historians in the eighteenth century to designate fifteenth- and sixteenth-century Italian civilization as it was expressed in literature and art. The French word for 'rebirth' is 'le renaissance'. In 1855, the historian Jules Michelet (1798–1874) published a 17-volume study of French history. He called the seventh volume 'Le Renaissance'. He generated a term that has been used ever since to specify a period of European history spanning at least the fifteenth and sixteenth centuries. In the nineteenth century, Jacob Burckhardt (1818–97), a Swiss historian, popularized the term for German-speaking audiences with his book *Die Kultur der Renaissance in Italien* ('The Culture of the Renaissance in Italy', 1860). As his title suggests, the Renaissance began mainly in Italy before it spread elsewhere in Europe. S.G.C. Middlemore introduced Burckhardt's tome to an English-speaking audience by translating it as *The Civilization of the Renaissance in Italy* (1878).[1] As with the expression 'Middle Ages', the concept of a Renaissance was not used in the fourteenth, fifteenth or sixteenth centuries to tag a time of cultural regeneration in Europe. It was employed much later to refer to a period when Christianity inspired a flood of intellectual and artistic creations by painters, writers, sculptors, architects and musicians. The Renaissance had its roots in the second half of the fourteenth century and thus overlapped with the High Middle Ages. It represents an important stage in Christian life and thought because Renaissance Christians who were not priests, monks or nuns bequeathed to all later generations literary and artistic compositions that expressed structurally (in buildings), aurally (with music), and visually (in fine art), Christian beliefs and ethical values.

The purpose of this chapter is to consider ways in which Christianity changed during the Renaissance. Towards the end of the fifteenth century, Spanish and Portuguese Christian explorers set sail from Europe and came across the Caribbean, awakening Europeans to the Americas and revising the geography of the Bible. New scholarship, thinking and art during the Renaissance, coupled with a revolution in geography symbolized by Columbus, and in astronomy by Copernicus, collectively proved an irritant for patristic and medieval dogmatic theology. The Renaissance was the primary seedbed for the growth of a civilization that flourished in the eighteenth-century Enlightenment, the first period since the beginning of the High Middle Ages that Christianity was subjected to widespread and withering critique in Europe, without fear of an Inquisition.

Christianity's Second Encounter with Antiquity

The Renaissance represented Christianity's second major engagement with the thought and civilization of ancient Greece and Rome. The first occurred over the first four or five centuries of Christianity's history. Aspects of ancient Greek philosophy were certainly known to medieval scholars. Theologians such as Aquinas and Scotus were keen on Aristotle's logic and metaphysics. Their primary work was articulating Christian doctrines for a medieval audience, and they used Aristotle to advance that aim.

The hallmark of the Renaissance was humanism: a culture based on a renewed interest in and intense scrutiny of ancient Greek and Latin literature. Roman authors such as Seneca, Cicero and Virgil were known to medieval scholars, primarily thanks to the painstaking labour of monks, who copied papyri onto parchment to be preserved in monastic libraries.

During the early fifteenth century, interest in Latin classics was reawakened in Italy. One of those involved in the reawakening was Poggio Bracciolini (1381–1459), a papal secretary. In his spare time while attending the Council of Constance (or Konstanz, contemporary Germany) between 1414 and 1418, he perused the contents of local monastic libraries. There he found two previously unknown works by Cicero and Quintilian's (c. 35–c. 100 CE) *Rudiments of Oratory* (*Institutio oratoria*). Throughout the rest of the fifteenth century Cicero's prose was so closely studied and imitated in Italy that it became the standard by which Renaissance humanists judged the worth of literature.[2]

Humanism involved more than a liking for ancient texts. It also involved a keen admiration for human dignity. This aspect is seen vividly in sculpture of the fifteenth and sixteenth centuries. Statues displayed prominently and publicly in towns are good indicators of what those who erected them esteemed. The ancient Egyptians, Etruscans, Persians, Greeks and Romans all loved to show off statues of their Gods and heroes. Their enthusiasm for displaying bodies publicly was rekindled during the Renaissance. A statue discovered in 1506 encapsulates vividly an enthralment with the dignity, beauty and powers of the human body that enthralled Renaissance Christians in Italy. The statue depicts Laöcoon flanked by his two sons, as they are writhing in their death throes. They are being squeezed before being eaten by two giant serpents.

This statue was discovered in the ruins of the palace of the Emperor Titus, who, as a general in 70 CE, loosed the Xth Legion on Jerusalem, which slew thousands of the city's inhabitants. Three Rhodians created the sculpture. According to various tales of Greek mythology, Laöcoon was a prince and priest. Because he opposed bringing the giant wooden horse secretly hiding soldiers in its interior (mentioned in Virgil's *Aeneid*) within the walls of Troy, the God Poseidon dispatched two immense serpents to travel across the sea from the island of Tenedos to kill Laöcoon and his sons. Pliny the Elder (c. 61–c. 112) admired the Rhodian sculpture more than any marble carving or painting.[3]

Medieval art was avowedly Christian in terms of its purpose and content. So too was Renaissance painting, music and sculpture. Renaissance art began to distinguish itself not merely by producing depictions of figures from antiquity, along with Christian saints, martyrs, kings and popes. During the fifteenth and sixteenth centuries, artists, following the ancients, were far more prone to display images of completely naked bodies than were their medieval predecessors.

Figure 18: Laöcoon and sons being killed by serpents, c. 60 CE

Dante and Giotto

Two Christians who straddle the transition from the Middle Ages to the Renaissance were Dante Alighieri and Giotto di Bondone. Both originally came from Florence. Dante was a poet and keenly participated in the politics of Florence. The second activity caused him to be banished from the city. As a precursor of the fifteenth-century

Renaissance, he stressed (especially in his *Il convivo*, 'The banquet') that Italian was a *literary* language, not just market-place babble. In a work of prose called *De monarchia* ('The monarchy'), he argued that a state should not only be autonomous but secular. In these writings, he presaged a primary feature of the Renaissance which was an enthusiasm for the *saeculum* – the every-day world of here and now in contradistinction to an anticipated otherworldly paradise or transcendental sphere. Medieval Christianity was theocentric – all people and all things have their purpose and reason for existence in God. Renaissance Christianity marks a trend among Christians to be more concentrated on themselves, their cities and their creative powers.

Giotto was a very different man. Originally a peasant boy, he developed a style of painting that differed from medieval portraiture. The most prominent and frequently encountered artistic images of the Middle Ages show the baby Jesus; Mary, extolled as his Virgin Mother; Jesus crucified or being crucified; martyrs being tortured; and saints radiating holiness (signified by haloes or other icons of honour). These figures are often portrayed as serene, static or staring heavenwards. Giotto altered that style, as can be seen in the frescoes he painted in the Scroegni and Arena Chapels in Padua:

> The figures gain bulk, resolve in space, and move across prop-like buildings or landscape whose lines and volumes add to the meaning of the scene. Above all, the figures have expression. They show love, fear, rage, and anguish, both in the arrangement of their features and in the inclinations and tensions of the stocky, mobile figures.[4]

Giotto was a vivid colourist. The allure of his pigments made the people he portrayed far more arresting.

Neither Dante nor Giotto could be called a Renaissance humanist in a strict sense. Dante, for all his excitement about the secular city, still espoused a medieval doctrinal schema of human destiny through purgatory, hell and paradise. He imagines and traces his own journey through all three in his massive *Divina commedia* ('The Divine Comedy'). In this work he shows that human beings, for all their abilities, can be caught in an infernal, sad, sullen, inert and inarticulate state, blind to the beauty of reality. As he says himself when commenting on hell:

'Sullen were we in the air made sweet by the Sun;
in the glory of his shining our hearts poured
a bitter smoke. Sullen were we begun;
sullen we lie forever in this ditch.'
This litany they gargle in their throats
as if they sang, but lacked the words and pitch.[5]

Boccaccio and Petrarch

It is with literature written in the latter half of the fourteenth century that a typically Renaissance enthralment with the human being is amply evident. Giovanni Boccaccio (1313–75) and Francesco Petrarca (Francis Petrarch, 1304–74) wrote with a marked engrossment for people.

Boccaccio, like Dante and Giotto, was a Florentine Christian, although with a difference. He was not afraid to expose the Church to withering ridicule and satire. Around 1453, he completed his most famous work, *The Decameron*. Its strange title is a conflation of two Greek words: *déka* ('ten') and *hēméra* ('day'). It consists of a series of short stories told by ten people who had lodged over a period of ten days in a villa outside the walls of Florence. In the course of their sojourn, each of the lodgers tells a pointed tale.

What, it could be asked, does any of this have to do with Christianity? Boccaccio wrote in the aftermath of the Black Death, the first outbreak of which in 1348 killed roughly half of Europe's population, sparing neither farmer and friar, nor nun and knight. The Black Death was caused by the bacillus *Yersina pestis*, which lodged in the stomachs of the fleas, *Xenopsylla cheopis*, and which in turn attached themselves to rodents that were common in the Central Asian steppes in the fourteenth century. The bacillus was deadly when it passed to humans.[6] In its wake, increasing numbers of Europeans were disenchanted with the Church. Why pay money for Masses, or gather in churches, when Christian prayers, priests and rituals all seemed ineffectual in the wake of the pestilence? This disaffection with Christianity was exacerbated during and after the Thirty Years War (1518–48), which demonstrated starkly that Christians did not love each other let alone anyone else.

The Decameron begins by describing the Black Death. It narrates the experiences of seven women and three men who sought to escape the plague in Florence by seeking refuge in a villa. Sharply echoing disgruntlement with Christianity, it pokes fun at monks, nuns and priests with bawdy satire. Love and lust dominate the work, as is reflected in the names of the lodgers. The three men, for instance, are called Panfilo ('thoroughly in love'), Filostrato ('overwhelmed by love') and Dioneo ('lusty'), while the seven women in the narrative bear names such as Filomena ('steadfast in love') and Fiammetta ('little flame'). In the midst of death, *The Decameron* is a celebration of comedy attending the lustful encounters between people, including ecclesiastical persons. Its overt demonstration that clergy can be corrupt appealed to Martin Luther in the sixteenth century. It proved to be very popular during succeeding centuries. In 1487, Sandro Botticelli depicted a scene from it in a painting. Hugh Hefner, the founder of the Playboy trademark, tried to render parts of it as pornography in the 1960s, while Pier Paulo Posolini released his film, *Decameron*, in 1971. Boccaccio's forays into comic literature do not detract from his more fundamental contribution to the Renaissance. He wrote a scholarly book in Latin called *De genealogiis deorum gentilium* ('On the Genealogies of the Gods of the Gentiles'), which explains protagonists in ancient mythologies. Its chief significance lies in its ready acceptance that people of his time had a great deal to learn from antiquity.[7]

Despite Boccaccio's love of irreverent humour, it would be a mistake to dismiss him as a Christian. In his *On the Genealogies of the Gods of the Gentiles*, he scanned Greek and Roman myths to see if they expressed beliefs and truths that were adopted by Christians. He was also thoroughly acquainted with penitential literature of his time; that is, with theologically motivated instructions on how repentant Christians were to confess their sins to priests. His familiarity with these texts is reflected in *The Decameron*'s fifth story of a man who disguises himself so that he might hear his wife's confession:

> When Christmas morning came, the lady got up close to dawn, prepared herself, and went to the church ... The Jealous husband ... arriving there before her ... quickly put on one of the priest's robes with a hood that came down to his cheeks, like those we often see priests wearing, and after pulling it forward a bit, he went down to sit in one of the pews.[8]

Petrarch was a contemporary of Boccaccio. They died a year apart. Both wrote in Italian and Latin. Although born in Arezzo, Petrarch spent his boyhood in Avignon while the papal court was there. From there he moved to Montpellier in Languedoc–Roussillon and studied law in the city's university. In adulthood, he owned the largest personal library in Europe, and from it acquired a formidable erudition. One of his works, cast in the form of a letter, is 'Ascent of Mont Ventoux'. It describes one of his attempts to climb a mountain. When he reaches the summit, he opens a copy of Augustine's auto-biographical work, *Confessions*, and discovers a passage that laments those who neglect the depths of their souls and seek illumination elsewhere. By enthusing over this passage, Petrarch presaged a domi-nating preoccupation of the eighteenth-century Enlightenment – the turn to the self as a reservoir of knowledge and wisdom.[9]

For all its interest in the human body and its self-determination, the Renaissance was not a secular development. Throughout the fifteenth and sixteenth centuries Europe remained a resoundingly Christian culture. Petrarch typifies a combined Renaissance enthusi-asm for Christianity and a keenness to reconfigure the ways people relate to the world around them. In his late work, *On His Own Ignorance and That of Many* (1370), he reveals his love of Ciceronian Latin to the extent that he laments the use scholastic theologians made of Aristotle. Petrarch disapproved of Aristotle's teaching that the world is eternal because he thought it contradicted the Christian doctrine that God created the world. In contrast, Petrarch argued, Cicero espoused a belief in creation. That affirmed, Petrarch was Christian enough to deplore Cicero's belief in pagan Gods.[10]

It is precisely in Petrarch's interest in Cicero that his interest in reconfiguring people's relation to their world appears. Such a recon-figuration was evident in the fifteenth-century republican state of Florence, which had developed a novel form of urban life that was artistically dynamic, politically self-governing and commercially vibrant. From Cicero, Petrarch imbibed a keen interest in the self-hood and experiences of authors, which is central to Renaissance humanism's engrossment with human experiences and dignity.[11]

Faith Through Art

An unmistakeable feature of the Renaissance was the way Christians expressed their faith through art. New styles in painting, architecture, sculpture and music all developed during the Renaissance, an epoch of breathtaking artistic fertility and innovation. This was the time when art criticism and connoisseurship gestated. The humanism that marked the Renaissance was

> in no guise a rejection of Christian faith in favour of an earlier paganism or an espousal of a purely human set of values and agendas, as the term tends to signify today. It was, rather, an affirmation of human intellect and creativity, but in the service of God.[12]

Medieval and Byzantine Christians also loved music and art, but monophony and organum dominated their music, and linear perspective in art had not yet been well understood and practised. One of the greatest bodies of medieval music was the Gregorian chant, a form of monophony ranging from simple syllabic and unaccompanied melodies to highly melismatic or florid vocal lines. It was a vast musical corpus, with several thousand melodies embellishing biblical and theological texts. 'Monophony' means 'a single voice'. It can involve a soloist vocalizing a melody or a choir singing it in unison. Monophony was the staple of the medieval musical diet in the churches of the West. Polyphony ('many voices') flourished during the Renaissance. It is a more ornate form of singing than monophony. It normally involves a choir divided between voices with a higher pitch singing in concert with lower-pitched voices. Polyphony typically begins with the announcement of a single melodic theme by a voice or cluster of voices at the same pitch, which is then taken over, repeated and varied in higher or lower vocal parts.

While polyphony was developed among musicians of the Renaissance, linear perspective was mastered by architects, sculptors and painters. It is related to the concept of artistic composition: placing objects depicted in an image in a proportional relation to each other. Perspective is a method of painting that represents three-dimensional people and objects on a surface of two dimensions.[13] With a sense of perspective, Renaissance painters were able to make the form of human bodies look far more lifelike and realistic than had previously been possible. Sculptors since antiquity were adept at recreating human forms with great realism. The understanding of perspective that emerged during the Renaissance allowed painters to follow suit.

Italy as it is now known was only formed in 1860 when Garibaldi finally reduced the Kingdoms of the Two Sicilies to submission. During the Renaissance, the territories it encompassed were a range of autonomous cities, some of which were republics, like Florence and Venice, while others were principalities. Many of them involved thriving mercantile production and exchange, which generated considerable wealth for them. Rome, Florence, Siena, Venice, Urbino, Ferrara and Mantua all flourished financially. The more wealthy of their inhabitants, like the Medici family in Florence, were thus well placed to finance the production of art.

Florence of the fourteenth and fifteenth centuries – periods referred to in Italian as the *Trecento* and *Quattrocento* – was a hothouse for artistic production. So too was the *Cinquecento*, or sixteenth century. Its sculptors first began to understand artistic perspective. The creations of Lorenzo Ghiberti (1378–1455) are cases in point. Pride of place in Florence's skyline during the Renaissance belonged to the city's magnificent cathedral, one side of which is a separate and elaborately decorated baptistery. The huge bronze doors at the baptistery's entrance are decorated with three large panels of bronze relief sculptures. The panels portray vignettes from the Bible. Ghiberti designed and made the second and third panels for the door. There is a marked difference in style between the two. The second door plaque recreates scenes from the Bible's New Testament, with people set against blank backgrounds. The third one displays figures from the Hebrew scriptures that are represented in relation to a more realistic portrayal of three-dimensional space.[14]

Filippo Brunelleschi (1377–1446) was a contemporary of Ghiberti and a Florentine sculptor and architect as well. He was the first person to have grasped in technical terms how spatial and linear perspective is conveyed in art. He studied the reflection of the bronze relief doors of Florence's baptistery on a flat mirror, from which he made a mathematical analysis of the forms he saw. He was able to identify a *vanishing point* – 'the furthest point of convergence of the main lines of the image, and constructed through this point the horizontal line that would be the horizon of the painting. All other lines formed rational relationships to the horizon.'[15] In this way, Brunelleschi was able to paint objects in spatial relation to each other as they appeared realistically, as in a mirror, to the human eye. Piero della Francesca's painting, *Ideal City*, is a clear attempt to convey in oil on a panel an image of a townscape as it would appear to ocular perception. The painting plainly exhibits the inspiration of ancient Greek and Roman architecture.

Figure 19: Piero della Francesca, Ideal City, *late fifteenth century, oil on panel, showing linear perspective*

A decisive impulse for the production of art during the Renaissance was patronage. Wealthy buyers of art such as popes, cardinals, and princes and their wives often commissioned the production of art, or employed artists on a full-time basis to work on decorating their residences with paintings and sculptures. In this way, too, musicians were engaged to compose for liturgies or court celebrations. Most of the larger expressions of art were the result of patronage. Once the papacy returned from Avignon to Rome, it set to work creating an environment of artistic splendour in the city. Through patronage, Pope Nicholas V (in office from 1447 to 1455) had the Vatican Palace redecorated. Sixtus IV (1471–84) commissioned builders to construct the Sistine Chapel. Julius II (1503–13) engaged Raphael to paint his apartments in the Vatican Palace, and Michelangelo to paint the ceiling of the Sistine Chapel. Prelates of this period became infamous for not observing the law of celibacy that their church required of all clerics. Alexander VI (1492–1503) had a daughter, Lucretia Borgia, and a son, Caesare.[16]

Through the patronage of popes, cardinals and princes, the creation of art during the Renaissance was breathtaking. Names of artists alone illustrate how painting and sculpture was used by Christians to express not only their faith, but also their delight in the world in which their contemporaries found themselves. This was the age of Fra Angelico (Fra Giovanni da Fiesole), Piero della Francesca, Andrea Mantegna, Sandro Botticelli, Andrea del Verrocchio, Michelangelo Buonarroti, Raphael (Raffaello Sanzio), Gentile, Bellini, Luca della Robbia, Antonello da Messina, Caravaggio (late Renaissance) and Leonardo da Vinci.

Women were not absent from all this artistic creativity. Among the women who attracted admirers for their paintings during the Renaissance were Caterina Vegri, Marietta Tintoretto (daughter of

Jacopo Tintoretto) and Sofonisba Anguissola. Most of the works of Anguissola are portraits. She became so popular late in the sixteenth century that she was regularly commissioned to paint portraits of her patrons.[17]

Patronage also accounts for a great volume of musical composition during the Renaissance. To the Christian repertoire of Gregorian chant, a vast corpus of polyphony was added during the sixteenth century. The technology of printing was a German invention during the fifteenth century, but it greatly enabled the dissemination of polyphony during the sixteenth century. Unlike monophony, polyphony needs to be printed. Making copies from an original manuscript for a newly composed polyphonic work is too arduous if the choir engaged to perform it includes a large number of varied voices. Monophony, unlike polyphony, can also be improvised, and so does not necessarily need all of its notes to be printed. Harmonic disarray would ensue were a choir to attempt to sing in a polyphonic style, with different vocal groups extemporizing a single melody synchronically in diverse ways.

A greatly celebrated master of polyphony during the Renaissance was Giovanni Pierluigi da Palestrina (1525/6–1594). He was born near Rome and died in that city in the service of the Giulia Chapel. He composed over a hundred polyphonic settings of the Mass and roughly 400 motets. His most popular Mass proved to be the Missa Papae Marcelli, published in 1567.[18] It is still performed internationally in churches and concert halls.

Christianity of the Populace

Art and music have received attention in this chapter not as a matter of indulgence, but because they were vital parts of Christians' lives during the fifteenth and sixteenth centuries. While they were often commissioned by clerics and nobles, they were created in the main by hard-working people who were devout Christian lay men and women. They deliberately created their works as tools of evangelism; that is, as media for disseminating the Gospel stories of the life and wonders wrought by Jesus as recorded in the Bible.

From Italy, the Renaissance spread to other territories of Europe, where its impact was initially felt mostly in cities. Desiderius Erasmus was an erudite enthusiast of Renaissance humanism. He promoted its study of texts of Classical Antiquity to produce an edition of the New Testament in Greek. The vast majority of his contemporaries could not read or write their own languages let alone Greek or Latin. During the fifteenth and sixteenth centuries Christians in Europe did not live in large cities like Rome, Florence or Paris. Nor were they able to live as connoisseurs of art and fine music. Their lives as Christians were typically led in small rural communities in towns, villages or working for manors and on clusters of farms. Although they had barely any chance in their lifetimes of seeing a sculpture by Michelangelo or the Palace of the Doge in Venice, their lives were richly endowed by religious symbolism and beliefs.

Men, women and children expressed their dedication to God and the Church, both in their homes and publicly in their local churches or manorial chapels. Their domestic religion frequently involved the recitation of the rosary with mother and father leading their children in communal prayer and meditation. Within their own doors they kept statuettes of saints and the Virgin Mary. During the day, while working in fields and preparing meals, they said prayers they had learned by rote.

People's domestic religious observance could be just as earnest and strictly regular as practices in monasteries. The story of the Renaissance Florentine merchant Giovanni de Paolo Morelli illustrates well how the home could serve as a site for intense religious devotion. In 1407, he was still heartbroken over the death of his young son a year before. He reproached himself remorsefully for having allowed his son to die without religious observances. In his home, he devised and performed a penitential regime for himself as a punishment for his neglect of his son. In his bedroom, 'before a painted image of the crucifixion with the Virgin and St John; in his nightshirt, barefoot, and with a halter round his neck like a public penitent, he addressed himself to each of the holy personages in turn, apologizing for his unpolished speech'.[19]

At the outset of the fifteenth century, Giovanni Dominici, a Dominican friar based in Florence, encouraged parents to display religious pictures in their homes. He also encouraged mothers to set up toy altars in their bedchambers so that their very young sons could play in imitation of priests saying Mass. One boy could pretend to be the priest with his brothers serving as acolytes. In this way, they could mimic and celebrate in their homes a pivotal Christian practice that they witnessed in church buildings.[20]

People's worship in churches was always communal, visual and oral. Their churches were their art galleries. They were adorned with statues and wall paintings, and often had stained glass windows. Ironically, reception of Holy Communion by the people was rare. The doctrine of transubstantiation held that the bread and wine used at Mass were transformed on a level *of reality* into the body and blood of Christ. Anyone who consumed them unworthily would be guilty of an horrendous blasphemy and thereby merit the perpetual torments of hell. One needed to be sure that one had not ethically transgressed so as to sever for ever a relation with God.

Sin and Confession

All of which raises the matter of sin and its confession to a priest – a mainstay of Christian practice during the Later Middle Ages and the Renaissance. During this time, clergy taught their people that there were three principal types of sin: original, venial and mortal. A venial sin was a minor affair, such as intemperate laughter, while a mortal sin, as its name suggested, was deadly – lethal that is to a person's life in relation to God, or severely harmful to others. Original sin was believed to be an inherited form of the sin of Adam and Eve, like the passing on through generations of a defective gene. Etymologically speaking, the word 'sin' comes from sport and, more particularly, from archery. Its origin is Greek. To sin is to miss a bull's-eye with an arrow. Transferred into people's daily life, sinning is deliberately choosing to be deflected from a goal by acting in a way that is inimical to God and harmful to people.

Thomas Aquinas taught that three factors determine whether an action is sinful or not, and whether it is venial or mortal.[21] All three need to be held in an equilibrium when determining the nature of sin. They are the action itself, the context in which it is performed, and the intention of the person doing it. These factors generate three interrogatives. First, is the action gravely and intrinsically bad? Second, did it take place in a setting of fear, drunkenness, ignorance or duress? Finally, was the intention motivating a person's action evil? For Aquinas, intention is decisive in establishing moral innocence or culpability. For him it is possible to act in a harmful way, yet to do so with a good intention. Were a person to prevent an attacker from killing himself or herself by killing the attacker instead in self-defence, the attacked person may be morally innocent if the intention of killing the attacker was self-defence and not delight in killing for its own sake.

Deciding what constitutes sin is never a simple matter. Each case is different because of utterly unique combinations of action, context and intent found in people's very different lives. The confession of sins to a priest was an obligation placed on Catholic Christians by the Fourth Lateran Council in 1215:

> All the faithful of either sex, after they have reached the age of discernment, should individually confess all their sins in a faithful manner to their own priest at least once a year, and let them take care to do what they can to perform the penance imposed on them. Let them reverently receive the sacrament of the eucharist at least at Easter unless they think, for a good reason and on the advice of their own priest, they should abstain from receiving it for a time. Otherwise they shall be barred from entering a church during their lifetime and they shall be denied a Christian burial at death. Let this decree be frequently published in churches, so that nobody may find the pretence of an excuse in the blindness of ignorance.[22]

The obligation to confess once a year could be interpreted to mean that it only applied *if* a person had committed a mortal sin. If not, there would be no real and urgent need. In any case, in each and every confession of guilt, for a person to be absolved from the consequences of sin by a priest acting on behalf of the Church, according to Catholic theology and law of the Middle Ages and the Renaissance, two essential prerequisites were required on behalf of the person confessing. He or she needed to be motivated by *contrition* (sorrow for sin) rather than *attrition* (a mere fear of punishment); and prepared to undertake the practice of a penance imposed by the confessor. Hence the name Sacrament of Penance.

Peculiar to the late Renaissance was the introduction of confessionals – panels separating priest and penitent – so that individuals could confess their sins without danger of either being accused of improper behaviour with each other. The Bishop of Verona, Gian Matteo Giberti, decreed in 1542 that confessionals were to be used whenever one of his priests heard a confession: 'Whenever he has to hear a woman in confession, we want there to be a panel between the priest hearing confession and the woman, with a little window in which there is a grate or a thin sheet of perforated metal; we call this panel a confessional.'[23]

Bishop Giberti was supported by Carlo Borromeo (1538–84), the Archbishop of Milan, who described the features a confessional should have in 1577 with his publication, *Instructions Concerning Ecclesiastical Building and Furnishings*. Borromeo's ideas were incorporated into the *Roman Ritual* (a description of liturgical rites) that was published in Rome in 1584, having been edited by Cardinal Giulio Antonio Santoro. A subsequent version of this text was published in 1614.[24] From then on, confessionals were compulsory items of furniture in Catholic churches until the Second Vatican Council in the twentieth century.[25]

The felt need for confessionals arose primarily because of the delicate matter of celibate priests hearing the sins of women. Before confessionals became obligatory in churches, priests heard confessions in public spaces such as the naves of churches, or in rooms set aside in monasteries of nuns. This was the scenario depicted in *the Decameron*. Whenever sins confessed involved sexual matters the priest was required to question the penitent to determine the nature, context and intent circumscribing the action confessed. Consequences could be perilous for both confessor and penitent. The latter could accuse the former of prurience, while the confessor could lose control and behave lasciviously or seductively with the penitent.

Attending Mass and confessing sins were sacraments of which Christians could avail themselves repeatedly during the course of a year-long liturgical cycle. Its zenith was Easter Sunday of Holy Week, which, in the Northern Hemisphere, coincided with the joyful celebration of spring after the vicissitudes of winter. Each day of Holy Week commemorated a day in the final week of Jesus. It ended with the celebration of his resurrection on Easter Sunday, the high point of the Church's year. Lent, a period of 40 days of fasting and penance, preceded the *Triduum*: the commemoration of the last three days of Holy Week. Easter is followed by 50 days of anticipation of the liturgical feast of Pentecost, which celebrates the divine gift of the Holy Spirit to the Church. A few months before Easter, Christmas Day was a popular celebration of Jesus' birth and, hence,

Figure 20: Woman confessing in an open space, frontispiece, Venezia, 1506

of the Incarnation. On other days and at other times during the year, Christians celebrated in their homes, and at Mass, commemorations of saints, martyrs, angels and archangels. Their religious lives formed a richly vivid web of historical memory, giving thanks for the past and joyful anticipation of a better future, culminating ideally in union with God and loved ones in paradise.

The Fires of Hell and the Pains of Purgatory

As anyone who suffers severely from guilt knows full well, it can gnaw away at any sense of enjoyment in living. A prominent part of Christians' lives in the West from about 1300 onwards was attempts to alleviate burdens associated with guilt and the fear of dreadful punishments by fire in either hell or purgatory. Nothing could be done for souls sent to hell. There they would suffer in torment in perpetuity. Neither the souls themselves, nor their living friends and relatives, could overtrump or reduce their punishment for mortal sin or original sin that had not been washed away by baptism. Following a teaching of Augustine, it was widely believed during the Middle Ages and Renaissance that all children who died before baptism, and anyone else who was never baptized, were ineligible to enter heaven. They either went to hell or suppurated in an imagined holding pen called limbo.

A third possibility became increasingly popular during the Middle Ages and was widely accepted by Catholics during the Renaissance. It concerned the possibility of having sins purged in a place Pope Gregory IV called 'purgatory'. A doctrine of purgatory took a long time historically to develop. It can be traced to Augustine, but it was articulated in precise terms by scholastic theologians between around 1100 and 1250. In 1274, the Second Council of Lyons published a profession of faith that expresses the basic idea of purgatory:

> if the truly penitent die in charity before having rendered satisfaction by worthy fruits of penance for the things they have committed or omitted, their souls ... are purged after their death, by purgatorial or purificatory pains, and ... for the alleviation of these pains they gain benefit from the suffrages of the living faithful, that is, by the sacrifice of the mass, prayers, and alms, and other works of piety which are customarily offered by the faithful for others of the faithful as instituted by the Church.[26]

Purgatory was thus a place where sinful souls were consigned in order to be purified of sin before they could enter heaven. Passage to heaven was assured, but the question was a matter of when. No one wanted a lengthy stay in purgatory because the method of purgation was fire. By the Renaissance, most Catholics believed they would need to spend time in purgatory. Only the most utterly blameless or innocent who had not regressed into sin after baptism could expect immediate entry into heaven.[27]

Indulgences

The doctrine of purgatory became a mainstay of Christians' lives in Western Europe from roughly the thirteenth to the sixteenth century. During the same time, belief in purgatory became allied with the practice of indulgences. Indulgences were remissions of time in purgatory, normally on payment of a fee to a priest. The living could pay priests to say Masses or a series of Masses to reduce the time the souls of deceased relatives and friends needed to spend in purgatory. A trental was such a series involving 30 Masses said on successive days. People living could obtain indulgences for themselves in preparation for their own inevitable sojourn in purgatory. Popes granted indulgences to individuals who undertook specified activities, such as joining pilgrimages, participating in crusades or giving alms to the poor. People could also leave money in their wills so that Masses could be paid for them upon their deaths to lessen their own waiting in purgatory. Wealthy people were able to provide for an enormous number of such Masses for themselves if they so wished.[28]

New and Broken Worlds

The entire sixteenth century was a renaissance for geography that has had major implications for Christianity ever since. It was the epoch when the Americas, South and North, were discovered, explored, populated and subdued by European Christian colonizers. The engine for geographical exploration during the Renaissance was Spain, followed by Portugal. By the late fifteenth century, Catholic Spain was religiously self-confident, politically strong and aesthetically fertile. Its merchants were ambitious, adventurous and energetic.

In 1469, King Ferdinand of Aragon married Queen Isabella of Castille. The two realms retained their own laws, but the union between the two Crowns gave birth to a politically strong and resolutely Catholic sovereignty.[29] The monarchs' armies defeated the Muslim stronghold of Granada in 1492. With edicts of 1501 and 1502, all Muslims in Granada's hinterland were expelled. On 31

March 1492, Ferdinand and Isabella ordered Jews to convert to Christianity or be expelled from Spain.[30]

In the same year, Queen Isabella decided to sponsor a maritime exploratory expedition to be led by Christopher Columbus. He was born in Genoa around 1451, but moved from there to settle in Portugal. After marrying a Portuguese woman, he hatched a plan to sail westwards across the Atlantic Ocean in the hope of reaching China. His primary motive was not to convert souls for Christianity, but to discover gold. Of this he made no secret. He offered his plan for a voyage to the Portuguese Court, which rejected it. Then he sought approval and financial support from the French and the English. Again he was rejected. Finally, he turned to Isabella of Castile, who agreed to help him. King Ferdinand did not stand in the way.[31]

Columbus set sail with two small caravels, the *Pinta* and the *Nina*, and a heavier square-rigged flagship called the *Santa Maria*. He disembarked on land in the same year he set sail. Until his death in 1506, he remained steadfast in his conviction that he had landed on islands to the east of mainland Asia. He never entertained the view that he had discovered a New World previously unknown to European geographers.[32] He had actually landed on an island called variously by the people who lived there, Haiti, Quisqueya, Bohío and Babeque, according to different regions of the island. The Spaniards called it Hispaniola. Today it is known as the Dominican Republic and Haiti.[33]

The Spaniards' arrival at Hispaniola was simultaneously a momentous discovery and a ghastly disaster. 1492 is a symbolic year which marks the seizure of South America by Spanish colonizers. The conquerors did not disguise their greedy glee for gold and they eventually managed to export shiploads of it back to Europe. To do so, they needed violently to subdue the local populations they happened upon. The Portuguese followed the Spaniards to South America and they in turn were followed by French, German, Dutch, English and Italian adventurers. Of these nationalities, 'Spain alone had the courage to hold a comprehensive debate on the ethics and morality of the European presence in the Indies. In the other countries of the old world, the right to occupy these lands was regarded as too obvious to be questioned.'[34]

What the colonizers did to the local people they met on Hispaniola sparked the Spanish debate. Columbus launched a military action

Figure 21: Giuliano Dati, Columbus arriving in the Americas, woodcut, 1497

against them in 1492 and took over a thousand prisoners. Of these, he sent 500 to be sold into slavery. Spanish theologians began to react decisively. Isabella and Ferdinand halted the traffic in enslaved bodies in 1510 and ordered that Indians sold and exiled cruelly in Spain were to be released.[35]

Meanwhile, back in Hispaniola, a small band of Dominican friars launched a preaching campaign against the island's governor, Diego Columbus (Christopher's son). In 1510, one of them, Antón Montesino, preached in the governor's presence and upbraided him for killing local people. In 1442, another Dominican, Bartolomé de Las Casas, published a brief book called *A Short Account of the Destruction of the Indies.* He addressed it to Prince Philip, the son of the emperor Charles V and the future King Philip II of Spain. To this day, Las Casas' account is harrowing to read. He begins it in a sober

way with little indication of the horrors he is about to describe and
which he had witnessed with his own eyes:

> Everything that has happened since the marvellous discovery of the
> Americas – from the short-lived initial attempts of the Spanish to
> live there, right down to the present day – has been so extraordinary
> that the whole story remains quite incredible to anyone who has not
> experienced it at first hand. It seems, indeed, to overshadow all the
> deeds of famous men of the past, no matter how heroic, and to silence
> all talk of other wonders of the world. Prominent among the aspects
> that have caught the imagination are the massacres of innocent
> peoples, the atrocities committed against them and, among other
> horrific excesses, the ways in which towns, provinces, and whole
> kingdoms have been entirely cleared of their native inhabitants.[36]

Las Casas then proceeds to document the spread of the conquerors to
provinces such as Nicaragua, Cuba, Guatemala, Venezuela and Peru.
He begins by describing what happened to the five kingdoms of
Hispaniola. In the fourth kingdom of Xaraguá, the Spanish governor
summoned local people to his presence. The governor is unnamed
by Las Casas, but was most likely to have been Nicolás de Ovando,
appointed in 1501. Over 300 people assembled, including men,
women and children. The Christian governor met them with 300
armed men and 60 mounted horsemen. The cavalry alone were
enough to slaughter the assembled people. The governor and his
soldiers hoodwinked the friendly and unsuspecting islanders into
assembling in a large straw building. He then had his men set fire to
it and burn alive everyone inside. All others in sight outside the straw
building were run through with swords or speared with lances.
Anacona, the Queen who ruled the people, was hanged. Horsemen
galloped through groups of children sprawling on the ground and cut
off their legs. Other children who were being helped to escape were
run through with lances. The governor ordered that anyone who had
managed to flee was to be captured to be sold into slavery.[37] This car-
nage was only a beginning.

Conclusion

Throughout the fifteenth century, Christians in Europe revelled in
the marvels of antiquity, built cathedrals, sang polyphonic Masses,

Figure 22: Inhabitants of New Spain roped together, tied to stakes and burned alive

and paid to release souls from purgatory. They did all this at exactly the same time as the more aggressive among them routed Jews and Muslims in the Iberian Peninsula, and set out from there to create in South America a living hell for Indians they regarded as heathen vermin. Other Christians who settled in South America were dedicated to resisting plunder, and inspired by the Gospel of Jesus Christ, argued that to kill natives was to crucify Christ over and over again. The story of Christianity throughout the Middle Ages and the Renaissance is a tensile dialectic of betrayals of the legacy of Jesus intertwined with radical attempts to live exactly as he did. Christians who were wealthy patrons of arts, monarchs and nobles saw in Jesus a prototype for their own excellence. The Cathars of France, the Dolcinians of Italy and the friars of Hispaniola glimpsed in exactly the same Jesus the archetype of an utterly poor, homeless and executed prophet of God. In the sixteenth century, the dialectic that is Christianity appeared in an entirely new and unexpected form – the Reformation.

Chapter VI

Reformation and Revolution

'Do you want to be shown, you senseless person, that faith without works is barren?'
James 2: 20

Few texts in the New Testament are as spirited in their defence of poor people as the Letter of James. It is addressed to the Twelve Tribes of Israel in the Diaspora and is most likely to have been written in the second half of the first century. In the Roman Empire, to recall, 97 to 98 per cent of its population were poor, often wretchedly so. James will not let his listeners and readers rest until they realize that they cannot be religious if they ignore the poor. He is as blunt as he can be: 'Religion that is pure and undefiled before God, the Father, is this: to care for orphans and widows in their distress, and to keep oneself unstained by the world' (James 1: 27). What about buying indulgences? What about supporting the papacy? On such practices, James has nothing to say. Over and again he returns to his theme:

> What good is it my brothers and sisters, if you say you have faith but do not have works? Can faith save you? If a brother or sister is naked and lacks daily food, and one of you says to them, 'Go in peace; keep warm and eat your fill', and yet you do not supply their bodily needs, what is the good of that? So faith by itself, if it has no works, is dead (James 2: 14–16).

In the second decade of the sixteenth century, Martin Luther began to think of the relation between faith and actions in a different way. When James warns 'Come now, you rich people, weep and wail for the miseries that are coming to you' (5: 1), Luther could advise all people, rich and poor alike, that they can be justified, saved or rendered righteous before God by their faith.

That might seem an innocuous idea to promote, but in the context of the sixteenth century it drove the second great schism within Christianity's history when Protestantism formed in contradistinction to Catholicism and Orthodoxy. Eastern and Western Christianity had fallen into schism in the eleventh century. With attempts of earnest Christians in northern Europe of the sixteenth century to change and challenge the Catholic Church, Protestantism soon came into being, forming a schism which, like that of the eleventh century, has never been broached. The initial attempts of these Christians challenging the leadership of the Catholic Church, and especially the papacy, blossomed into the major historical movement of the Reformation, one of the two principal themes of this chapter. The other concerns sciences.

While the Reformation was a religious revolution with political consequences, it was accompanied by a burgeoning of new scientific knowledge that helped to generate the cultural features peculiar to the modern age, paramount among which is a demonstrated capacity of empirical sciences to explain the structure of the visible cosmos in the light of knowledge unknown to anyone in pre-modern periods. The previous chapter hinted at the origins of a scientific revolution in the figure of Columbus. In unwittingly discovering the island that is now home to Haiti and the Dominican Republic, Columbus both altered the known geography of his contemporaries in Europe and *brought into question the unquestioned authority* that the Bible enjoyed during the patristic era and Middle Ages, when it was regarded as a reliable repository of information about the world that people inhabit. Columbus, of course, did not see himself either as a saboteur of biblical authority or as a prophet of geography, but he stands as an historical and cultural symbol of advances in knowledge that were unique to modernity.

In contemporary Western academies it is customary for students to be taught that modernity began in Western Europe among philosophers such as René Descartes and Immanuel Kant. Both are described as leading a revolution in thought by focusing on the mental powers of an individual thinking subject. Alternatively, students are commonly instructed that the roots of modernity are found either in the eighteenth-century European Enlightenment, or the Industrial Revolution of the nineteenth century. The Argentine historian and theologian Enrique Dussel argues for a different view. For him, the roots of modernity are to be found elsewhere. He links modernity to Columbus and his discovery of previously unknown territory.[1] In the perspective typified by Dussel:

> Modernity does not begin with René Descartes, Immanuel Kant, and the ideas of other famous philosophers, but with Christopher Columbus, Hernando Cortés, and – we might add the North American perspective – continues with the founding fathers of the United States of America. Columbus's 'I conquer' precedes the Cartesian 'I think therefore I am' by almost one hundred years – and both attitudes reverberate in the affirmation of the United States's Manifest Destiny in the new continent. In all of these models, other people are subordinated to the expanding powers of the modern self.[2]

The Reformation

The Reformation surged forth in two waves: first, around 1520, in German-speaking territories; and then from about 1550 in the Dutch Republic, Eastern Europe, France, England and Scotland.[3] Intertwined propaedeutic questions immediately present themselves in relation to the Reformation – what sparked it, in what did it consist, and why was Martin Luther moved to conclude that the key to religious justification before God is faith, not faith *and* works? The answer to these questions lies in a sermon. The Reformation was ignited when a priest's sermon stung another priest. One priest involved, Martin Luther, reacted with fury to a sermon the Dominican priest, Johann Tetzel, had been preaching in Saxony during 1517. Tetzel's sermonizing was an attempt to hawk indulgences. It unleashed the Reformation. It was 'because of one priest's bad sermon on indulgences and another priest's response to it that the papacy lost its hegemony in Europe and that the unity of the Western church was forever undone'.[4]

Tetzel was part of a campaign in Germany. He wanted to support Pope Leo X's plan to build the huge basilica of St Peter in Rome. The youthful Cardinal Albrecht of Mainz (1490–1545), a man still in his 20s, cooperated with the Curia in Rome to sell indulgences in Germany for the dual purpose of contributing to the construction of St Peter's, as well as the costs involved in his installation as the Archbishop of Mainz.[5] Willingly joining this drive to raise money,

Tetzel proved to be an unrefined and unsubtle preacher. He did not disguise the motive behind the selling of indulgences to people who wanted to reduce the time souls spent in purgatory. His preaching went along these lines:

> Listen now, God and St. Peter call *you*. Consider the salvation of *your* souls and those of *your loved ones* departed ... Listen to the voices of *your dead relatives* and friends, beseeching *you* and saying, 'Pity us, pity us. We are in dire torment from which *you* can redeem us for a pittance.' Do *you* not wish to? Open *your* ears ... Remember you are able to release them, for *as soon as the coin in the coffer rings, the soul from purgatory springs*. Will *you* not then for a quarter of a florin receive these letters of indulgence through which you are able to lead a divine and immortal soul into the fatherland of paradise?[6]

'*You* can redeem us for a pittance' and '*as soon as the coin in the coffer rings, the soul from purgatory springs*' are statements that blatantly link the payment of money to saving souls from suffering in an afterlife. The very word 'redeem' is still used in monetary exchanges. If, for instance, a person has hocked a watch in a pawn shop in order to raise cash quickly, the watch can only be *redeemed*, or repossessed, through the payment of a fee. To argue that souls mired in the dire torment of purgatory could be released for a pittance is to suggest that salvation or ultimate justification is a mechanical matter, and that God can be bought for a crass payment of cash. The entire practice of buying indulgences, as envisaged by Tetzel, was impelled by the idea that humans can secure their eternal salvation by their own earthly actions. It was this notion that stung Luther into a furious riposte that culminated in his rejection of the papacy and the Catholic Church.

To depict Christianity in the sixteenth century as having undergone a Reformation and as having split between Catholic and Protestant factions occludes two situations. First, much of Christian life, thought and practice in the sixteenth century stood in historical continuity with Christianity as it was lived during the Middle Ages and Renaissance. And second, there were multiple Reformations in the sixteenth century, such as Lutheran, English, Scottish and Catholic attempts to reform the Church. This was the primary period in the history of Christianity when the number of different types of Christians – denominations – began to proliferate far beyond the number of principal types during the Middle Ages. What all these endeavours shared was a focus on, and fretfulness about, a question: 'What is the Church?' Is it fundamentally constituted by people of equal rank, or is it encapsulated in a hierarchy that governs people? Related to the pivotal issue of the essential nature of the Church was the question of death: how to prepare for it, what will happen after it, and what can be done, if anything, by the living to help the dead.

On these two matters – the character of the Church and the reality of death – the Protestant Reformation (including multiple forms) was guided and governed by two great principles – the doctrines of justification by faith, and of the primacy of the Bible in the life of the Church. Of all issues that were contested by Catholics and Protestants throughout the sixteenth century, often with lethal enmity, these two were pre-eminent, and they are both linked to death and the nature of the Church. To say that an individual is justified, saved or redeemed before God by the profession of his or her faith takes issue with the notion that securing indulgences can contribute to the well-being of anyone after the moment of death. To regard the Bible as the supreme authority in the Church undermines the notion that indulgences are indispensable to the Church's life, because the Bible does not mention indulgences. It also directly destabilizes the view that the pope is the Church's supreme authority. Death and its after-effects viewed in relation to the essence of the Church are the architectonic themes dominating Christianity's evolution during the sixteenth-century Reformations.

The sixteenth century not only produced a Catholic Reformation, but also a Catholic Counter-Reformation, especially in the second half of the century. The difference between the two rests in a distinction between internal reform and external rebuttal. The Catholic Reformation sought to reinvigorate established practices and structures in the Church. It aimed to improve the education of the clergy and the instruction of Catholics, so that they would better understand their beliefs in an age of heated controversy. The Counter-Reformation was primarily moved to refute and resist Protestant teachings and customs.

Just as there has never been a single form of the Reformation, neither has there prevailed a monochrome Protestantism. There were and are many kinds of Reformed Christian traditions and groups of Protestants. Speaking of the Reformation in the singular is a useful convention. It can serve both as a general term for the sixteenth century in Europe considered as *a period* of far-reaching religious renovation, and more specifically for specifying mutations within northern European Christian communities, especially those located in Germany and Switzerland. These variations soon became apparent in regions of The Netherlands, Poland, Hungary, France and Scotland.[7] In neither sense did the Reformation take hold of Spain or Italy.

The Reformation was not planned, either carefully or cursorily. It unravelled according to a sequence of unanticipated events. Luther was a Catholic who wanted to devote his life to a different kind of Church. When he challenged Johannes Tetzel, he did not yet know that from being a celibate friar and priest he would end his life as a married Protestant with children. He was not aware at that stage that he would be excommunicated by the Pope and vilified by the Emperor Charles V, incurring the wrath of Church and Empire.

The story of Christianity in the sixteenth century is distinctive in respects apart from the European Reformation. This was a time when Christians arrived in large numbers in North America. They also established missions in Asia and Africa. While they brought with them European disputes to all of these regions, Christianity could no longer be described in purely European or Middle Eastern terms. North American Reformations can thus be distinguished from their European counterparts.

While the Reformation was primarily an ecclesiastical and theological revolution, it entailed more than propositional disputes. On the eve of the Reformation, only about 5 per cent of Europe's populace could read. Ideas pivotal to the Reformation were disseminated among illiterate people through songs, psalms and new ceremonies. Alterations in rituals and emphases according to different rituals entailed a radical change in style of furniture in churches, and the general layout of furniture. The pivotal change in the design of church buildings was that the areas occupied by the assembly of worshippers became a primary spatial focus. In Medieval and Baroque churches, the altar in a sanctuary, an ambo (lecturn/pulpit) and a baptismal font were the principal spatial foci. All attention had to be drawn to the liturgical action performed by a priest, deacon or bishop. Altering furnishing entailed changing the way people understood their relation to God. Martin Luther had much to contribute to such a change.

Martin Luther (1483–1546)

The dedication of medieval religious orders to scholarship and the preservation of ancient texts continued throughout the sixteenth century. It produced outstandingly learned Christian thinkers who taught in universities. Martin Luther was among them. He was born in 1483 in the small town of Eisleben, which lay in the principality of Mansfeld. As a boy he was educated in Eisenach, Mansfeld and Magdeburg. His father, Hans, worked as a miner and earned enough money to pay for a splendid education for his son. His ambition for Martin was for him to study law, so in 1501 Martin was dispatched to the University of Erfurt to begin studying arts. As his studies advanced, an intense experience moved him to change the course of his life. In 1505, he was badly shaken while outdoors in a thunderstorm. Impelled by abject fright, he vowed to St Anne, Jesus' maternal grandmother, that he would enter a religious order if she protected him. Surviving the tempest, this is precisely what he did. He joined a strictly observant convent of friars in Erfurt, known as Eremites (or Hermits) of Saint Augustine. Their name was misleading. Luther was neither a monk nor an eremite, but a friar. Eremites are hermits. Hermitages in Tuscany were unified by Pope Alexander IV in 1256 to form a band of friars, who are the historical antecedents of sixteenth-century and contemporary Augustinian Friars. In Erfurt, Luther's convent of friars lived in strict observance of the *Rule of St Augustine*.[8]

The historian of Christianity, Diarmaid MacCulloch, underscores how fiery yet engaging Luther was:

> There is no doubt that Luther was a passionate, impulsive man, who felt his theology rather than beginning with logical questions and answers about God, resulting in a theology full of paradoxes or downright contradictions. In any century in which he was born, Luther would have guaranteed a richly memorable night out, whether hilariously entertaining or infuriatingly quarrelsome.[9]

Luther was ordained to the priesthood in 1507. Once a priest, his order set him on a path to become a theologian. His initial theological studies were undertaken in his convent at Erfurt. By his early 20s he was already fluent in Latin, which he had studied as a boy. He stood out among his contemporaries in the convent to the extent that he was chosen to travel to Rome on business for his order. He saw Rome for the first time in 1510. The following year, the Augustinian Eremites sent him to a newly created university in the town of Wittenberg in Saxony.[10] Luther remained there until his death in 1545, and it was there that Protestantism was born. The original use of the term 'Protestants' (in Latin, *Protestatio*) dates from 1529, when five princes of the Holy Roman Empire met in the Diet of Speyer with the intent of resisting Catholicism.[11] When Luther arrived in Wittenberg, it was governed by the Elector Friedrich (the Wise) of Saxony. As an Elector, he had a vital say in the affairs of the running of the Holy Roman Empire. He supported Luther as the Reformation unfolded.

In Luther's conventual education with the Augustinians, he had been taught according to humanist principles of learning that were so highly esteemed during the Renaissance, and which stressed the importance of studying ancient classical languages. An interest in languages was about all Luther shared with humanists of his time because he was not overly optimistic about humanity's capacity to be good in inclination and achievement. He studied Plato, the Church Fathers, and because of the tradition of his order, Augustine. From Augustine, he imbibed a heightened respect for the Bible as an authority in theology, as well as in Christian living. In universities of the Later Middle Ages, the supreme authority for theological discourse and study was the Bible, which is why individuals destined to teach theology began their preparations with *sacra pagina* – the study of the sacred page. Most religions of the world have bodies of texts that their devotees regard as sacred and hence eminently worthy of close intellectual investigation.

Luther became a busy man soon after he arrived in Wittenberg. His appointment in the university was to lecture on sacred scripture. He was required to deliver public commentaries on biblical books such as the Psalms, and the Letters to the Hebrews, Romans and Galatians.[12] Notes from his lectures still survive. Apart from teaching, he preached regularly in the town's church; became involved in the governance of his order in Saxony; and eventually became the dean of the university's theology faculty. Amid all this, he studied and wrote intensively. He was more than capable of following his own inclinations. As a young university teacher he was required to study and teach the ethics of Aristotle, who had been a towering philosophical authority for medieval theologians. Luther differed from many of them because he disliked the ethics of Aristotle intensely.[13]

His study of the sacred page as a professor at Wittenberg helped him to address an intense personal anguish he felt as a young man about ever being able to please God in order to be redeemed. He was needled by the gnawing doubt of whether he would ever prove to be anything other than utterly inadequate before God, no matter how scrupulously he attempted to live by rules of a strict Augustinian life. He found the remedy for his intense personal anguish in a single verse of a single letter in the Bible. In Paul's Letter to the Romans, Luther set upon and took to heart two successive verses: 'For I am not ashamed of the gospel; it is the power of God for salvation to everyone who has faith, to the Jew first and also to the Greek. For in it the righteousness of God is revealed through faith for faith; as it is written "The one who is righteous will live by faith"' (Rom 1: 16–17).

It is not immediately obvious what Paul might have meant by these verses, especially when they are read in an English translation of the original Greek. It has six key terms: gospel, God, salvation, revelation, faith and righteousness. Verse 16 seems the more comprehensible of the two verses. Its thrust is the idea that the gospel is a powerful instrument in achieving salvation. What could Paul have intended by speaking of God's righteousness being revealed 'through faith for faith'? The reference to Hebrew scripture which follows the expression 'faith through faith' is crucial. It is a quotation from the prophet of Israel, Habakkuk: 'The one who is righteous will live by faith' (Hab 2: 4). This text is one of only two in the entire Tanakh that link the notions of faith and righteousness. Israel had long been troubled by a fretfulness as to whether it had been or would be abandoned by God because of its sins. The prophets of Israel often lamented Israel's betrayal of God. Psalms of lament in the Hebrew scriptures also speak of God's Israel; for instance, Psalm 87: 3. Such psalms and the prophets lie behind Paul's theology in the Letter to the Romans. Verses 16 and 17 encapsulate the heart of Paul's theology: 'God saves all (both Jew and Greek) in the same way (by faith) by the same means (the gospel), thus demonstrating God's righteousness (God's fairness and fidelity).'[14] God's righteousness is not neatly identifiable with God's justice. It implies a divine commitment, faithfulness, largesse or graciousness.[15] Because of their sins, humans, by their own terms, deserve to be punished strictly according to justice. Despite their wickedness, God constitutes them as deserving, meritorious or righteous. Humans do nothing. They are saved by a disposition of God – *if* they have faith in the gospel. The Letter to the Romans is dominated by the theme of God's righteousness.

Paul's phrase 'through faith for faith' (in transliterated Greek, *ek pisteos eis pistin*) is tricky, because faith (*pistis*) is a notoriously fluid word in his writings. It can refer both to human fidelity or elemental trust, and to God's dedication (faithfulness) to humans. It seems that God's faithfulness to people can be recognized in their response of faith in God.[16]

Habakkuk's prophetic teaching, 'The one who is righteous will live by faith', cocooned in the two verses of Romans 1: 16–17, became the backbone of both Luther's theology as he matured and of his challenge to papal authority. In his terms, to be righteous, to be justified before God, one did not need to perform meritorious actions. All that was needed was faith – steadfast commitment to God. This idea was taken up as a battle cry during the Reformation, expressed in the Latin adage *sola fide*: *faith alone* renders a person righteous. The axiom *sole fide* was linked to the second great pithy proclamation of Luther's Reformation, *sola scriptura*: it is *scripture alone* that determines that in which faith consists. The assertion of *sola fide* dissipated in a stroke the necessity or usefulness of giving alms to the poor, obtaining indulgences, going to confession, embarking on pilgrimages, or undertaking severe penances. Nothing rectified a fractured relation with God except a faith that acknowledged God's gracious faithfulness to humanity. The insistence on *sola scriptura* was more than a broadside against papal power and privilege in Luther's age. It undercut the authority of papal and conciliar teaching over several centuries if their concepts and terminology were alien to the Bible.

On 31 October 1517, Luther circulated 95 theses concerning indulgences. Cardinal Albrecht received a copy, and acknowledged it as such by referring to it as a 'treatise and theses by an impertinent monk in Wittenberg touching the holy business of indulgences'.[17] Indeed it did. Luther mounted three principal arguments against the practice of indulgences. First, he pointed out that were the pope to become aware of the dire poverty of the German people, he would prefer that the project to build St Peter's would never be realized.

Second, he questioned the pope's assumption that he enjoyed jurisdiction over souls in purgatory. Finally, he pointed out that trying to
elude punishment was a fruitless venture. Sin merits horror, from
which God alone can rescue a sinner.[18]

Luther needed to be careful because he issued his theses at an
extremely precarious time in Europe. Between 1494 and 1559, rival
groups in Europe became locked in a series of wars. In 1494, the
French monarch launched an invasion of Italy which, at the time,
was exceptionally populous. Spain reacted swiftly, not wanting
French domination to establish itself in the prize of northern
Italy. By 1519, the royal court of Valois in France had fallen into conflict with the royal house of the Habsburgs. Both wanted to
control Europe. Their conflict provoked outbreaks of war that lasted
until 1559.[19] Luther's life could not escape consequences of this
conflict.

Because of his theses, he was delated to Rome. From then on he
became snared in difficult public debates. In 1519, he entered into
public dispute with Johannes Eck. These disputations lasted for ten
days, from 4 to 14 July. Luther did not retract his views. By then he
had begun to query the highest authorities in the governance of the
Catholic Church, which were the papacy and episcopal councils.
Pope Leo X responded in 1520 by issuing the bull *Exsurge domine* (15
June) that declared Luther to be a heretic and forbad believers from
reading or promoting his beliefs. It also threatened him with excommunication.[20] The Latin title of the Pope's bull means 'Rise up
Lord'. Luther burnt it at the gates of Wittenberg, together with writings of Johannes Eck, in December 1520. The following year,
Charles V, the Holy Roman Emperor and a Hapsburg, entered the
fray. He met with Luther at a gathering of the Empire's Diet, or governing body, during April of 1521. By then Luther had published
extensively, disseminating his views. In the presence of the Emperor,
he was asked whether he would recant or not, and then given a day
to consider his response. Luther's answer was 'no'.[21] The Emperor
reacted by giving himself time to consider his reaction. He was a very
young man, still in his teens. Despite his youth, he was a level-
headed ruler. He allowed Luther to leave Worms, but issued a declaration condemning him as a heretic. Luther now had reason to fear
for his safety. Within days he was back in Wittenberg. Friedrich the
Elector protected him, and housed him in a fortified castle looking

Paſſional Chriſti und   Antichriſti.

Figure 23: Protestant engravings, Passional Christi und Antichristi, *Wittenburg, 1521.*
Christ suffers under the weight of his cross in the left engraving. The Pope, called the
'Antichrist', enjoys the comfort of being carried in a litter on the right

down on the city of Eisenach. Luther stayed there, absent from public life, for ten months.

Luther's Reformation had begun, and was not about to dissipate. When he emerged from his isolation in Eisenach, he set to work reforming the Church in German territories, beginning mainly in his own Saxony. The Lutheran reform that ensued involved the training and appointment of pastors for congregations, the transformation of forms of worship and the abolition of many Catholic ritual practices, the composition of Lutheran rituals for churches, the structuring of school education and systems of social care, and the establishment of structures for the newly reorganized Church.

Catholic Reformers

Luther was not a voice crying alone in his efforts to reform the Catholic Church: religious orders, including the Eremites of St Augustine, had earnestly embarked on zealous programmes of religios reinvigoration in the fifteenth century. By then, Franciscans and Dominicans had established convents throughout Europe, and

Dominican houses of study flourished in Europe's university towns and cities. The friars, because of their mobility, adapted far more readily to expanding urban populations during the fifteenth and sixteenth centuries than did monastic foundations whose members were required to take a vow of stability, obliging them to spend their entire lives in one monastery.

When Luther was a friar, one of his mentors was Johann von Staupitz, the vicar general of the Augustinian Eremites. Like Luther, Staupitz could be highly critical of papal authority. Unlike Luther, he never abandoned the Catholic Church, but in effect 'gave Luther several of the most central insights of the Lutheran reformation'.[22] One of these was an objection to indulgences; another was a steadfast confidence in divine mercy.

Several scholarly Catholics of the fifteenth century had presaged the work of Luther in their own adamant dislike of indulgences. Prominent among these were John of Wesel and Wessel Gansfort, Dutch advocates of a *Devotia Moderna* ('new devotion'), a form of religious living based on contemplation, especially on the sufferings of Jesus. It is exemplified in Thomas à Kempis' *The Imitation of Christ*. The *Devotio Moderna* emerged among the Dutch during the fourteenth century and from then spread to Germany, Italy and France. Many teachers at Paris' Sorbonne University also denounced abusive practices related to indulgences.[23]

Desiderius Erasmus (c. 1469–1536)

Luther engaged an intellectual sparring partner in the figure of Desiderius Erasmus, a fervent though irenic Catholic. Erasmus was also one of the most learned people of his age. He was a Renaissance humanist in intellectual disposition. Like Luther, he was an Augustinian, though a canon, not a friar. He left his canonry in 1495 to study at the Sorbonne and then at Oxford. He was so adept at classical Greek that he was appointed to teach it in Cambridge.[24]

Erasmus was greatly vexed by Luther's challenges to Catholic leadership and worship. He was particularly troubled by Luther's understanding of human will and its potencies. In 1524, he published a tract called *De libero arbitrio* ('On free will'). Erasmus argued in a humanist vein that human beings are distinguished by their reason. Relying on it, they are free to choose to act in either a good or a bad way. The point is, either way, their decision is based on a free choice. They are not in any way coerced to act in a particular way. Any view of free will is pivotal to how Christian faith is perceived. For Erasmus, humans do not live like puppets whose movements are determined by a divine Puppeteer. Luther reacted sharply. In 1525, he responded with his own tract on human volition, *On the Bondage of the Will*. His view of how Christians live displaced Erasmus' emphasis on freedom with an accentuation of bondage. Humans are not sovereignly free when faced with practical choices. They will be bound to act in a good or despicable way, but when they become aware of God's gracious and benevolent disposition towards them, they are obliged not to rebuff it.[25]

On the question of will, Erasmus and Luther were never reconciled. They were united in both being religious reformers and both wanting the Bible to be the primary engine for reform. Erasmus was not shy to criticize practices he disliked in the Catholic Church. A principal aim of his publications was a biblically-based renewal of the Church's theology and popular piety.[26] German reformers did not fail to consider Erasmus as an ally, a response that troubled him, because he had no intention of abandoning his Church. In Spain, his books were placed on the *Index librorum prohibitorum* ('The Index of Forbidden Books').[27]

Erasmus had been at work since the second decade of the sixteenth century studying the Bible in a new way. The pith of his approach was to try to discern the literal meaning of biblical texts. He was not opposed to figurative, allegorical or metaphorical interpretations of scripture, but wanted to know what the texts at their point of origin really meant. This involved a way of reading that was not typical in the early stages of the sixteenth century. To ascertain the literal sense of a biblical passage requires minimally at least two methodological steps. First, the *original terminology* of the text needs to be examined in the language of its initial composition. This entails philology, a study of the meanings of words in different languages, and textual criticism, an analysis of divergences between different copies of an original text. A second step needs to consider the *history* of the text being examined. Where was it written? For whom was it composed? Is it the work of a single or several authors? Can the identities of its authors be known? Has it been edited or altered by later generations to suit their interests?[28]

Erasmus was a harbinger of modern biblical analysis in seeking the literal meaning of scripture through textual, linguistic, and historical analysis. The fruits of his labours appeared in 1516, when he published the *Instrumentum Novi Testamenti* ('Apparatus of the New Testament'). Printing with moveable type was pioneered in Europe by Johann Gutenberg (c. 1397–1468), who produced the first printed Bible in 1455. Erasmus' publication of 1516 is the first printed version of the New Testament in Greek. It also contains Erasmus' translation of the Greek into Latin. With this New Testament, Erasmus launched a challenge to reform both the study of the Bible in his age as well as theology. The method for biblical reform proposed was close attention to the Greek text. The instrument for a revolution in theology he countenanced was *ad fontes*, a return to biblical *sources* rather than speculative disputation in theological discussions. He wanted biblical and theological reform to inform two others: a change in popular piety to focus it more on the Gospels; and a reform of the clergy. Erasmus was highly critical of monasticism in his day. He was critical of monks who seemed more interested in money, honour and filling their bellies than with being disciples of Jesus.[29]

For all Erasmus' questioning of Catholic practices, he never aligned himself with the Lutheran Reformation. Writing to Archbishop Warham in 1521, he revealed how disquieted he was by it:

> The condition of things is extremely dangerous. I have to steer my own course, so as not to desert the truth of Christ through fear of man, and to avoid unnecessary risks. Luther has been sent into the world by the genius of discord. Every corner of it has been disturbed by him. All admit that the corruptions of the Church required a drastic medicine. But drugs wrongly given make the sick man worse … For myself I am a man of peace, and hate quarrels. Luther's movement was not connected with learning, but it has brought learning into ill-repute, and the lean, and barren dogmatists, who used to be my enemies, have now fastened on Luther, like the Greeks on Hector.[30]

Despite Erasmus' misgivings about religious reformers in Germany, he remained committed to irenicism. An instance of his willingness to concede points to the reformers is found among his disquisitions on music. In 1533, Erasmus published *Liber de sarcienda ecclesiae*

Concordia ('On Restoring the Harmony of the Church'), which comments on the rite of Mass and music used to accompany it. Therein he is willing to concede that it is acceptable to correct a superstition or impropriety if it has crept into the Mass. What he is unable to admit is that the Mass should be condemned outright. Having described the different stages of Mass, he continues to comment:

> What is there in this that is not pious and worthy of veneration? Whoever is offended by the mean crowd of hired priests should expel the unworthy ones and keep the worthy. Whoever dislikes the sequences, especially the inept ones, may omit them; the Roman Church does not recognize any sequences. Likewise the songs they sing these days in many churches after the consecration of the body and blood of the Lord – songs for peace or against pestilence or for a successful crop – may be omitted without any detriment to religion. All this has been added onto the ancient usages.[31]

City Reformations

Luther was a prolific writer. He continued to publish and disseminate his ideas for the rest of his life. By the time of his death, 'approximately 700 works in his name were circulating throughout the German lands in over 4000 editions'.[32] In Wittenberg, his work was assisted by learned colleagues such as Philipp Melanchthon, Justus Jonas, and Johannes Bughagen. In Switzerland, the direction of the Reformation assumed new forms, forged by John Calvin and Huldrych Zwingli. Neither was a disciple of Luther.

Zwingli had actually fallen out with Luther over what transpires during the Eucharist. He was based in Zürich, but met Luther at Marburg in 1529. Luther rejected the Aristotelian distinction between substance and accidents, when it was applied to explain a transformation of the blessed bread and wine during liturgical celebrations of the Lord's Supper. The Catholic doctrine of a real presence of Christ in the bread and wine was retained by Luther, but not by Zwingli. Instead, Zwingli proposed that Christ's presence in the Eucharist is not material or physical.

Zwingli was a radical reformer indeed. He could easily be regarded as an iconoclast. In Zürich, he was the priest in charge of the Grössmunster, which was a Carolingian building that was finished in 1215, with two Gothic towers added in the late fifteenth century. Its interior was richly decorated. Zwingli directed a committee in methodically destroying all of the church's images and removing all of its art. The committee set to work in June and July of 1524.

By contrast, Lutherans in Germany were initially content to modify existing churches less drastically. A distinctly Protestant style of church architecture in Germany still survives. It is located in Torgau, and is the Schloss-Hartenfels Chapel. Luther dedicated it to God on 5 October 1544. Compared to a Catholic church of the late Renaissance, it is an essay in straightforward simplicity. Simply described, it has a rectangular shape with galleries for worshippers and white-plastered walls. Grey stone constitutes the building's other main colour. It is furnished plainly with an altar, pipe organ, pulpit (with some ornamentation) and a baptismal font.[33]

Pipe organs were a vital part of large Protestant churches. They were powerful instruments, well suited to accompanying and sustaining singing congregations. With so many Christians still illiterate during the sixteenth century, Luther and other reformers composed hymns to instil their ideas in the minds of believers who could learn the hymns by heart. Composing for the organ and choirs became the chief burden of the composer Johann Sebastian Bach, a Baroque master of contrapuntal composition and melodic invention.

John Calvin (1509–64)

In Geneva, the Reformation followed a different course under the leadership of the theologian, John Calvin. He stands among a second generation of reformers. He was born during 1509 in the town of Noyon, which lies in the French region of Picardy. He studied arts in the University of Paris before undertaking higher studies in law in Bourges and Orléans. In Orléans, he was taught methods and languages to study texts critically in their historical contexts. From there he returned to Paris and began to associate with a circle of friends who were critical of the Catholic Church. One of them was Nicolas Cop, who, on being appointed as Rector of the University of Paris, delivered an inaugural speech espousing Lutheran principles. The result was that he, Calvin, and their friends had to leave France.[34]

Figure 24: The Schloss-Hartenfels Chapel, with the pulpit centre-left

An unmistakeable aspect of the lives of prominent Protestant Reformers was that they spent most of their time in a single city. While Wittenberg was the primary site for Luther's labours, and Zwingli was based in Zürich, Calvin settled in the city state of Geneva. He was driven, like all the leaders of the Protestant Reformation and their adversaries, to answer the question 'what, fundamentally, is the Church?'. His answer to that question constitutes one of his two primary contributions to the Reformation. The other is his treatise on Christian faith, called the *Institutes of the Christian Religion*.

This large exposition of Christian faith follows the structure of the Apostles' Creed as it elaborates Calvin's understanding of what is entailed in being a Christian. It was first published in six chapters in 1536, but by the time its final edition was issued Calvin had expanded it to include 80 chapters.[35]

Luther had elaborated a view of the Church that eliminated a distinction between sacred priests and ordinary Christians. In its place he spoke of a Priesthood of All Believers: every baptized Christian has the privilege and responsibility of striving to encounter God without the aid of a celibate cultic figure. The other Protestant Reformers chimed with this view, but developed structures for their city communities that varied according to their particular preferences. In Zürich and Geneva, the Reformation was not remembered as Lutheran. Because of the peculiarities of Zwingli's and Calvin's views of the Church, it came to be known as the Reformed Church.

In Geneva, Calvin proposed more than a new structure for the Church. He also announced a conception of how a Christian society could be constituted. His proposal for an ideal church and society is articulated in his *Ecclesiastical Ordinances*, which were published in 1542. The government of Geneva accepted it as a plan for their own ambitions to reform the life of the city. Calvin's Church was not to be overseen by a bishop and operated by priests. He was convinced that the New Testament did not sanction the offices of bishops and priests as they had developed well after the Christian scriptures were composed. He daringly proposed a fourfold structure of Christian ministry for those in need. This involved the work of ordained pastors; elders who were not clerics; doctors, in the sense of teachers, to educate the young; and deacons, to practise charity in the community. Deacons are mentioned in the New Testament, so Calvin was content to keep that title for someone who serves in and for the Church.

The application of his ideas in the city of Geneva was more worrying because it involved the establishment of a court called the Consistory. The task of the Consistory was to police the morals of the citizens. It was presided over by the Church's elders. It interrogated and punished the inhabitants of Geneva on a wide spectrum of offences, ranging from witchcraft to participating in dances.[36]

Calvin's model for a Church proved highly attractive to others and was eventually imitated in other countries including England and Scotland. In the seventeenth century, Dutch Calvinists took it to South Africa. It was implanted in North America in the third decade of that century.

The People's Christianity

Like all other periods in Christianity's history, the Reformation was the story of masses of illiterate and faceless people who did not enjoy the learning and fame of their normally male leaders, but who daily strove to live as authentic Christians in their homes, on their farms, and in the grubby dark back streets of their cities. The Reformation had a major impact on all of them and was especially uplifting for women and children who were Christians, because it taught them to esteem anew marriage and family life. Medieval theology clearly instructed that clerics are sacred persons, superior to other human beings in kind and degree. Their celibate state is holier than that of married people because it conforms more closely to Jesus' way of living, and because it does not involve the distraction generated by the pursuit of carnal delights. Or so it was argued.

The Reformers swept away both the obligation of celibacy for clerics, and the distinction between sacred and secular persons. An effect of this was that women could more easily regard themselves as disciples of Jesus by creating a loving and religious community with their husbands and children.

Children too were cherished by Reformed and Lutheran Christians and their care for children was shown in two ways apart from supporting them in their homes. To begin with, Christians were to be baptized, even while infants, so that they could enjoy the benefits of entry into the Church. In the second place, no effort was to be spared to educate children in the stories and principles of the Bible that spurred on the Reformation.

In the Reformed cities of Europe, people's piety and patterns of worship were thoroughly transformed:

> the cult of saints, prayers to the Virgin Mary, images and statues, processions and pilgrimages, memorial masses, and the calendar of religious feasts disappeared, despite occasional popular reluctance. Liturgical space and language, preaching, and participation in the Eucharist were also transformed. The Lord's Supper replaced the Latin Mass, and, in the process, the sacrificial understanding associated with the medieval Mass gave way to a shared eucharistic celebration.[37]

Changes in the lives of people who joined the Reformation were far-reaching. Among Lutherans and Calvinists, the communion cup holding the wine used at the Lord's Supper was circulated during ceremonies for all to drink. In the preceding centuries, drinking from chalices (cups forged in precious metals) was reserved for clerics, for fear of spilling the Blood of Christ if given to the people. The art of preaching dominated Protestant meetings for worship, and even the structure of the Lord's Supper was included in an overarching framework focused on the delivery of a usually long sermon. In place of the daily medieval Mass, the Lord's Supper came to be celebrated far less frequently and ceased to stand as the principal form of weekly worship. It came to be celebrated minimally four times a year, in mid-September, and at Christmas, Easter and Pentecost.[38]

Anabaptists

During the convulsions of the Reformation, Protestants occasionally turned on each other vehemently. One group, who came to be known as Anabaptists, scoured the New Testament and found no signs of a practice of baptizing infants. In this light, they argued that adults who had been baptized as infants could not have been baptized at all. They stood in need, as adults, freely to decide to be initiated into the Church by baptism. Hence the name Anabaptists – those who re-baptize. They were roundly denounced by Luther, Zwingli and Calvin and suffered severe persecution by Protestants and Catholics alike. They call to mind the Dolcinians of medieval Italy, who were often hounded to their graves for emulating the Gospels strictly.

Island Reformations

Meanwhile, on the throne of England was one of the most outstandingly well-educated monarchs of the sixteenth century, Henry VIII. Henry was a son of Elizabeth of York and King Henry VII. He became heir to the throne when his older brother, Arthur, died in 1502. The boy Henry had been taught music, mathematics, Latin, Spanish and French by his tutors.

As a young monarch, Henry married Catherine of Aragon, who had previously been married to his brother, Arthur. Catherine was the niece of Charles V of Spain, who, in league with Pope Leo X, denounced Luther. A marriage between Catherine and Henry served to strengthen a convenient political alliance between Spain and England. Like many royal couples of their time, Henry and Catherine were keen to have a son to succeed as king. No such boy was ever born to them. Henry became frustrated and turned his attentions elsewhere. He became intimately involved with Anne Boleyn and decided to marry her. A six-year struggle between him and the papacy ensued in his battle to have his marriage to Catherine annulled. Anne Boleyn became pregnant in December 1532. The following month, Henry secretly married her, but without having secured a papal dissolution of his marriage to Catherine.

Henry's quest to have his marriage to Anne recognized was impelled by a biblical text. The Book of Leviticus, in the Tanakh, teaches this: 'You shall not uncover the nakedness of your brother's wife; it is your brother's nakedness' (18: 16); and again: 'if a man takes his brother's wife, it is impurity; he has uncovered his brother's nakedness; they shall be childless' (10: 21). It is easy to see how these two verses would needle Henry's deeply religious conscience. He was indeed childless, and he had married the wife of his dead brother. He had previously published a rebuttal of Luther with a defence of Catholic sacraments and papal authority.

Henry and Anne never received papal permission for their marriage. It was declared valid by a new Archbishop of Canterbury, Thomas Cranmer, who had been appointed by Henry in August 1532. In 1534, Henry signed into law a Supremacy Act that declared him to be the supreme head of the Church in England. To deny this supremacy was treasonable and punishable by death, as Henry's Lord Chancellor, Thomas More, discovered. He was beheaded on 6 July 1535. He was declared a saint by Pope Pius XI in 1935.

By 1534, Henry was in schism with Rome. For the next five centuries, Christianity in Great Britain was primarily expressed in Reformed traditions with major Catholic structures retained. Unlike Calvinists, the Church of England, as devised by Cranmer, retained a line of bishops to show that it stood in historical continuity with the ancient Catholic Church.

In the sixteenth century there were three Reformations, in what is now called the United Kingdom of Great Britain and Ireland. In England, the Reformation took time to be established and was driven by a succession of monarchs. A Reformation in Ireland failed, but a third Reformation, in Scotland, proved successful. All three Reformations were united in their deference to Calvin. The Reformation in Scotland differed from that in England, to the extent that in following Calvin it accepted his theology as well as his patterns for Church organization.[39]

In England, Henry VIII had certainly severed juridical association with the Church of Rome, but he was not nearly as recognizably Protestant as Calvin or Zwingli. Henry retained patterns of worship in Latin, required his clergy generally to be celibate, and issued Ten Articles (of Religion) in 1536 that retained doctrines of purgatory and transubstantiation. It was during the reign of his son and successor, Edward, that the Reformation in England began to look more Protestant. Parliaments during Edward's reign suppressed chantries (chapels for Masses for the dead to be celebrated), and introduced worship in English with the publication of the Book of Common Prayer. With all this, the Reformation was still not firmly in place. It took time to win over the hearts of the people, and the next sovereign, Queen Mary, vigorously re-established Catholicism as the religion of the land. During her short reign (1553–58), the Archbishop of Canterbury, who had served Henry and Edward, was burnt at the stake in Oxford (1556). In 1563, while Elizabeth I was Queen, 39 Articles were promulgated. They tabulate doctrines that regulated the lives of members in what now could be called a Church *of* England, or an Anglican Church.[40]

In Scotland, kirk sessions were created. The word 'kirk' is the
Scottish equivalent of the English term 'church'. The sessions were
like Calvin's court in Geneva and regulated the religious and moral
lives of the people. Sessions first emerged in towns of the lowlands,
but soon spread to rural parishes. Each session included a local minister, who collaborated with a circle of about a dozen lay elders, or
presbyters. Crucially, the local community of Christians had a say in
deciding how their church was to be directed. By the late sixteenth
century, parish sessions became involved in a larger network of pres-
byteries (gatherings of elders). The members of these then took part
in even broader provincial synods, and finally in a national general
assembly.[41]

As with Calvin's Geneva court, kirk sessions could be very rigorous in their oversight of parishioners' lives:

> Absentees from Sunday sermons were fined, and while elders took
> attendance, others were designated 'searchers' to prowl the parish
> during the service and detect absentees. Boys found playing golf were
> whipped; drinkers in alehouses paid heavy fines. Town sessions
> enforced attendance at weekday sermons as well, ensuring that the
> Protestant message became firmly embedded in the minds of the
> people. Parents were told to instruct their children in religion, supple-
> menting the regular Sunday afternoon catechism in the kirk.[42]

All this transpired with the consent of the people at local levels. John
Knox (c. 1513–72) became a prominent leader of the Scottish
Reformation and was largely responsible for the contents of a
Protestant Scottish text for worship, *The Book of Common Order*
(1556–64). Knox also developed an intense hatred of Catholicism.[43]

A Quick Guide to some Protestant Denominations

Anabaptists   A nickname, meaning the 're-baptizers', given to a variety of
Protestants who emerged during the sixteenth century, including Thomas
Münster (c. 1489–1525). They refused to baptize infants and argued that adults
baptized in their infancy need to be baptized again with a profession of con-
scious belief.

Anglicans, Evangelical   Members of the Church of England who adopt
principles and beliefs of the Protestant Reformation.

Baptists   Emerged in the early seventeenth century and now form one of the largest Protestant denominations. They profess that committed baptized Christians form the unifying principle of the Church and that only believers should be baptized. General Baptists hold that salvation is available to all people. Particular Baptists restrict it to a predestined elect or few.

Calvinists   Followers of a system of beliefs, doctrines and customs first enunciated by John Calvin (1509–65) in Geneva.

Charismatics   A general term encompassing Christians, especially in the twentieth and twenty-first centuries, who live and worship by making central to their lives the gifts (charisms) of the Holy Spirit listed in the New Testament.

Congregational Church   Began in sixteenth-century England and led by Robert Brown, who wished to be independent of the Church of England. Congregationalists espouse Trinitarian doctrine and advocate reverence towards the Bible, but they wish to safeguard the independence and autonomy of local churches.

Episcopalians   Stem from the sixteenth-century Church of England in England, but emerged in North America after English colonization and in communities wishing to worship with Anglican rituals. They accept the authority of bishops.

Evangelicals   A broad term encompassing Protestants stemming from Anglican, Baptist, Methodist, Calvinist and Lutheran traditions who stress the centrality and indispensability of the Bible and the gospel in Christian lives.

Lutherans   Follow the system of beliefs, doctrines and customs espoused by Martin Luther (1483–1546), espousing especially the priesthood of all believers, and the unparalled authority of the Bible.

Mennonites   Founded by Meno Simons (1496–1561) and seeking to emulate Christian practices of the ancient Church. Contemporary Mennonites tend to be strict pacifists.

Methodists   Formed in eighteenth-century England on principles and beliefs enunciated by John Wesley (1703–91) and Charles Wesley (1707–98), and generally espousing a belief that Jesus Christ died for all people and not just a few.

Moravians   Originated in Bohemia and Moravia (contemporary Czech Republic) after John Huss (1373–1415). These Christians emphasize piety in their lives and worship, as well as the authority of the Bible.

Pentecostals   An international movement that began in the USA in the early twentieth century and now constitutes the most rapidly growing of all Christian denominations. They stress and celebrate the gifts they believe the Holy Spirit bestowed on believers on the feast of Pentecost.

Presbyterians   Members of churches founded originally in Scotland on Calvinist principles by John Knox (1514–72), and advocating a form of local church government by presbyters or elders.

Religious Society of Friends   Otherwise known as Quakers and emerging in the seventeenth century. They form resolutely egalitarian communities and normally observe silence when they meet until one or more of their number are emboldened to speak on behalf of all.

Salvation Army   An international organization founded by William Booth (1829–1912) in London and best known for their outdoor evangelical activity of band recitals and extensive material charitable care for poor and homeless people.

Catholic Reformations and Counter-Reformations

Among Catholics, multiple initiatives for reforming the Church were underway long before the Protestant Reformations sprung into action after Luther. The Dominican Girolamo Savonarola was burnt at the stake in Florence in 1498 for his attempts to rid the churches of abuses. The Fifth Lateran Council (1511–17) also attempted to purify the life of the Latin-Rite Church. A new order of regular clerics, or clerks, was founded with papal approval in 1540 by Ignatius of Loyola (1491–1556). It was called the Society of Jesus. Its members, popularly known as Jesuits, threw themselves into educational and missionary work. One of them, Francis Xavier (1505–52), baptized tens of thousands of people in India. Other religious orders blossomed and attempted to reinvigorate their church. Matteo Serafini da Bascio (c. 1495–1559) founded the Capuchin order of

Franciscan Friars. The brown hoods of their habits inspired the name of the now popular form of coffee known as cappuccino, with its distinctive topping of nutmeg or chocolate. St Cajetan (1480–1547) established the Theatines, an order of clerks regular like the Jesuits, in Rome.

Other zealous reforming Catholics took as their primary motive the desire to resist Protestant Reformers, and thus formed a Counter-Reformation. Its centre was Italy, but Peter Canisius and other Jesuits devoted themselves to combating the Protestant Reformation so as to ensure that Germany, Austria, Poland and England were confirmed as Catholic countries. Other significant participants of a Counter-Reformation were St Philip Neri (1515–95), St Charles Borromeo (1538–84), Mary Ward (1585–1645) and St Francis de Sales (1567–1622).

The Council of Trent

When Martin Luther first fell out with Pope Leo X, he wanted a general council of bishops to resolve their disagreement. He had to wait for almost three decades before a council was convened. When the Council of Trent met for its first session in 1545, the rift between Lutherans and Catholics appeared too deep to heal, and so it was. This council met in a string of sessions between 1545 and 1563. They legislated for far-reaching reforms in the Catholic Church. Its impact on Catholic life lasted for 400 years, until the Second Vatican Council (1962–65) ushered in a new understanding of, and era for, the Catholic Church. It produced a catechism, improved the education of clergy, and revised the Breviary, a collection of psalms, readings, and prayers to be recited daily by monks, nuns and clerics. It also published a new form of the *Missale Romanum* ('Roman Missal'), with detailed rubrics or directions for the celebration of Mass that was later called the Tridentine Rite.[44]

Scientific Revolutions

The reformations and revolutions of the sixteenth century involved a major sea change in science, and more specifically in astronomy and cosmology. It was associated principally with the Polish priest, Nicolas Copernicus (Mikolaj Kopernik, 1473–1543).

Copernicus was born in Prussia on 19 February 1473. He studied classics and mathematics in the Polish University of Kraków between 1491 and 1494 before studying astronomy in the University of Bologna. From there he studied medicine in Padua (1501–5), and earned a doctorate in canon law in the University of Ferrara in 1503. When his studies were complete, he settled back in Poland.

Copernicus was never ordained, a priest even though he was appointed as Canon of the cathedral of Frombork in 1506 by his uncle, who was the local bishop.[45] Astronomy was not necessarily his primary intellectual interest, but it is for his revolution in understanding the constitution of the earth's solar system that he became famous, or infamous, *as a Christian*. From studying the motions of planets, Copernicus realized that the earth could not possibly be the centre of the universe, as both Aristotle and the second-century CE Egyptian astronomer Ptolemy had taught. To look at the sun in the sky naturally gives the common-sense impression that the earth is immobile, and that during the course of the day the sun circles the earth. Copernicus' revolution in astronomy, as every school child now knows, was to reverse that impression and argue that the earth revolves around the sun, and is thus not the centre of the universe as it was generally conceived in the sixteenth century, and as it had long been envisaged since Aristotle and before.

What does any of this have to do with Christianity? Everything. Humans' understandings of their world determine what they believe and how they behave: 'we always shape our values in significant measure in accord with our notion of the kind of universe we live in. What we believe about the nature of nature, how we evaluate nature drives our sense of duty.'[46] Before modern astronomy, human beings had no notion of galaxies.[47] They happened to inhabit one, the Milky Way galaxy, but they assumed that their earth was the inert centre of the universe with the sun and planets swirling around it, the abode of God above the circles of planets. It was only in the twentieth century that it was discovered that there are 100,000 million galaxies in the observable universe, each with 100,000 million solar systems, and that the universe is expanding.

Biblical, patristic, and medieval theologians all assume that the earth is the centre of the universe. On that basis, it is much easier to regard human history and the life of Jesus as important to the purpose of the universe. In arguing that the earth orbits the sun,

Copernicus contradicted Aristotle, who had argued that only bodies in the heavens above the earth could have perpetual circular motion. All Christian theology before Copernicus presupposed what Copernicus set aside.

This may seem a slight matter today, but in the sixteenth century Copernicus' heliocentricity could easily be judged as an assertion that what Christian doctrine taught about the world is false and unworthy of belief. This explains why Copernicus hesitated before publishing his ideas. They were offered to a general readership in 1543 in the book, *De Revolutionibus Orbium Coelestrum* ('On the Revolution of the Celestial Spheres'). Copernicus was presented with a copy on the day he died, 24 May 1543.

In the generations that followed Copernicus' death, his work was vindicated by calculations worked out by the Danish astronomer Tycho Brahe (1546–1601), as well as by Johann Kepler (1571–1630). In 1609, Galileo Galilei (1564–1642), a younger contemporary of Kepler, built an instrument, a refracting telescope, the type of which was unavailable to Copernicus.[48] By observation he confirmed the central argument of Copernicus. He was placed under house arrest in Rome by the Inquisition but he escaped the fate of Giordano Bruno, who, in 1600, was burnt at the stake in Rome's Campo de'Fiori. His crime? He had accepted Copernicus' views and argued not only that the universe is infinite in extent, but within that infinity it is possible that there are manifold worlds.[49]

The revolutions in astronomy and cosmology ignited by Copernicus continued in the field of physics, and more specifically in mechanics, during the seventeenth century. In 1668, the 26-year-old Isaac Newton (1642–1727) was appointed as the Lacasian Professor of Mathematics in Cambridge. He lived in Cambridge for the next three decades of his life. His greatest work was *Philosophiae Naturalis Principia Mathematica* ('The Mathematical Principles of Natural Philosophy'), in which he proposed a universal law of gravity and three laws of motion that account for the movement of celestial bodies in an exclusively scientific way, without reference to either God or theology. A new view of the world was set to become entrenched in the West and principles of modern science, some of which were articulated by Galileo, slowly began to exercise people's minds:

Before the age of science, religious belief was based on faith, cultural tradition, and a confidence in the revealed truth in the scriptures and teachings of holy men and women specifically selected by God. Science began to erode these beliefs by showing that many of the traditional teachings, such as that of a flat Earth at rest at the center of a firmament of stars and planets were simply wrong, people began to look to science itself for evidence of a supreme being that did not depend on any assumptions about the literal truth of the Bible or divine revelation.[50]

Conclusion

Orthodox Christians were left politically and religiously unsettled by the Protestant Reformation. They continued serenely to worship with icons and developed a form of liturgical music that is choral and richly harmonic. Among Catholics, Baroque art, architecture and music flourished. Because of the Protestant Reformation, the repertoire of beliefs available to Christians expanded in new directions. Masses for the dead, doctrines of purgatory and transubstantiation, and a cult of saints and the Virgin Mary were augmented by beliefs in the priesthood of all believers, in the centrality of baptism and the Lord's Supper, in justification by faith, and the authority of the Bible alone in the lives of Christians. A major belief that arose among Calvinists was in predestination, which holds that not all human beings will be saved because their ultimate destinies were predetermined by God before their deaths. During centuries that ensued, a repository of beliefs and styles of living among Christians grew incessantly.

Part 4

Enlightenment and Modernity

Chapter VII

Christianity Transformed

'*Welcome those who are weak in faith, but not for the purpose of quarrelling over opinions.*'
Romans 14: 1

When two trains collide at great speed, the combined force of their impact unleashes death and destruction. When two debaters joust with each other over a contentious issue with sophisticated and confidently expressed arguments, their very conflict demonstrates that doubt attends the question they contest. Collision causes devastation; disagreement breeds uncertainty.

By the beginning of the seventeenth century, Christianity was plagued by violent disagreements. For the next three centuries its hold over people's lives was transformed because its own believers, and those observing them, became more unsettled and uncertain about what constitutes Christianity's essence. Because Christians could be seen to hate each other, Christianity became a victim of its own disaccord. It lost its previous medieval, Renaissance and Reformation cultural hegemony in Europe because of the scepticism it spawned.

This chapter takes up the story of Christianity on the eve of the birth of the modern age. By the end of the nineteenth century, Christianity had been transformed from a dominant controlling culture of Christendom to a religion forced to negotiate with and within nation states, enthused by freedoms of religion, speech and conscience. From the seventeenth until throughout the nineteenth century, Christianity's medieval and feudal network of rural parishes and monasteries saw its members drawn to expanding cities, whose scientists were demonstrating that the world was not constituted as had been previously thought and taught, and whose politicians were increasingly motivated to relegate Christian institutions to social margins.

Blood drenched the history of Christianity in the early stages of the seventeenth century. By this time, Eastern Orthodox and Catholic Christians did not usually slaughter each other. Catholics and Protestants did, on a massive scale. A war between the two types in Europe began in 1618, and lasted for 30 years until 1648. Wars with at least a partial religious motivation were waged in central Europe before and after those dates, but the Thirty Years War was particularly destructive, especially for the populace of Germany. It was a continuation under an altered guise of the long-standing feud between the Valois and Habsburg dynasties, although by this time French Bourbons had succeeded the Valois. One of the causes of the war was the acceptance by the Protestant Elector Palatine of the Rhineland of the Crown of Bohemia, an act of defiance directed at Austrian Catholic Habsburgs.[1] During the last half of the sixteenth century and the first half of the seventeenth, Catholicism and Protestantism were like two trains colliding and two debaters debunking each other.

How can people who are meant to love each other, as well as their enemies, let loose deadly armies on those who deserve their service and affection? The scandalizing shock of bloodletting by and among Christians during the first half of the seventeenth century was that it was carried out in the name of Jesus. When Christians demonstrate in their behaviour that they have nothing to do with Jesus according to what is remembered and known about him, they corrode all hope that they will be regarded admirably by those they hope to convince and convert. Their own violent aggression on the eve of modernity was one factor contributing to the collapse of Christendom. During and after the Thirty Years War, Christian denominations and sects proliferated, each convinced that it was the *only* authentic form of Christianity. People do not normally devote their lives to a religious group unless they are convinced it is the best among others.

Conflict always disturbs children. Catholic children of medieval Germany only knew children of similar religious dispositions. They could play with youngsters like themselves. After the traumas of the Reformation, children in central Europe needed to distinguish between their good selves and lesser alien types of their own age, whose parents raised them with new and different religious allegiances.

Despite all the conflict among and between Western Christians in the first half of the seventeenth century, it is easy to overlook that they remained united in the religious rudiments they professed. Christians in North Africa, Sweden and Poland, as well as Catholics and Protestants everywhere may well have been at odds about the authorities of the Bible and the papacy, but they all believed that God had created the world, that Jesus Christ was the harbinger for them of salvation, and that baptism was a necessary requirement for initiation into the Church.

In the three centuries preceding 1900, Christianity was transformed in several other ways apart from losing its cultural hegemony in Europe. From 1700 to 1900, its missionaries moved north, east, west, and south from Europe to introduce Christianity in newly discovered lands such as Australia, New Zealand, and the vast reaches of Canada and North America. Christian missionaries during these centuries continued to work in South America and Africa. This was an age of energetic colonialism. Jesuits excelled in establishing missions in Asia and South America. The nineteenth century was a high point for Protestant missionary endeavour in several corners of the globe. Orthodoxy took hold of the people of Russia, and its distinctive mode of devotion, the icon, flourished.

The rest of this chapter falls into three parts, each of which corresponds to either the seventeenth, eighteenth or nineteenth centuries. The second is pivotal for Christianity's later development because it involved the Enlightenment, which was the most serious intellectual and cultural threat to Christianity's viability since antiquity. Its seeds were planted especially in the seventeenth century, with innovations in philosophy, science, biblical scholarship and political theory. The chapter will need to account for the fate and fortunes of Christians in the nineteenth century, as their world was colonized, industrialized and secularized.

Moves to America

A major result of warfare in Europe during the seventeenth century was that it triggered waves of emigration elsewhere, notably to North America. Christianity on the large landmass of North America is nearly 400 years old. It was introduced there by Christians seeking a new and freer life. In 1620, a group of English Protestants set sail from Plymouth in the South of England and made their home in a town they created and named as Plymouth.

It was on the eastern seaboard of what is now called Massachusetts in the USA. These intrepid travellers are remembered as the founding Pilgrim Fathers. By religious disposition, they were Congregationalists. Their origins lay in Norwich, England, in the late sixteenth century, when Robert Brown led a congregation in seeking greater religious autonomy from the Church of England – hence the name 'Congregationalists'. In 1638, they were followed to their settlement, a *New England*, by Roger Williams. He established a Baptist community on Long Island. Baptists now form one of the largest Christian Protestant denominations, and are a major religious force in the USA. They originated in England in the seventeenth century and, like Congregationalists, wanted to be independent of the Church of England. They are united in their belief that a person needs to be a fervent believer in order to be baptized.

Baptists were followed to New England by members of the Religious Society of Friends, who were more popularly known as Quakers. Their origins also lie in seventeenth-century England. The person who inspired their formation in 1647 was George Fox (1624–91). He was seized by a verse from John's Gospel: 'The true light, which enlightens everyone, was coming into the world' (Jn 1: 9). This meant for him and for his subsequent followers that the heralded true light of John, the Inner Light, was available to anyone, regardless of any religious commitment.

He preached this view on foot in northern England, and the associates he attracted were initially called 'Children of Light' or 'Children of Truth'. They also become known as 'Friends' in view of another text from John: 'You are my friends if you do what I command you' (Jn 15: 14). For their time, they were amazingly free in their thought and behaviour. They refused to countenance war, to attend churches, to swear legal oaths, or to favour people on the basis of sex or social respectability. In the tradition of the Reformation, George Fox would not acknowledge a mainstay of the medieval Church, which was the necessity of a priest to mediate sacramentally between God and people. In the latter half of the seventeenth century, the Friends held monthly, quarterly and annual meetings. Silence was a highly distinctive aspect of their gatherings when they assembled in meeting houses for worship, meditation and prayer. Seated as a unified group without a prelate presiding, they would normally remain silent until one of their number was moved, they believed, by God's Spirit to speak for the benefit of all. The experience of the Inner Light, or divinely impelled inspiration to speak, led some of them to shake or quake, giving rise to the name Quaker.[2] Like most Christians of their time, they espoused a Trinitarian understanding of God.

Fox encountered public hostility in England and was imprisoned eight times from 1649 to 1673. Undaunted, and upon final release, he travelled to North America, the Caribbean islands and countries of Europe, especially The Netherlands.[3] In North America, Quakers proved to be very influential. As was the case in England, their religious sensibilities attracted people involved in business. Towards the end of the seventeenth century, they founded the Quarter state of Pennsylvania under the leadership of William Penn. Because they taught that the Inner Light was accessible to all, they allowed women to preach.

Puritanism

The culture of Congregationalism that established itself in New England in 1620 was also Puritan in religious commitment. Puritanism arose in England during the reign of Elizabeth I (1533–1603). It could be a severe and exacting way of living, and was certainly an intense expression of Protestantism. Puritans regarded the Church in England of their time as riddled with corruption, and sought to excise from its life any practice or belief that was without foundation in the Bible. Their theology was strictly Calvinistic. They insisted on the paramountcy of gathering for worship on Sunday, but they rid their mode of adoring God of ornate vestments and music sounded by pipe organs. Their dress was extremely sober, normally black and eschewing colour and ornate fabrics. Dancing and frivolity, expressed in games such as those involving cards and gambling, were alien to their lives.

Puritanism took hold of the new budding colonies in New England. It policed the sexual practices of people, often to the detriment of women. Of known public trials for fornication (unmarried sexual encounters), which was considered a crime in the state of Massachusetts, women were often regarded as the natural culprits of the offence. Records kept in the county courts indicate that bridal pregnancies were as high as 40 per cent in towns of New England.[4] Such a pregnancy occurred when a woman gave birth within the first seven months of marriage, indicating to others that she had become pregnant before she had married. At this time, the offspring of bridal pregnancies were socially stigmatized as bastards.

The case of Martha Root illustrates the plight of several other women among eighteenth-century Puritans of New England, who were victims of a duplicitous ethical standard that relegated culpability to them, and impunity to the men who contributed to making them pregnant, when none of the men and the women was married to each other. Martha Root had sexual relations with the 20-year-old man Elisha Hawley. She became pregnant while single, which was a crime in the law of Massachusets. A state statute of 1642 stipulated that available suitable punishments for people convicted of fornication were corporal punishment, a fine or court-ordered marriage. Courts were at liberty to impose one or all three of these penalties on a couple.[5]

Martha Root gave birth to two girls, one of whom died in 1747. When accused, she named Elisha Hawley as the father. She was brought before the Hampshire County Court of General Sessions in November of 1747, but did not name the father of her surviving child. She assumed all guilt, and Elisha's name did not even appear in court records. Why did she act thus? Because 'Joseph Hawley, Elisha's bother and a young lawyer eager to make a reputation for himself, negotiated privately a settlement with Martha for the child's maintenance'.[6] By assuming complete culpability she could provide for her daughter.

A high regard for families among North American Puritans is based on an understanding of people that differs from that which later modern societies of the West expected of their citizens. English Puritans of the seventeenth century, in contrast to many aristocrats, insisted on strict marital fidelity between husbands and wives, together with a submission of wives, children and servants to household patriarchs.[7] Closely-knit familial units were transported to Massachusetts Bay by the Puritans seeking relief from duress in England. A law of the new colony required all citizens to live in households. People who lived alone were obliged to join a household. As Ava Chamberlain has observed; 'it was not until the eighteenth century that the concept of an individual defined by inherent rights rather than reciprocal relations begin to challenge the essentially communitarian organization of colonial society'.[8]

New Lands for an Old Faith

The transformation of Christianity in the seventeenth century by its extension to North America was not limited to Puritanism. Spanish missionaries started to work among North American Indians in 1526, almost a century before the Pilgrim Fathers established their New England. In 1565, a Catholic community flourished at St Augustine in Florida. The contemporary state of Maryland in the USA began as a Catholic colony in 1634.[9]

Christianity had also been long established in Mexico before it was implanted further north on the same continent. Catholicism arrived in Mexico in the person of Amerigo Vespucci when he landed near Tampico in 1497. Spanish communities who followed him settled in Mexico in 1518. Franciscan friars arrived in 1522. Mexico could boast the foundation of a university in 1551, which was conducted according to Christian principles, well before the arrival of Congregationalists further north.[10]

Pronounced veneration of Mary, the mother of Jesus, was an aspect of Catholic Christianity as it developed in Mexico that deserves consideration. There are two main reasons why this is the case. First, veneration of Mary as the Virgin Mother of Jesus proved similarly popular throughout South America. Secondly and more subtlely, enthusiasm for the Virgin Mary sheds light on why Catholicism became so readily popular among Mexicans who were the heirs to very ancient cultures and religious cults that knew nothing of Christianity.

The first inhabitants of the Americas were immigrants from Asia around 40,000 years ago. They became far more numerous in South than in North America. One calculation concludes that populations of tribal groups in the Americas rose in such a way that there were ten times as many people in the South than the roughly 3 million in the North.[11] Unlike the North, civilizations in Central and South America built very large cities. Contemporary Mexico City stems from one of them. The Aztec, or Mexica, civilization of Central America was ruled from its capital of Tenochtilan, the original

Mexico City. The language of this civilization, Nahuatl, has survived until today among the 1.5 million or so people who speak it.[12]

A larger civilization, the empire of the Incas, was governed from its capital of Cuzco, the contemporary Cusco in Peru. It included regions of what are now called Peru, Ecuador, Northern Argentina and Chile, Bolivia, and Colombia. Its language was Quecha, which is still spoken by about 10 million people. This civilization and that of the Aztecs further north had no contact with Europeans before the fifteenth century, unless some of their peoples encountered wandering Vikings around 1000 CE.[13] Christianity was introduced to them principally by Catholic Spain.

The sun formed the principal focus of worship for the Aztecs and Incas, but their people were also fond of Goddesses, and this may explain why they adapted readily to a cult of the Virgin Mary. One of the principal forms of Catholic devotion in Mexico today has a history of 500 years. It is centred on the Virgin of Guadalupe, who has also been known and venerated by Mexicans over five centuries as Our Lady of Guadalupe.

The name 'Guadalupe' is Spanish, and refers to a hill in a suburb of contemporary Mexico City. Its Aztec name was 'Tepeyac'.[14] According to pious accounts, the veneration of the Virgin of Guadalupe stems form a morning of 1531 on the Feast of the Immaculate Conception, which celebrates that Mary was born without original sin, such was her dignity as the mother of Jesus. On that morning a local man, Cuauhtlatoatzin, reported seeing a celestial lady on the spot of a shrine from which the Goddess Tonantzín used to be worshipped. He took the appearance of the woman to him as a vision of the Virgin Mary, but it was quite distinctive. He reported that Mary had skin that was darker than was normal for Spaniards, and she spoke his own language. A poem in the Nahuatl language, the Nican Mopohua, depicts Mary as the one who would cure sorrows, miseries and misfortunes of people after listening to their laments.[15]

Large numbers of the local population converted to Christianity after hearing this story. Veneration of the Virgin of Guadalupe became popular during the seventeenth century among Creoles. Its commemoration 'has become Mexico's most popular religious event and there are many other such celebrations of the Virgin-Mother across Latin America, which include Our Lady of Copacabana

Figure 25: Altarpiece of Our Lady of Guadalupe, Mexico City, with exuberant Baroque decoration

(Bolivia), the Virgin of Luján (Argentina) and the Virgen de la Caridad del Cobre (Cuba)'.[16]

Catholicism was introduced to the large region of Brazil by Portuguese, rather than Spanish, settlers. The territory was claimed for Portugal by Pedro Alvares Cabral in 1500. In the sixteenth century, any attempts by Protestants to settle in the area were eliminated by the Portuguese. In the first half of the seventeenth century, Dutch Protestants established a foothold in Brazil, but after a series of violent conflicts they were forced to withdraw.[17] The Portuguese colonizers exploited the rich resources of Brazil by exporting large volumes of its sugar to Europe during the seventeenth century, as well as gold and diamonds during the eighteenth. Enslaved Africans were transported to work in Brazilian fields and mines because so many indigenous people were killed by conquerors and their diseases, as well as by the surfeit of back-breaking toil demanded of them.

Jesuits established a mission among Indians in Brazil during 1549. It was only in the nineteenth century that a Protestant church was able to be rooted in Brazil. German Lutherans arrived there in 1823, and were able to stabilize a church in 1837. In the early stages of the seventeenth century, Jesuits tried to protect Indians from the predations of European colonialists in southern Brazil, as well as in Argentina, Uruguay and Paraguay, but in the eighteenth century their society was temporarily suppressed by the papacy. Their imposed inability to operate enabled colonialists to exploit Indians without fetters.[18]

The historian Enrique Dussel designates the years from 1511 to 1553 as a period of 'prophetic theology' in South America. This was the period in which the Dominicans Antón Montesino and Bartolomé de las Casas laboured tirelessly to defend the inhabitants of Hispaniola from annihilation at the hands of the conquerors. Dussel ties the end of a period of prophetic theology in South America to the early 1550s, when universities were established in Mexico City and Lima in Peru. A period of three centuries followed thereafter, when a 'theology of colonial Christendom' was used by Spanish and Portuguese colonizers to subdue Indian peoples, rob them systematically of their resources, and destroy vestiges of the ancient civilizations. This baneful stage of South America's history began to change in 1808 and 1831, when the nations of the regions became politically independent of Spain and Portugal.[19]

Iberian Catholicism

It would be difficult to overestimate the formative influence of Spain and Portugal on the historical evolution of Christianity. From the late fifteenth century onwards, these two competing empires were responsible for transporting Catholicism to the Caribbean, the Philippines, Mexico and South America. Brazil is the primary recipient of Portuguese Christian influences.

In 1846, Ernesto Salvado, a gifted concert pianist and Spanish Benedictine, set up a monastery in the austere conditions of arid land in Western Australia. He and his monks called their monastery New Norcia, in homage to Saint Benedict's foundation.[20] He introduced Catholicism to Aborigines he met, and learnt Aboriginal languages.

The first Catholic priest arrived in the Philippines in 1521. He was followed by Augustinian missionaries, who settled in 1565 on some of the 7107 islands that constitute the contemporary Republic of the Philippines. Dominican friars arrived next, and in 1611 founded the University of Saint Thomas in Manila. Before becoming a republic in 1946, the Philippines endured a long period of foreign control from the sixteenth to the twentieth centuries. The islands became a Spanish colony in 1564. They declared their collective independence from Spain in 1898, only to have the USA take control of their affairs.[21] Filipinos had to wait until after the Second World War until they were able to direct their nation according to their own sovereignty.

At the beginning of the twentieth century, the population of the Philippines included about 76 million people. Of these, about 82.4 per cent were Catholics. Their lives as Catholics still bore the marks of Spanish civilization. The first Spanish missionaries to arrive in the Philippines did so in the immediate aftermath of the Council of Trent. Once settled, they set to work preaching to local people with the aim of baptizing them. Their theology and patterns of worship were directly determined by the Council of Trent.

The two primary influences the missionaries exerted among the locals were a teaching about human salvation and a system of sacraments to assists quests for salvation. One of the most difficult points of dispute during the Reformation was whether faith alone renders a believer justified in relation to God. Trent decreed that although justification depends on a 'predisposing grace of God through Jesus Christ', humans can respond by 'giving free assent to and cooperating with this same grace'.[22] For Trent, being saved involves faith *and* works:

> But no one, however much justified, ought to think that he is exempt
> from the observance of the commandments, nor should he use that
> rash statement, forbidden by the fathers under anathema, that the
> commandments of God are impossible of observance by one who is
> justified ... Therefore, no one should yield to complacency in faith
> alone, thinking that by faith alone he has been established as an heir,
> and that he will obtain that inheritance even if he has not suffered
> with Christ so as to be glorified with him.[23]

Spanish missionaries, wherever they settled, preached a gospel of salvation through faith and actions. Again following Trent, they initiated newcomers into the Church with sacraments of Baptism, Confirmation, Penance and the Eucharist. The first two of these were experienced once in a person's lifetime, but the last two could be celebrated regularly. At other stages in converted Christians' lives, the missionaries encouraged them to participate in three additional sacraments: marriage (for those not wishing to be clerics), holy orders (for deacons, priests and bishops) and extreme unction (for those close to death).

The Jesuits, originating in Spain, proved to be exceptionally intrepid missionaries. Two Japanese men were ordained Jesuit priests in 1601. A Spanish Jesuit, Pedro Paez, introduced Tridentine (stemming from Trent) Catholicism to Ethiopia in 1603. His confreres set up a mission in Thailand in 1607. In 1624, the Jesuit missionary Alexandre de Rhodes settled in Cochin, China. The following year another Jesuit, Jean de Brégeuf, started to live among Huron natives in Canada. Christianity was introduced to Tibet in 1626 by Antonio del Andrade, yet another Jesuit.[24]

Baroque Christianity

Throughout the seventeenth and eighteenth centuries, Christians of all nationalities continued to express their beliefs concretely; that is, they used art, architecture and music as vehicles for preaching the Gospel to which they had dedicated their lives. During this time, Orthodox Christians persisted in producing icons in very large numbers. Their churches were richly decorated with paintings and mosaics. The furniture within them was ornately decorated, especially their iconostases – screens separating sanctuaries from naves on which icons could be displayed.

At the same time, Carthusian and Cistercian monks built abbey churches whose sublime beauty lay in utter simplicity, free of ornate decoration. Their fondness for austerely bracing surroundings for worship reminded them that their liturgies were not attempts to entertain people in comfortable domestic surroundings. Through their rituals they worshipped God by repeatedly keeping alive the memory of the slaughtered prophet, Jesus of Galilee. A distinctive feature of their worship was that they used their entire bodies in demonstrations of obedience and penitential subservience to God. Through prostrations on the ground and frequent profound inclinations (bowing of the head down to waist level) before each other and altars, they expressed loving and humble service to God and the people of God's creation. They shared with English and New England Puritans a distaste for what they regarded as superfluous ornamentation in dress and worship. Unlike Puritans, they denied themselves marriage. This immured them from the pleasures of sexual partnership, but it also rid their lives of the joys, hardships, responsibilities and sufferings attendant on raising children.

As monks of strict regular observance and Puritans attempted to live without ostentation and extravagance, a new style of art developed that sought to declare Christian beliefs and values precisely through the medium of extravagance. It came to be dubbed 'the Baroque', from the Portuguese adjective, barroco, meaning extravagant. By the end of the sixteenth century, the artistic styles characteristic of the High Renaissance were largely spent, and gave way to Baroque art. Throughout the sixteenth century and in the early stages of the seventeenth century, Italy was pre-eminent among nations with its art, sculpture, architecture, and music. In painting, its discovery of linear perspective was imitated throughout Europe, with flourishing schools of art in Spain, the Low Lands and Germany. The Baroque style was the last great artistic export of Italy to the rest of the world.[25] Wherever Spanish and Portuguese explorers and missionaries went after 1600, they took Baroque architecture with them. Baroque taste in music gave birth to opera, with Jacopo Peri's

Figure 26: Velázquez, Christ Crucified, *oil on canvas, Baroque, 1630,*
Prado Museum, Madrid

Euridice of 1600, Claudio Monteverdi's *Orfeo*, composed in 1607, and his masterwork, *The Coronation of Poppea* (1642).

In what did the Baroque consist? Its primary characteristic was exuberant ornamentation. It sought to recreate beauty and splendour in song, architectural space, sculptured figures and paintings. It was extravagantly sensuous and the very antithesis of ascetic control. It is exemplified in the sculpture and architecture of Gianlorenzo Bernini (1598–1680), and the paintings of Michelangelo Merisi di Caravaggio (1571–1610) and Diego Rodríguez de Silva y Velázquez (1599–1660).

The large oil painting by Velázquez, 'Cristo crucificado' (*Christ Crucified*), typifies both Renaissance linear perspective and Baroque effusiveness of emotion. It also exemplifies an archetypal image of Christian piety over many centuries – the Crucifixion. It aims to stimulate faith by arousing emotions. The body is young and shapely, but not horribly disfigured. Its darkened background thrusts it into focus. A shadowed left armpit is one of the many tools used to achieve linear perspective, and makes the image all the more lifelike. The painting's emotive force stems primarily not from wounds of torture, but from the dangling hair covering the right side of a man's head who was killed in the prime of his life.

By contrast, Bernini's *Ecstasy of Saint Teresa* radiates light. It too seeks to stimulate faith by exciting emotions, but it does so by engaging a spectrum of blissful, erotic, frenzied and hallucinogenic sentiments.

Rome was the point of origin of Baroque architecture in the late sixteenth century. An example there of an emergent Baroque style is the Jesuit church, Il Gesu ('the Church of Jesus'). Unlike Gothic cathedrals, its interior is a large space that is not obstructed by pillars or side isles. Everyone in its nave was able to see its visual focal point, which is a richly ornate marble altar in its sanctuary. The eyes of worshippers are also drawn to its painted ceiling

> that draws the imagination beyond the limits of the here and now. In the Gesu the ceiling was painted by Andrea Pozzo towards the end of the seventeenth century. It shows the Jesuits spreading the gospel to many different peoples, as they are drawn up into the central encounter between St Ignatius Loyola, the founder, and the figure of the savior himself, who holds his cross as he blesses Ignatius.[26]

Figure 27: Bernini, The Ecstasy of Saint Teresa, *marble, 1645–52, Cornaro Chapel altar, S. Maria dell Vittoria, Rome*

This and other Baroque buildings were constructed to excite visual senses as well as imaginations. They were meant to provide the setting for artistically splendid liturgies. Their interiors exude triumph and confidence, as they seek to stimulate their worshippers with a foretaste of paradise. In this sense they expressed Catholic sacramentalism: the belief that material things can be loci or media for humans to encounter divine life.

The Baroque impetus to thrill senses and imaginations is also captured in new musical styles, typified by operas and oratorios. The complex contrapuntal texture of intertwining contrapuntal lines and melodic lines was increasingly overshadowed by a new style of *monody*, meaning 'one song'. This method of composition involved the creation of a melody for a single voice accompanied by one or more instruments. Both singers and instrumentalists developed advanced skills in improvisation, again to stimulate audiences with a sense of unpredictable excitement. As with architecture, Baroque music was richly and emotionally decorative.

From Italy, Baroque expressions of Christian beliefs in music, spaces and imagery were mimicked in other countries of predominantly Catholic culture, and introduced locally wherever missionaries of the seventeenth century landed.

The Enlightenment

By the end of the seventeenth century and throughout the eighteenth century, the extravagant self-confidence of a Baroque Church had begun to lose its grip on the minds and hearts of many Europeans. Intrepid explorers and indefatigable missionaries heightened the awareness of Europeans that they inhabited a planet with a large range of starkly diverse peoples, tribes and civilizations. Travellers returning to Europe in the seventeenth century brought back tantalizing news about ancient civilizations in China and Egypt. A major result of such thrilling discoveries of other peoples and cultures was that it began to destabilize a common view among medieval and Reformation Christians that foreigners with religions apart from Christianity were heathen inferiors. The period between roughly 1650 and 1800 has come to be called the Enlightenment. It was a time especially in Europe, North America and the UK when a new awareness took hold of both Christians and people who had abjured religion. What enlightened or awakened a growing awareness was the realization that Christianity was one religion among many, and that Christians could be unsteady in any conviction that their religion was uniquely true and therefore superior to all others. This awakening

> marks a seismic change in the history of Christianity for it effectively marks the end of the possibility of maintaining 'Christendom' as a totalizing concept embracing and unifying all aspects of known

society (even though the reality of that 'Christendom' had already been decisively fractured by the Reformation).[27]

The Enlightenment began among intellectuals, but ended up as a major period of cultural and historical change. What motivated and impelled it was the intellectual temper of scepticism. Pyrrho of Elis (c. 365–c. 275 BCE) was famed among ancient philosophers for his tendency to be doubtful about intellectual propositions, rather than credulous. His intellectual bent gave his name to the frame of mind known as Pyrrhonian scepticism, or simply Pyrrhonism. It can be a devastatingly unsettling form of questioning for anyone who is confident that absolute truth is known absolutely. It is the polar opposite of dogmatic thought. As Christianity became more dogmatically confident, to the point of killing its opponents and own doctrinal deviants, ancient Greek sceptical postures receded into obsolescence. Christians have never been and could never be forbidden to think, but they have frequently been muted so that they do not say what they think. Inquisitors and Reformers alike burnt, hanged or impaled people if their ideas deviated from defining tenets of either Catholicism or Protestantism. Inducing fear is an excellent instrument for silencing new thought.

Knowledge of Pyrrho, and his style of sceptical calling into question all assertive declarations, became more widespread in Europe during the seventeenth and eighteenth centuries.[28] It triggered doubt and uncertainty about dogmas and certitude in the minds of many questioning individuals from the sixteenth century onwards.[29] Yet doubt achieves nothing unless it is aided by circumstances that enable it to be voiced. The Enlightenment was an age during which a coalescence of factors emboldened questioners to challenge Christianity's religious hegemony in Europe and its conquered territories, with the cumulative result that Christianity thereafter never again exercised a controlling supervision of what people could think, say and do.

With its scepticism, proponents of the Enlightenment began to consign previously non-debatable dogmas to a lesser, devalued realm of private opinion. During the beginnings of the Enlightenment, the majority of people in Europe and its colonies believed in angels, hell and a Triune God. While scepticism was the centrepiece of its mental constitution, a rediscovery of another feature of ancient

Greek life – democracy – enabled its realization in politics. The Enlightenment culminated in the French Revolution, which involved the guillotining of a French king, Louis XVI. His violent death in quarrelsome times served as a symbol of the collapse of imperial and regal government stemming back to Rome of the Claudian emperors. Since the French and North American Revolutions of over two centuries ago, every nation of the planet has had to decide whether or not to adopt a democratic form of government. Many still resist it, but it represents the political modus operandi of most independent states. Its cornerstone, captured in Article 3 of the French Revolutionaries' *Declaration of the Rights of Man and the Citizen* (1789), asserts, to paraphrase, that no one shall exercise sovereignty over the people without the consent of the people.

The idea that a collectivity of people ought to decide who exercises sovereignty on their behalf is not at all inimical to Christianity. It resonates well with organizational principles of Dominicans, Presbyterians and Quakers. What it does jar with is papal monarchy, and with it a hierarchical exercise of authority found among Catholic, Orthodox and Anglican Churches. Hierarchy technically does not mean a stratified pecking order of superiority, with top dogs ranked above underdogs. It means 'rule by priests'. Priests did indeed rule and govern all others in pre-Enlightenment France, as is captured in the figure of Cardinal Richelieu (1585–1642).

Intellectually and politically, the Enlightenment represents the first major period since the Fall of Rome that a free-thinking and democratically arranged culture flourished *independently* of the control of Churches. Several historical changes can be adduced to explain why and how Christianity, or rather Christendom, lost its cultural supremacy in the territories where it had previously held sway. With the Reformation, the papacy was forced to relinquish power in large regions of the heartlands of Europe. The Reformation also heralded acrimonious disunity among Christians that expressed itself most shockingly in wars waged involving religious motivations. Incremental fragmentation characterized relations between Protestants, Catholics and the Orthodox, but also among Protestants as well. Added to the proliferation of Protestant denominations that enfeebled Christian unity, merchant classes that had formed on the eve of the Enlightenment became moneyed and confident enough to challenge the social control enjoyed by preachers, so that they could preserve and promote their own interests.[30]

Above all, the engine that drove the Enlightenment was powered by new forms of knowledge that shed light upon, or enlightened, the previous dark recesses of human ignorance and superstition. The revolutions in geography, astronomy and physics, typified by Columbus, Kepler and Newton, were followed in the seventeenth century by new patterns of thought among philosophers, more advances in the therapeutic practices of medicine, and the beginnings of a critical or analytical study of the Bible.

The Bible itself was an unchallenged sovereign authority throughout the Patristic era, the Middle Ages, the Renaissance, and the Reformation. Its authority, together with the entire edifice of pre-modern Christian doctrine, was placed under the microscope of Enlightenment scepticism. The result of scrutiny was a widely disseminated conviction that the Bible, from its beginning to its end, is the product of human minds and hands recording their thoughts and beliefs in the Middle East of antiquity. It was an historical artifact like any other body of writings. It could be venerated because it was composed with more chronological proximity to the prophets and Jesus than anyone alive in the eighteenth century enjoyed, but after the development of modern biblical criticism it became much more difficult to regard the Bible as an infallible record of God's will and commands. Why? Because it contains historical errors and direct contradictions. It is ignorant of information discovered by early modern sciences. This does not mean that it was regarded universally as devoid of authority, prophetic power and wisdom. It simply lost its authority among many devotees of the Enlightenment, who had been seduced by the unsettling potency of sceptical questioning.

Many Christians were champions of the Enlightenment. They were keen to rid their lives of the paralysing shackles of dogmatism. They were tired of venomous strife between warring Christians, and they were eager to profit from new knowledge, as well as to be able to decide who ought to manage their societies. Christians, too, joined in the French Revolution with glee.

The eighteenth century proved to be a period of religious enthusiasm and creativity, as well as democratic revolution and philosophical questioning. Christianity was brought to Australia soon after Captain Cook took possession of the land for the English Crown in 1770. In 1730, in the settlement of Northampton, Massachusetts, an evangelical or Bible-based revival began among Protestants. It spread from there to other American colonial settlements. It was called the First Great Awakening.

Two men in England, John Wesley (1703–91) and his younger brother Charles (1707–88), met with friends in Oxford with whom they formed what they called the *Holy Club*. They came to be known, disparagingly at first, as Methodists, because their routine in trying to live as Christians and read the Bible struck others as overly strict in its method. In 1736, the Wesley brothers sailed to North America. John began missionary work among tribes in Georgia, while Charles worked as a secretary to a general. Vitally for John's religious development, he met Moravian Christians in America. These stressed the indispensability of personal conversion to the Gospel and heart-felt piety in prayer. Returning to London, John sought out the company of Moravians. He was so engrossed by their form of Christianity that, in 1738, he underwent a religious conversion, which emboldened him to form groups of like-minded evangelical Christians. They secured their own building, which had previously been used for the business of government, and began weekly meetings, called classes, for people who converted to their cause. By 1743, rules had been drawn up for a Methodist Society. John and Charles Wesley were members of the Church of England, and Methodism was initially internal to that Church. Only on the death of John Wesley, in 1791, did Methodist societies begin to regard themselves as an independent Christian denomination.[31]

Rosendo Salvado

In a book presenting Christianity it is instructive simply to tell stories of Christians, rather than give accounts of endless historical change and intellectual revolutions. The story of Rosendo Salvado (mentioned above) illustrates well the missionary fervour that characterized many Christian Churches during the nineteenth century. He was a Spanish missionary to Australia. When Captain Cook arrived on the east coast of Australia, he had stumbled on a massive land mass, with about half a million inhabitants who spoke a variety of 250 different languages.[32] A penal colony was established around Botany Bay where Cook landed, and Richard Johnson (1753–1827) was appointed colony chaplain. The new settlers in the region included transported convicts, military officers and their marines, as well as free adventurers. The convicts came principally from three Christian denominations: the Church of Scotland, which was Presbyterian in temper; the United Church of England and Ireland; and the Catholic Church.[33]

Rosendo Salvado lived for 50 years on the south-west corner of Australia, and devoted his life to trying to evangelize Aborigines of the region. During all those years, he attempted to build an oasis of European culture on the edge of the Gibson Desert among gum trees, black snakes, screeching cockatoos and Aboriginal nomads. He was a talented person, who managed during his life to become a pianist, organist, Benedictine abbot, bishop, builder, explorer, missionary, scholar and linguist.

Salvado was born in Spain in a town called Tuy on 1 March 1814. He died in Rome during 1900. As a young man he entered the Benedictine Monastery of St Martin in Compostela, where he studied music and philosophy. In 1835, the Spanish government closed all religious communities in Spain. Salvado was thereby forced to abandon his country because of aggressive anti-clerical legislation. In 1838, he moved to a Benedictine monastery at Cava, about 12 miles, or 20 kilometres, to the north of Naples. In this monastery, he hatched a plan to establish a mission among Australian Aborigines. In the fourth decade of the nineteenth century, the missionary activity of the Catholic Church was rather enfeebled, and still reeling from the after-effects of the French Revolution. Rosendo, and a Benedictine friend from Compostela, Joseph Serra, sent word to the only bishop in the newly founded Swan River Colony of south-west Western Australia, asking for permission to be received as missionaries. The bishop, John Martin, agreed.[34] The two monks were then dispatched to the colony by Pope Gregory XVI.

Salvado and Serra set sail with a few other missionaries from England, in a ship called *Elizabeth*, in 1845.[35] In the same year, Friedrich Engels wrote about the condition of the working class in

England. The monks arrived in Fremantle, near Perth, in January 1846. From there they went to Perth, a town named after Perth in Scotland. Recovered from their journey, they decided to walk into the bush and establish a mission at a place they called New Norcia, after the birthplace of the founder of the Benedictine Order. New Norcia is about 82 miles, or 132 kilometres, to the north-east of Perth, in what are known as the Victoria Plains. It is an exceptionally arid place. Salvado published an account of his travels and engagement with Aborigines in a text called *Historical Memoirs of Australia* (*Memorie Storiche dell'Australia*). Surprisingly, he wrote in Italian. The *Memoirs* are replete with original discussions of race, religion, theology and religious beliefs.

After months of attempting to sow crops in the dust of New Norcia, Salvado and three other missionaries in his band were in danger of starvation. Salvado sent word to Perth that he would like to give a public piano recital to raise money for food. He walked for several days to reach the town. When he arrived his feet were bleeding because his boots were worn out. The boots, so-called, were made out of a wooden base and kangaroo hide begged from Aborigines. In Perth, the Governor organized an audience to assemble in the main hall of the local law courts. Protestants, Jews and Catholics all attended to see what this unusual monk was like. Piano recitals were rare in penal colonies of the time! Salvado had to play from memory since he had no musical scores with him. For three hours he entertained his listeners by extemporizing excerpts from recent Italian operas, and by musically imitating Aboriginal corroborees. Happily, he earned enough money to stave off starvation.

Back at New Norcia, he built a monastery and schools for Aboriginal children. On another trip to Perth, he was given two bullocks, a dray, and a piano.[36] He set out to take them back to New Norcia. His journey turned out to be much more perilous than he had envisaged. In his *Memoirs*, he describes the following scene:

> When I got to seven miles from the Mission I found myself in another area of marshy ground, a good deal worse than the earlier one. The bullocks sank into the mire right up to their bellies, and the dray disappeared up to the axle, and to make things worse, not only was the rain coming down in torrents, but the fury of the wind was breaking

off big branches from the trees, and there was continuous thunder and lightning.[37]

The more Salvado tried to extract the bullocks, the deeper they sank. What he did next is unforgettable, and for some, unforgivable. In his own words:

> Then I began to fear for the life of the poor animals, and after a moment's reflection, decided to make one last attempt.

> I lit a fresh fire, and pitilessly jabbed a lighted brand fair and square on their sensitive hind parts. Feeling that they were being burned alive, the two bullocks with incredible efforts and terrible bellowing finally managed to extricate themselves ... Extreme dangers call for extreme measures; the situation was so bad that I stood to lose my team.[38]

Salvado lived and laboured in a larger historical context of augmenting colonialism, nation-state imperialism, secularism and slavery. Most of Salvado's colonial co-explorers in Australia regarded Aboriginies as exceptionally ugly and lazy. Salvado disagreed and notes:

> The physical and moral character of the Australian Aborigine has been falsely represented, for many think of him as the most degraded member of the human race. He is thought to be puny, deformed, and not very different from the brute beasts, some going so far as to say that he is indistinguishable from the ourang-outang. Quite a number of people deny that the poor native has a rational soul.[39]

Salvado cited a local magistrate, who observed that Aborigines, male and female, were well built, muscular, with beautiful limbs and lively black eyes.[40] He never spoke of them as savages or underlings. He observed that he had found natives with physical beauty and dignified gait. He even commented: 'Some boys of six or seven years of age, in particular, had limbs of such distinction and beauty that they surpassed the finest creations of Greek sculpture.'[41] Unlike missionaries on the eastern coast of Australia, he bothered to learn Aboriginal languages. Initially, he attempted to live as a nomad among Aborigines.

Salvado was a gifted linguist. He spoke Galician, Castilian, Italian, French and English, and a variety of Aboriginal dialects. He was the first person to import into Australia, and to study there, Minge's Greek and Latin Patrologies. He participated in the First Vatican Council between 1869 and 1870. While he did not make an intervention in the Council's debates on papal infallibility, he did submit a paper on missionary endeavours. He was consecrated a bishop in 1849. In 1867, Pope Pius IX raised New Norcia to the status of an abbey *nullius* (exercising ecclesiastical jurisdiction in the region), and Salvado was installed as its first Lord Abbot.

Protestant Missionaries

The story of Rosendo is only one of a multitude of others that recount the extent to which missionaries were prepared to endure physical danger and deprivation, to preach to peoples unfamiliar with Christianity. The nineteenth century was a golden age for Protestant missionary endeavours. Many groups of Protestants were founded in the eighteenth century specifically for the purpose of conducting foreign missions. Their collective aim was to convert the world to Christianity. These institutes worked indefatigably throughout the nineteenth century. Having contributed to missionary work in Australia, Henry Martyn went and laboured in India from 1805 onward. Robert Morrison began similar efforts in China in 1807, Adroniram Judson in 1813, Samuel Marsden in New Zealand in 1814, Karl Gützlaff and Jacob Tomlin in Siam in 1828, and John Williams in Samoa in 1830.[42] The primary recipient of Protestant missionary attention during the nineteenth century was Africa. It proved much more difficult to make any impression in South America.

The famed explorer David Livingstone delivered a speech among students in Cambridge in 1857. In the course of his address, he stated: 'I go to Africa to try to make an open path for commerce and Christianity; do you carry out the work which I have begun?'[43] Livingstone met an eager audience and lit a fuse among generations of undergraduates determined to follow his lead of bringing Christianity to new worlds amenable to European commerce. As the twentieth century began, missionaries from the West had extended their reach enormously into Africa and Asia. By 1910, 60 years after Livingston's speech, 'there were some 19,000 foreign Protestant missionaries in the field, supplemented by nearly 100,000 native workers'.[44]

Papal Infallibility

One of the more perplexing of all Catholic dogmas for Protestants is a nineteenth-century teaching of the First Vatican Council that the Pope can occasionally teach infallibly. This dogma is all the more baffling for Christians of any kind because infallibility – the capacity to act and speak without error – is traditionally regarded as an attribute of God. Since humans are finite and perspectival in everything they can see, perceive, and experience, it seems decidedly odd to assert that one of them enjoys a divine attribute.

The First Vatican Council, or Vatican I, was the only General Council of bishops held during the nineteenth century. It was convened in 1869 by Pope Pius IX (in office from 1846 to 1878), and ended precipitously in 1870 because of the outbreak of the Franco-Prussian War.

The Council was called in troubled times for the Catholic Church. It had survived the French Revolution and withering assessments of the Enlightenment, but now needed to negotiate with large urbanized and industrialized nations of the world that were increasingly enthused by democracy.[45] In response, the Council promulgated two decrees: 'Constitution on the Catholic Faith'; and 'Constitution on the Church of Christ'. The teaching on papal infallibility is contained in the second, and states:

> we teach an as divinely revealed dogma that when the Roman pontiff speaks *ex cathedra*, that is, when in the exercise of his office as shepherd and teacher of all Christians, in virtue of his supreme apostolic authority, he defines a doctrine concerning faith or morals to be held by the whole church, he possesses, by the divine assistance promised to him in blessed Peter, that infallibility which the divine Redeemer willed his church to enjoy in defining doctrine concerning faith or morals. Therefore, such definitions of the Roman pontiff are of themselves, and not by the consent of the church, irreformable.[46]

It is crucial to note regarding this text that it does *not* state that the pope is infallible.[47] It speaks of the Roman pontiff possessing 'that infallibility which *the divine Redeemer willed his church to enjoy*' (emphasis added). The notion of infallibility is thereby linked to the will of Jesus Christ and the Church. The dogma of infallibility asserts in effect that, under very limited circumstances, the pope may enjoy the influence of infallibility which is an attribute *of God* and only God.

The Salvation Army

While Pius IX was trying to steady unnerved Catholics after the Enlightenment, another Christian, William Booth (1829–1912), was trying to fill hungry bellies in London. Booth began his ecclesiastical career as a Methodist preacher, but left that ministry to undertake evangelical preaching and social work in impoverished areas of East London. In 1865, he established a foundation for his work, the Christian Mission, in Whitechapel. He soon attracted disaffected Anglicans and Methodists. His associates in charitable work adopted the name of Salvation Army in 1878, and in 1880 began to wear military uniforms, such was the intensity of their battles to bring food and Christ to down-and-out street dwellers. Its leadership also adopted a military style with the person in charge called a General. From London, the Salvation Army grew into an international web of evangelizing Christians, present in sections of Europe, the USA, Australia, New Zealand, India and South Africa.[48]

In all these countries, Salvation Army members organized themselves into their basic units of corps which were led by officers such as lieutenants and brigadiers. Such officers presided at marriages, preached, and occasionally served as military chaplains.

The Salvation Army's doctrines are contained in their *Articles of War*. They include an insistence that the Bible alone determines Christian beliefs and practices; an affirmation that God is Triune; and a conviction that all people can be saved. They differ from many other Christians in that they reject baptism and celebrations of the Lord's Supper.[49] They see in the Mass, or Eucharist, an endless source of acrimony among Christians.

The primary religious motivation impelling the work of the Salvation Army is the conclusion that a person will be better disposed to listen, as the Gospel is preached among them, *if* they are housed, fed, clothed and purged of parasites. It is not difficult to see in such a rationale a direct resonance with the life and observations of Jesus.

Charles Darwin

No other name captures the travails of Christianity, in its process of transforming extensively during the eighteenth and nineteenth centuries, as Charles Darwin. He had no known intention of baiting the Church or corroding orthodoxy, but one of his ideas, among the greatest notions in the history of science and humanity, pulled the foundation stone from beneath the edifice of pre-modern Christian doctrine. It was called the evolution of species by natural selection.

Christians at the outset of the nineteenth century almost universally believed in the literal truth of the creation narratives in the Book of Genesis. According to these ancient stories, God created humans in the image of God on a separate day from all other animals. Indeed, in 1800, humans could barely have thought of themselves as animals at all, which they are. Because only humans can speak with perfect, past perfect, future perfect and pluperfect tenses, they seemed to many before Darwin to be distinct from animals. The Bible also evinces that God providentially cares for humans (Mt 10: 29–31). As for all other animals, God, so early nineteenth-century Christians generally believed, created them in such a way that they always maintain their distinct forms which do not alter over the course of centuries.

Darwin taught differently. What if the history of living organisms is a haphazard, unpredictable and violent story of predation, in which species change into other species over time? And what if most species that have ever lived no longer do? Did God not care for them after all? These queries were not irrelevant to Darwin. As a young man, he earned a degree in divinity from the University of Cambridge, which surprises those who think of him exclusively as a biologist. Even though he had studied theology at university level, he was not particularly enraptured by it, and his overriding fidelity was to follow the consequences of his life-long investigations of fossils and living organisms. These led him in 1859, after considerable personal anguish, to publish *On the Origin of Species by Means of Natural Selection*.

The lynchpin of this book's thesis is that all the variegated forms of life now observable are not fixed within immutable species, but are interrelated by having developed over vast periods of time from a common source of simpler life forms. Darwin's thesis was not merely a clever idea. He could illustrate it with tell-tale signs: bottled samples of animal specimens he had collected after years of travel, including research among the Galapagos Islands.

The question Darwin needed to unlock was how one species could change into another if all species share a common ancestry from a single type of life form. He observed that animals produce many more offspring than are able to survive and breed themselves. Those that manage to survive among the siblings are likely to be the strongest, healthiest and most suited to manage within a surrounding environment. They will then pass on to their own offspring those physical features that enabled them to endure. As some of their features differ from those of their parents, their own offspring will develop strengths peculiar to them, so over large stretches of time a species could change, even alter into another.

The key to Darwin's whole pattern of thought about life was the insight that only the strongest and healthiest of offspring survive. The process by which they manage to do so he names in the final paragraph of the fourth chapter of *On the Origin of Species*. He dubs it natural selection. Among offspring, the characteristics of the strongest act as a mechanism which selects them, or enables them to survive and pass on their features.

One and a half centuries after the publication of Darwin's account of biological evolution by natural selection, contemporary genetics, unknown to him, have confirmed its central thesis. Life emerged in oceans around 3000 million years ago, when chemical molecules grouped together to form individual cells. Cells formed bacteria, and from these came multi-celled organisms out of which emerged insects. A chain of organisms developed from these: reptiles, dinosaurs, birds, and then mammals.[50]

All these forms of life are the biological origin of humans, and hence Christians. That is the point of speaking about Darwin in a book on Christianity. Even though his ideas seemed to undermine Christian doctrine for many of his contemporaries, most coped. It was easy for Christians to argue that in view of evolution by natural selection in a massive web of life, God's creation is all the more wondrous. What remained and remains deeply troubling for them is the observation that most species that have ever been are now extinct, and that animals, insects and reptiles of all kinds survive in a ruthless battle of killing and eating one another.[51] This is not a very benevolent situation in which to be.

The True Gospel of Jesus Christ Asserted

While Christian life was in the process of far-reaching transformation during the centuries preceding the twentieth, bold thought on Jesus complemented novel views on biology to forge new ways of talking about old doctrines. Christian missionaries of the eighteenth and nineteenth centuries normally preached a gospel of doctrinal orthodoxy. They were compelled to, because the missionary societies that equipped and dispatched them were concerned to instil in everyone they could a form of faith that was traditionally familiar to them. The views of missionaries were closely vetted before they could set sail. At the same time as their thought was being monitored to gauge whether it conformed to ecclesiastical orthodoxies, other more intellectually daring and innovative Christians decided it was time to interpret the identity and significance of Jesus Christ with patterns of thought that differed from dogma. One such thinker was the Englishman Thomas Chubb, a Deist who did so roughly mid-way through the eighteenth century.

Chubb was an enthusiast of the Enlightenment. He was a self-taught man, but unlike many religiously inclined thinkers he was prone to be consistently logical when he pondered the essence of Christianity. In 1738, he published a book in London that helped to launch an entirely new phase in the history of reflection on Jesus Christ. His book was called *The True Gospel of Jesus Christ Asserted*. At its outset, Chubb explains that in his tract he has '*rendered the gospel of Christ* defendable *upon* rational principles' (p. viii).[52] His alignment with the Enlightenment is plainly in view. In sections III–V of Chubb's book, he asserts in what lies the true Gospel of Christ. In Section VI, he begins to explain what is extraneous to the Gospel, and this turns out to be doctrines formulated by other people apart from and after Jesus was alive, and these included Saint Paul (p. 48).

Theology before Chubb was governed by the belief that the Bible is a divinely inspired text that reveals God to humankind. Chubb breaks new ground by arguing that such a belief rests on an unprovable presumption: 'To say in this case that St John was *divinely inspired* in writing his history, is (for any thing that appears) groundlessly to presume a point which is void of proof' (p. 48). The St John to whom Chubb refers to here is the person traditionally thought to have composed the Gospel According to John; that is, John the son of Zebedee. With the stroke of his pen, Chubb ruled out appeals to divine revelation as a foundation for theological interpretations of Jesus Christ. Five decades later, Immanuel Kant, the greatest philosopher of the Enlightenment, followed suit with his book, *Religion within the Limits of Reason Alone* (1793). Modern theology had been born. Orthodox dogmatic thought assumes the truthfulness of a pre-given divine revelation, whereas modern theology, while not always inimical to the idea of revelation, places itself under more of an obligation to offer reasoned arguments for why anyone should be inclined to be convinced that anyone or anything is a revelation of and from God.

No text in the history of Christology has been more influential than the first three verses of John's Gospel: 'In the beginning was the Word, and the Word was with God, and the Word was God. He was in the beginning with God. All things came into being through him, and without him no one thing came into being' (Jn 1: 1–3a). Commenting on these verses, Chubb makes a distinction between what and to whom Jesus preached, and the opinion of John. Thus, what Jesus had to say was one matter; what any of his disciples taught was another. Referring directly to the opening of John's Gospel, Chubb says:

> These propositions, for any thing that appears to the contrary, are only the *private opinion* of St John, who wrote the history of Christ's life and ministry, and they are no part of Christ's gospel; viz. that gospel which he preached to the poor, and which he charged his Apostles to publish to the world (p. 47).

Daringly, Chubb concludes:

> whether Christ was the *Logos* or Word, whether he was with God, and was God, or whether he made all things in the sense in which St *John* uses those terms, or not, is of no consequence to us, because these points are no part of Christ's gospel, and they are what the salvation of mankind is not in the least concerned with (p. 47).

The true Gospel of Jesus Christ in Chubb's eyes is the message he delivered to poor people he encountered. This message has three main aspects. It proclaimed that people will be pleasing to God when they repent of their evil ways so that their sins can be remitted or forgiven by God (p. 32). In Chubb's words: 'to preach the *gospel*, and to preach the doctrines of *repentance* and *remission of sins* is in Christ's account the *same thing*' (p. 35). In addition to repentance and remission of sins, Chubb notes a third aspect, which is God's choosing of a time when God will judge people's action (p. 38). Referring directly to the scene of divine judgement in Matthew's Gospel (Mt 25), Chubb points out that the rule by which God shall proceed in passing judgement on human beings is a law of charity, or benevolent affections of actions shown towards those in need (p. 40).

At the heart of Thomas Chubb's account of the essence of Christ's Gospel is the kingdom of God that Jesus Christ preached to the poor. Anyone who feeds the hungry, clothes the naked, looks after orphans and widows, or visits prisoners, will enter God's kingdom. This leads Chubb to observe in prose that is striking for its time: 'The *banner* of a Christian, is not the *picture* of a cross hung upon a pole, or made upon a man's forehead; but it is a *virtuous* and unblameable conversation, or a mind and life conformed to the gospel of Christ' (p. 60). Then Chubb launches into an illustration of how people who seek power, wealth, and honorific titles like 'Reverend', 'Right Reverend', and 'Most Reverend Fathers' have nothing to do with the Gospel (pp. 61–62). As he says:

> Christ did not lay the foundation of friendly societies to answer the purposes either of *pomp*, or *wealth*, or *power*. He never intended among his Disciples and followers, *some* should be *singled out* from their *brethren* to be possessed of great revenues, live in stately palaces, wallow in luxury and café, or sordidly heap up riches to raise a family, lord it over those by whose labours they are maintained, clothed in pompous and antick [antique] dresses, placed on thrones or garnished stalls and seats of honour, affirm and exercising dominion over their brethren; and that *others* should labour to maintain them, be subject to them, bow down before them, and call them Rabbi, Rabbi (p. 60; brackets added).

Thomas Chubb wrote *as a Christian*, not as a nihilistic gainsayer. He is refreshingly liberating for anyone who has become tired of doctrinal or theological platitudes. According to his view of the true Gospel of Jesus Christ, the medieval notion of purgatory, Luther's doctrine of justification by faith, Trent's theory of transubstantiation, and Chalcedon's dogmas of two natures in Christ, are all human *opinions* subsequent to and *created* after Christ's preaching of a Gospel involving a conversion from unloving neglect to affectionate practical care of the poor.

Conclusion

The nineteenth century was for Christianity an age of vertiginous change. It generated increasing secularization, ambitious colonialism, unstoppable urbanization, sophisticated scientific and technological accomplishments, the continuing gestation of feminism, and in response, an unbridled diversification among Christians. It was also still an age of Christian dukes, earls, barons, marquesses and viscounts. Their fortunes changed during the twentieth century, during a chain of social and political revolutions. In the midst of these and because of these, Christianity mutated even more.

Chapter VIII

Christianity in a Globalized World

'Brother will betray brother to death, and a father his child, and children will rise against parents and have them put to death; and you will be hated by all because of my name. But the one who endures to the end will be saved.'
Mark 13: 12–13

Christianity now shares many similarities with Christianity of the early centuries of the Common Era. It forms a minority of human beings in a pluricentric world of nations, ethnicities, religions and world-views. It has also changed starkly over the course of its history. In 1900 CE, there were about 558 million Christians in the world. A century later they numbered 2000 million, or 2 billion. By 500 CE, 22 per cent of human beings believed in Jesus Christ, but a thousand years later a lower proportion of 19 per cent counted themselves as Christian. During Christianity's first 18 centuries, more that 90 per cent of its adherents were Caucasian by race.[1] As the twenty-first century began, a third of humankind was Christian. Christianity expanded enormously in the world's poorest countries between 1900 and 2000 CE. In those ten decades, their numbers grew from 83 million to 1120 million. In the decades after 1900, Christianity was widely accepted among Africans, Filipinos and South Americans.

This chapter focuses on Christianity as it evolved in the twentieth century. By then, the world had become far more globalized than in any previous era. New technologies made it even more so by the beginning of the twenty-first century. This means that its members were interconnected in a global network with each other, and all other people, by means of air travel, satellites, television, computers and telephones. They lived in a force field of mixed races, religions and cultures. Twentieth-century Christians included peasants in Russia, Maoris in New Zealand, farmers in Ethiopia, kings and queens in Europe, traders in Canada, and missionaries in Korea.

Growth, triumph and ceaseless diversification were all dimensions of Christianity's story in the globalized world of the twentieth century, with its mixing and mingling of populations, but they were only part of its history. The last century was also a period of large-scale numerical defections from Christianity. Some of these were enforced; others were freely undertaken. Millions of Christians were persecuted and killed in Russia, and Communism in Eastern Europe did its best to trample Christianity under foot. Secularism tempted Western Europeans as never before to abandon church-going, and materialism everywhere provided for many a more alluring goal in living than penitence and fasting. Combined forces such as revulsion at religiously motivated violence, and an inability to perceive that Christianity remained truthful to its origins, collaborated to generate a skyrocketing increase during the twentieth century of people who wanted either to have nothing to do with religion, or to be free to declare confidently that there could not possibly be a God. People who declared themselves to be irreligious or atheistic amounted to 3.2 million individuals in 1900, but that number had increased to 697 million by 1970, and 918 million in 2000.[2]

So confident were gainsayers of Christianity at the outset of the twentieth century, the impression could easily be gained that it was poised to expire. By then, Christianity had accumulated enough decriers to give to a general public an impression it would end up like Tutankhamen – a mummified corpse. Enthusiasts of Feuerbach, Nietzsche and Freud could hope that Christianity would falter, as more and more people concluded it was a creation of the imagination, morally repressive, or conducive to mental illness. As the century wore on, Christianity's gravediggers were to be disappointed as it flourished in new forms and dynamic expressions of faith, love and hope.

For those who remained delighted to be Christians during the twentieth century, a good way of focusing on what their faith entailed for them is to focus on death. This is not a cheery thought, but it uncovers what matters most for Christians, and has preoccupied them over 20 centuries. For them, Jesus was rescued and raised from death by God to a heavenly mode of existence. According to any Christian during the Middle Ages and Reformations, preparing for death was decisive. The hour of death was a crucial time when eternal destiny was determined. In the Middle Ages, Christians even

spoke of the *ars moriendi* – the art of dying. How is a Christian to prepare gracefully for the moment of death? Is their best option to live
by a standard of faith *and* works, or by faith *alone*? And once people
are dead, is there any way those still living could influence how they
are regarded by God?

Around 500 years after Luther had fulminated against payments
for indulgences, two French composers, Gabriel Fauré and Maurice
Duruflé, thoroughly captivated their audiences with musical settings
of the Requiem, or Catholic Mass for the dead. With these works,
they at least signalled to their twentieth-century listeners that they
thought people today could and should pray for the dead. A
Requiem Mass is a liturgy originally performed in Latin, and is so
named after a commendation for the dead, *requiescat in pace* ('Rest in
peace', commonly abbreviated to RIP). Fauré composed his *Requiem*
(Opus 48) between 1887 and 1890 while he was director of the choir
of the Parisian church, the *Madeleine*. It soon became known internationally and remained popular in performance and recordings
throughout the twentieth century and after. Duruflé finished his
(Opus 9) in 1947, only two years after the end of the Second World
War. Both works set the Mass for the dead with scores calling for
choirs of mixed voices and instrumental accompaniment. Duruflé
made deliberate use of the Gregorian chant in his setting, and
included entrancing solo performances for mezzo-soprano and bari-
tone voices.

Combined, these two works were symptomatic of Christianity's
continued power to captivate people's belief that there is hope for the
living and the dead. The essence of their attraction was the same as
that of Baroque art – emotion, or the ability to arouse strong feelings
to match cognitive conviction. Another major symptom that the
confident predictions of Christianity's embalmers at the dawn of the
twentieth century were to be frustrated was a new permutation
in Christianity's evolution. This unforeseen change emerged clearly
in the first decade of the century, and now numbers anything from
an eighth to a quarter of all Christians worldwide. It is called
Pentecostalism, and grew from Evangelical Protestantism.

As an expression of Christian faith and action, Pentecostalism
looks to the Bible for its inspiration. There, in the second chapter of
the Acts of the Apostles, can be found a striking story of what happened to a group of Jesus' followers who had gathered indoors after

his death. On the 50th day after the events recalled as Jesus death and resurrection, the Acts of the Apostles records:

> When the day of Pentecost had come, they were all together in one place. And suddenly from heaven there came a sound like the rush of a violent wind, and it filled the entire house where they were sitting. Divided tongues, as of fire, appeared among them, and a tongue rested on each of them. All of them were filled with the Holy Spirit and began to speak in other languages, as the Spirit gave them ability.
>
> Now there were devout Jews from every nation under heaven living in Jerusalem. And at this sound the crowd gathered and was bewildered, because each one heard them speaking in the native language of each. Amazed and astonished, they asked, 'Are not all these who are speaking Galileans?' (Acts 2: 1–7).

The author of Acts then gives examples of devout Jews 'from every nation under heaven' present in Jerusalem for the events being narrated. They include Medes, Elamites, Parthians, Cretans and Arabs, and people from Judaea, Cappadocia, Mesopotamia, Pontus and Asia, Rome, Phrygia and Pamphylia, Egypt, and regions of Syria. Acts attributes the extraordinary ability of the apostles gathered in Jerusalem to speak intelligibly in a host of languages to the presence *in them* of God's Holy Spirit. While doing so, it makes no attempt to conceal an alternative explanation: 'All were amazed and perplexed, saying to one another, "What does this mean?" But others sneered and said, "They are filled with new wine"' (Acts 2: 12–13).

Pentecost is a very good illustration of how Judaism remains in Christianity's spine. For Christians, it is a celebration of the Holy Spirit's presence in the apostles assembled in Jerusalem 50 days after the resurrection. It shows that Judaism is part of Christianity's supporting backbone because the observance of Pentecost was originally a Jewish harvest festival called Shavuot ('weeks'), the feast of Weeks, or Pentecost. It involved a 24-hour-long festival that extended over the sixth and seventh day of the month of Sivan, which was the ninth month of the Jewish year. It celebrated the end of a wheat harvest that began at Passover and continued for seven full weeks during Spring. Shavuot commenced on the 50th day after Passover.[3]

Christians have celebrated Pentecost since the infancy of the Church. Throughout their history many have sought to reinvigorate their lives in forms of worship, rejoicing in the presence of the Holy Spirit in their lives. Such enthusiastic bursts were found, for example, among Pietists and Methodists. In the twentieth century, the numbers of Christians styling themselves as Pentecostals grew to staggering proportions with an equally striking rapidity. Their growth was accompanied by a sibling movement of Charismatics among Protestants and Catholics. The name of 'Charismatics' comes from the Greek work for 'gift', or 'grace', which is 'charisma'. In the New Testament there are lists of gifts which the Holy Spirit bestows on individuals (1 Cor 12: 4–11, 20–30; Eph 4: 1–12; and Rom 12: 6–8). These include the abilities to work wonders, to prophesy, teach, and to speak in tongues. The last gift enables a person to speak in a language not previously known to them.

In the twentieth century, an early manifestation of Pentecostalism is represented by the Bethel Bible School in Topeka of Texas, USA. There, on 1 January 1901, a gathering of students is said to have begun speaking in tongues as they were led in prayer by Charles Fox Parham (1873–1929). He had left the Methodist church in 1895 after recovering from rheumatic fever. He interpreted his recovery as a divinely wrought healing, so he began a Christian ministry centred on healing others.[4] Shortly after, Parham began preaching about the Holy Spirit in Houston of the same state. A distinctive feature of his preaching was an emphasis on baptism in or with the Holy Spirit – Spirit baptism, for short. This emphasized that people felt regenerated or born again once they experienced the presence of the Holy Spirit within them. Advocacy of Spirit baptism was not an attempt to supplant sacramental rituals of baptism, but was more simply a name applied to the experience of people emboldened anew to commit themselves to the Gospel. In Houston, William Joseph Seymour (1870–1922) listened to the preaching of Parham over the course of a month. This in itself was a feat because he was forbidden to worship in the same room as Christians who were not of African descent. Segregation according to racial type remained common in the USA until the 1960s, and continues in many metropolitan suburbs in a de facto way. Seymour managed to hear the preaching of Parham through a door that was partially open. He was adamant that the Holy Spirit could perform miracles for Christians in his community.[5]

In 1906, Seymour moved to Los Angeles to begin work as the pastor to a small community of African-American Christians. His contact with them was not a happy one because they rejected him once he started preaching that the phenomenon of people speaking in tongues was a symptom of Spirit baptism. With a group of like-minded friends he began to meet for prayer in the house of Richard and Ruth Asberry in Los Angeles. He lived in the house of Edward Lee, who, during a session of prayer, asked to have hands laid upon his head by Seymour. When Seymour obliged, Lee is said to have collapsed on the floor apparently unconscious and to have begun speaking in tongues. Later in the same evening, others in the assembly experienced the same manifestations of what they took to be the Holy Spirit's presence within them.

In less than a week, Seymour moved into an old storage building at 312 Azusa Street. The religious fervour and style of worship that was adopted there are often tied to the beginnings of North American Pentecostalism. It was certainly the most significant nucleus of Pentecostal revival on the North American continent in the first decade of the twentieth century. The manner of worship characterizing Azusa Street was transported throughout the world and shares many of the features of Pentecostal worship internationally today.

The yeast feeding the massive and rapid growth of Pentecostalism in the twentieth century is Pentecostal worship. This is not hierarchically arranged, clerically managed, or elaborately formulaic or ritualistic. Like Baroque art, and the Requiems of Fauré and Duruflé, the power of its attraction stems from aroused emotions. Allan Anderson describes the worship of Azusa Street in these terms: 'With sawdust-sprinkled floors and rough planks as benches, daily meetings commenced at about ten in the morning and usually lasted until late at night. They were completely spontaneous and usually emotional, without planned programmes or speakers.'[6] Common occurrences among worships at such meetings were singing in tongues and collapsing to the floor in trance-like states known as being 'slain in the Spirit' or being 'under the power'.[7]

A century later, it is unclear how many Christians align themselves with Pentecostals or emphasize gifts of the Spirit in their lives (Charismatics). The British sociologist, David Marin, estimates that 'Pentecostalism and its vast charismatic penumbra' include a quarter of a billion, or 250,000 Christians.[8] Two North American Researchers, David Barrett and Todd Johnson, are confident that there are many more. They calculate that in 2001 there were more

Figure 28: The Azusa Street storage building/church, Los Angeles, c. 1928, before its demolition

than 523 million Pentecostals and Charismatics.[9] Patrick Johnstone and Jason Mandryk are more restrained. They conclude that, in the year 2000, Charismatics numbered 345 million, of which 115 million were Pentecostals.[10]

Like all other Christians, Pentecostals are not all of one type. Some align themselves resolutely with capitalism and preach a gospel their detractors besmirch as 'pay to be saved' or 'wealth is health'. Others insist that the primary purpose of their care for others is to convert them. Still more conclude that Christian mission must involve practical care for weak, infirm and hungry people. What all Pentecostals share is a conviction, whether articulated or not, that Christianity is not reducible to cognitive consent to doctrines expressed as propositions. Their religion is a commitment of the heart, a joyful revelry in what they experience as the dynamism of God's Holy Spirit in their lives. They dance, sing and gyrate with all of their bodies. Even so, for many of them, ecstatic phenomena such as speaking in tongues, collapsing bodily, or prophesying, are far from being daily occurrences.[11]

Scattered internationally, there is now a cluster of major types of Pentecostalism. One is often called classical Pentecostalism, and is represented by churches known as Assemblies of God. These communities include about 2.6 million people in the USA, and 48 million others dispersed in 191 other countries.[12] Other Pentecostal churches have no association with North America. The Pentecostal Winners' Chapel originated in Nigeria during 1983, and was present in 38 African countries by the year 2000. In 2001, it boasted an auditorium that could seat 50,400 worshippers.[13] A third significant expression of Pentecostalism can be identified with the Charismatic Renewal Movement that began in the USA in the 1960s. It includes Catholics as well as Protestants. This type of Pentecostalism sprang into being in 1960 at St Mark's Episcopal Church in Vah Nuys, California, when worshippers began to speak in tongues. From there it spread to university campuses, including those of Yale and Stanford. It emerged among Catholics in the mid-1960s, and grew to the extent that in 1974 Notre Dame University in Indiana was host to a gathering of 30,000 Charismatics.[14] A fourth species of Pentecostalism could be tagged as 'Neo-Pentecostalism'. Christians of this identity are outgrowths of Pentecostal denominations, but on a smaller scale and without the structural organization of a major denomination. The pastors of these churches did and do not normally receive a formal education in theology or in seminaries. They are frequently entrepreneurs who have converted to Christianity with such enthusiasm that they wish to target teenagers and young adults who were not raised in Pentecostal traditions. Finally, there are Christians who are not drawn to any ecclesiastical denomination, and wish to avoid being labelled as 'Pentecostal' or 'Charismatic', but want to live their lives according to a model they perceive in the life of Jesus and the early Church, celebrating individuals' specific divinely bestowed gifts. The primary feature of this model consists of what they take to be manifestations in their lives of the Holy Spirit's power.[15]

Pentecostalism is exceptionally popular in South Korea. In Seoul, the capital of South Korea, a single church building boasts a congregation that totals 700,000 worshippers. It is the Yoido Full Gospel Church. It is entirely impossible for so many worshippers to meet in the same building for a single session. They pray there in shifts, with one assembly arriving as another leaves.[16]

Ecumenism and the World Council of Churches

Manifest vitality among Christians at the outset and conclusion of the twentieth century could not conceal a painful and embarrassing problem besetting Christianity as a global reality. If Jesus had wanted his followers to be one, why could those who regarded themselves as such throughout the twentieth century not manage to agree or be unified in what being a follower entails? Worse than that, why did they often intensely dislike each other? Fretfulness over questions such as these was the motor driving ecumenism during the twentieth and into the twenty-first century.

Ecumenism is a strange term in English. It comes from the Greek, *oikoumene*, which designates 'the inhabited world'. It is related to the English word 'economy', the equivalent of which in ancient Greek referred to managing the affairs of a household. Modern ecumenism seeks to forge an international family of Christians who are united in hope, love and faith.

A conference of Christians met in Edinburgh in 1910. It was called the World Missionary Conference. It presaged the birth of twentieth-century international ecumenism in a significant respect. While its participants met to foster denominationally collaborative missionary work abroad, they deliberately avoided listing for discussion any theological matters they expected would elicit dispute and disaccord among them. In so doing, they demonstrated their desire to establish and maintain unity among themselves, but detailed discussions of central questions could not be forestalled permanently, as if to support the pretence that they did not divide denominations substantively.

To straddle the hurdle represented by potentially divisive issues, a Faith and Order Movement was created among Protestants to examine and discuss questions stemming from sacramental theology (ordination and sacraments) and ecclesiology – theology centred on the nature, mission and extent of the Church. An international conference to promote the work of the Faith and Order Movement met in Lausanne, Switzerland, during 1927. In included delegates who were Old Catholics (Catholics who separated from Rome after 1724), Protestants, and representatives of the Orthodox. Catholics of the Latin Rite did not participate. The deliberations of this group were matched by a similar initiative – the Life and Work Movement. Its brief was to consider practical issues such as education, economics and ethics, as Christians attempted to relate to the modern world in which they found themselves. This group met for the first time in 1925 in Stockholm. Both the Faith and Order, and Life and Work, organizations called for the formation of a World Council of Churches as a means of unifying Christians. Their desires were frustrated by the outbreak of the Second World War. Finally, the World Council of Churches assembled formally for the first time in Amsterdam during August 1948.[17] Delegates represented Christians in 44 countries. The only major Church not to be represented was the Catholic Church of the Roman Rite. That Church was finally admitted to the World Council of Churches' Faith and Order Commission after the Second Vatican Council had committed itself to the importance of ecumenism.

The Ordination of Women

An unmistakable facet of Christianity in the twentieth and twenty-first centuries was the growth of willingness in Churches for women to be ordained as ministers, preachers and priests. By the late twentieth century, some Churches had begun to ordain women as bishops. In the first decade of the twenty-first century, female bishops were preaching and ordaining men and women in New Zealand, Australia, Canada, USA, Germany, and Sweden but not in the UK.

The modern practice of ordaining women began among Protestants. The extent to which women were formally ordained in the early Church is disputed.[18] The leadership of the Catholic Church in Rome currently argues that Jesus never ordained women. It also teaches that women could and should never be ordained in the universal Church if Jesus never countenanced such a practice. Because Jesus never ordained anyone, either men or women, other Christians have felt emboldened to extend full gender equality to women in all dimensions of the Church's life, including its officially sanctioned ministry. In the modern period, women were first ordained in 1853 by Congregationalists. Thereafter, a host of other Churches began to ordain women. The Advent Christian Church did so in 1863, and the Disciples of Christ in 1888. These were followed by Churches such as the Church of the Nazarene (1908), the Baptist General Conference (1918), the Cumberland Presbyterian Church, the Assemblies of God (1935) and the Methodist Church (1956). The Episcopal Church (the North American equivalent of the Church of England) first ordained women in 1976.[19]

Russia

The worst persecution ever inflicted on Christians occurred throughout most of the twentieth century in Russia. It was far more murderous and brutal than any oppression wrought against Christians in ancient Rome. It lasted roughly from 1917 to 1989, and began when the imperial ruler of Russia, the Tsar, was dethroned by Bolsheviks in the revolution of 1917. Overnight, the Orthodox Church lost the imperial sanction it had enjoyed since the early Middle Ages. With the Bolshevik seizure of power, successive Communist governments sought to repress and obliterate the influence of the Church in the lives of Russians. To that end, governments closed monasteries and seminaries or took over such buildings for their own administrative purposes. Church buildings were either systematically vandalized or entirely destroyed. Severe persecution of Christians during the 1930s brought the Church to its knees. Between 1937 and 1938 alone, more than 100,000 Christians were shot.[20] The Second World War found Russia's Communist government preoccupied with international conflicts, and violence against Christians subsided, but it began in earnest once more in 1959 under Nikita Khrushchev, who was determined to crush the influence of Orthodoxy in Russia. Because the Church had for many centuries aligned itself with imperial reign in Russia, Communists inevitably wanted to eliminate it as they had the rule of the Tsar.

The worst phase of deadly violence unleashed against Christians occurred under Joseph Stalin. During his purges (*chistka*), the episcopate in Russia was very nearly obliterated. At one stage, only four bishops remained in office in the entirety of the vast lands of Russia. One estimate records that between 1917 and 1943, Communists killed almost 300 bishops and 45,000 priests. Hundreds of thousands of lay Christians were tortured and murdered.[21] Anyone who attended churches while being employed by the state risked the forfeiture of their jobs or imprisonment. Communists forbad anyone under the age of 16 from receiving a religious education.[22]

Orthodoxy in Russia was never eliminated and regained its strength once Communist rule ended in 1989.[23] In other countries in Europe where Communists came into power, such as Bulgaria, Yugoslavia and Romania, Orthodoxy was similarly repressed, but not eliminated. The worst attempt to squash it was in Albania. All religious observance in Albania was legally forbidden in 1967. It became 'the only country in the world that outlawed religious practice altogether in its Constitution of 1976'.[24] Such repression ended in 1990, when Communist rule in Albania collapsed. In Russia, during the seven decades of animosity that the Orthodox Church endured since the revolution of 1917, individual Christians managed to survive by different means. Large numbers of them simply abandoned Christianity, but the majority of Russians remained privately Christian and devout, but publicly discreet about showing any signs of their faith. Throughout the purges, elderly women (*babushkas*) doggedly continued to worship where and when they could.[25]

World Wars

One of the bleakest and most baffling of phases in Christianity's long life was the first 50 years of the twentieth century. It was bleak because of the millions of unnecessary deaths that occurred during the two world wars of this period, and baffling because Christians not only killed each other in their millions, but millions of defence-less Jews as well. At this time, more than 95 per cent of Europeans and North Americans were Christians. In Germany around 1993, more than 98 per cent of its population was Christian, and less than 1 per cent Jewish.[26] How and why, then, did Christians homicidally turn on each other throughout the First World War, and through their fighting, embroil people of other religions as well? And why did Christians in Germany during the Second World War exterminate around 6 million Jews?

The first of the two questions allows for a penumbra of explanations. Christians are religious people – or are meant to be – but as so, they live, work, socialize and argue like anyone else. Also like any human being, they submit to anger, envy, greed and pride. Throughout the history of the human race, the three most dangerous perils its members have had to face continually have been arrogance, aggressive violence and greedy acquisitiveness. The outbreak of war can be caused by any one, or a combination of all, of these three factors. Wars can also be ignited by individuals as well as by societies acting as nations. The First World War began with a declaration of war by the Christian German Kaiser, Wilhelm II. He was opposed by other Christian monarchs and their armies. While most of the killing was done by Christians during this war, their homicidal actions were the consequence of their betrayal of Jesus' Gospel.

As for the twentieth-century mass killing of Jews by Christians in Nazi Germany, it was ultimately the consequence of irrational thinking about Jews, Judaism and Jewishness. The source of this irrationality lies in the first few centuries of Christianity's existence. Originally, Christianity was not anti-Jewish, anti-Judaic or anti-Semitic. Before Christianity began, Jesus and his circle were all Palestinian Jews. Those Jews who were first called 'Christians' in Antioch still accepted the religious authority of Moses and the God of Abraham. As Gentiles gradually joined Christian circles, most Jews did not. This immediately caused a grave problem for early Christians. Because the vast majority of Jews in the first centuries of the Common Era ignored and did not believe in Jesus, they were thus 'the very incarnation of disbelief in Jesus'.[27]

Here is where Christian *irrational* thought about Jews begins. An *historical* or *empirical* account of why most Jews were disinterested in Jesus could easily be given in terms of major disputes and divisions between all Jews in the first century CE. Those who first followed Jesus and their immediate descendents constituted a Jewish religiosity that regarded itself as a better way of living *as* Jews, and hence distanced themselves from other types of Judaism, such as those represented by Sadducees or Essenes. These other types, in turn, wanted nothing to do with those Jews who proclaimed Jesus as their Messiah.

Throughout subsequent history, irrational explanations for Jewish indifference to Jesus and his heritage began to predominate among Christians. They have taken three forms and have frequently proved lethal for Jews. With permutations they appear in patterns of thinking that argue, first, that Jews are blindly obdurate, and are incapable of perceiving the true identity and superlativeness of Jesus; second, that they are guilty of deicide because by being 'Christ-killers' they killed a divinity; and third, that Jews have and must inevitably suffer as a divinely imposed punishment for their sin of deicide.[28]

The result of antipathy to Jews and Judaism among Christians reached such an extent in the thirteenth century that Jews throughout Europe were relegated to a legal status lower than that of serfs. Their degraded legal standing set them apart from their contemporaries.[29]

By the time of the outbreak of the Second World War, anti-Semitism was rife among Christians throughout Europe. Churches there proved ill-prepared for a second global war. They may have wrongly thought that the German political regime after the First World War would not turn out to be as bad as that of Communist Russia. Their trusting thought 'along with the very widespread anti-Semitism in Europe at this time, is the only explanation for the churches' failure to denounce as clearly as they might have done Nazi racial policies'.[30]

The nightmare of Nazism began in 1933, when Adolf Hitler became Chancellor of Germany. Once installed, he set to work passing laws requiring German Protestants to align themselves with a state-approved Reich Church. The Protestant leaders of the Reich Church were known as 'German Christians', but they met resistance from other Protestants such as Martin Niemöller, who organized opposition to them in 1933 by founding a Pastors' Emergency League. In 1934, the Swiss Reformed theologian Karl Barth helped to form a 'Confessing Church' in opposition to the Reich Church. The talented young German Lutheran theologian, Dietrich Bonhoeffer, joined Barth's initiative. His opposition to Hitler and Nazism was such that he was hanged by the Gestapo in 1945 as the Second World War drew to a close.

When it did, the full extent of Nazi savagery against Jews was uncovered for the world to see. The Nazi regime began to hound Jews in Germany with quite specific forms of discrimination soon after they came to power. As they did, they deliberately looked for justification for their actions in similar statutes and laws passed against Jews in ecclesiastical decrees. In this way, the order of the Christian Synod of Elvira (306) forbidding Christians and Jews from eating together, appeared again on 30 December 1939, when the Nazi Minister of Transport informed the Minister of the Interior that Jews were forbidden to eat in restaurant cars on trains. The Fourth Lateran Council of 1215 decreed that Jews must display a distinctive sign on their clothing. This was used again in the Nazi ordinance of 1941, ordering the same measure. The Council of Vienna's (1267) sanction that Christians may not participate in Jewish festivities was mimicked in a Gestapo order banning friendly relations by anyone with Jews

(24 October 1941). More seriously, the decree of the Council of Breslau (1267) that Jews must live in sequestered areas was used by Nazis to issue a similar decree on 21 September 1939.[31]

Nazi methods of discriminating deleteriously against Jews mutated into a comprehensive slaughter of them. A German army invaded Russia in June 1941 and was followed by a military force known as *Einsatgruppen*. These were groups of executioners intent on killing those the Nazis wished to exterminate, which were mostly Jews. By the end of 1942, the rounding up and killing of Jews in urban ghettos had turned into the mechanized murder of them in death camps.[32]

A New World

After the horrors of the Second World War, people scarred by it slowly began to hope that they might be able to build a much better world. Signs of regeneration and growth of mutual respect among humans began to proliferate. International organizations were established to help those struggling with sickness, illiteracy or famine. UNESCO was created in 1945, and the World Health Organization (WHO) in 1948. The European Convention on Human Rights was enacted in 1954. In 1959, the General Assembly of the United Nations condemned apartheid in South Africa and racial discrimination in any form anywhere else.

The immediate post-war years were not free from anxieties. By this time, atomic weaponry had been invented, and nations scrambled to develop programmes to produce them. Civil war erupted in Greece in 1946, and a similar war began in China in the same year. A Chinese army attacked Seoul in 1951.

Despite disturbing continued political skirmishes after the Second World War, new scientific discoveries and technologies engendered some hope in humans of the time that a better world was forming. A pilotless jet-propelled plane was built in Australia in 1950. The following year electricity was produced from atomic energy in the USA at Arcon, in the state of Idaho. In 1952, radioactive carbon ($C14$) was employed to date archaeological discoveries. Forms of socially permissible human behaviour were also changing because of new discoveries. Again in 1952, George Jorgensen became the first person to undergo a sex-change operation through which he became she – Christine. In the same year, the first oral contraceptive pill (made from phosphorated hesperidin) was produced in the USA. A polio vaccine, devised by Jonas Salk, became generally available in 1954. The Soviet Union launched into orbit a satellite called *Sputnik I* in 1959. One of the most startling inventions of the twentieth century, one that would transform methods of communication internationally, was the devising of the silicon chip in 1959.

The Second Vatican Council

That was the year when an affable and diplomatic Italian, Pope John XXIII, took everyone who became aware of him, especially Catholics, by complete surprise.

It might seem hyperbolic to say so, but it is still the case that the Second Vatican Council was historically the most significant gathering of Christians in the twentieth century. It was by far the largest and most internationally representative of all the councils in the history of Christianity. Yet it was what it said and did, not who participated in it and from where, that signifies its historical importance. Its participants were bishops of the Roman rite, other prelates and bishops in union with them, together with their theological advisors and some Protestant observers.

It is not immediately apparent why Vatican II was so significant in Christianity's history, not only for Catholics, but also for the Orthodox, Protestants, Jews, atheists and all of humankind, whether religious or otherwise. In the age of modernity, roughly the last three centuries, general councils of bishops have been an exceptional rarity. Since the Council of Trent in the sixteenth century, there have only been two: Vatican I (1869–70) and Vatican II (1962–65). This means that in a period traversing 400 years, encompassing the childhood of modern science and the Enlightenment, as well as wars and political revolutions around the world, Catholic bishops and their analogues in other Churches in union with them, only met twice, once in the nineteenth century and again in the twentieth.

There is an obvious reason why the convocation of Catholic councils are so rare in the modern era. They are dangerous. Perilous, that is, for papal monarchy and the appendages that support it, and for those who are allergic to modernity's esteem for democracy, the recognition of individual and collective human rights, the acceptance of full social equality between genders, and freedoms essential for openness of speech, unfettered sexual practices and diverse styles of living.

When bishops are dispersed intercontinentally they can easily be ordered what to think and do from Rome. When they are convened and actually meet each other face to face, they soon come to know each other and discover that they have a collective voice and authority because they are dealing with much the same conundra. Acting as a group, they can assert their authority, which is certainly greater than that of the staff in the Vatican's Curia. Individually in isolation, they can be artfully neutered and manipulated by the Curia, but not so when they are assembled.

Vatican II was historically the most significant Christian event of the twentieth century because its participants worked well to transform the Catholic Church in ways that ended the era of Tridentine Catholicism that had endured for four centuries. The legislation of Trent dominated the lives of Catholics and determined their relations to other Christians and adherents to other religions until the sea change of Vatican II. Since Trent, Catholics were compelled to worship in Latin. The laity were not permitted to drink the consecrated sacramental wine at Mass, which they believed had become the Blood of Christ. Jews were described as 'perfidious' in the liturgy of Good Friday. It was a mortal sin for Catholics to eat meat on Fridays, or to be absent from Mass on Sundays and Holy Days of Obligation. Adolescents who masturbated were instructed that because they had sinned so gravely, they would go to hell if they did not repent and confess. Catholics were forbidden to worship with Protestants and encouraged only to marry other Catholics. Tridentine Catholicism was generally inimical to modernity, democracy, new philosophies and higher biblical studies, Darwinian theories, freedoms of speech and individual rights, and the recognition of the full-gender equality of females with males in the life of the Church.

Vatican II was an ecclesiological revolution, which is to say that it turned official Catholic thought on the nature and purpose of the Church on its head. Angelo Giuseppe Roncalli was elected Bishop of Rome in October of 1958, and took the name John XXIII. He was the first pope to be named John since the fourteenth century. He wasted no time in sparking initiatives for the radical reform of the Catholic Church and its place in the world only three months after his election. 'Radical' in this context means reforming the

Church by focusing on its historical roots, from the Latin, *radix*, 'root'. 'Radical' does not mean 'fashionable', 'newfangled' or even 'progressive'. To be radical is to dwell on what matters most, and to regard all else as negotiable, changeable or peripheral. Vatican II was a radical Council, not a modish exercise in experimentation. It was intellectually informed by many previous decades of research by monks, friars and scholars into the liturgy of ancient Christians, their beliefs, and pre-Reformation understandings of the Church. It also made important concessions to Reformers that Trent had been unwilling to do. Always to be kept in mind when pondering the Second Vatican Council was that it transformed the lives of ordinary Christians in their manifold millions.

John XXIII met with a small group of cardinals in Rome on 25 January 1959, in the church of St Paul's outside the Walls. He took them completely by surprise by informing them that he was going to summon an ecumenical council and call for a synod of the diocese of Rome. Revealingly, he informed rather than consulted them that his motives for calling the bishops from around the world to a new council were primarily pastoral; that is, he wanted to help people in their daily lives, instead of denouncing people and churches as heretics. Vatican II is rare among councils in that it did not publish anathemas – declarations that certain people are to be cut off from the life of the Church. He told the assembled cardinals in 1959 that his decision to call a council 'was formed by the recollection of certain ancient ways of making doctrinal statements and certain wise practices of ecclesiastical discipline that in ages of renewal in the history of the Church have yielded especially effective results for the strengthening of religious unity and the kindling of a more intense Christian fervour'.[33]

Roncalli was advanced in years when he was elected Pope. He recorded in his journal the huge task he had been elected to undertake:

> When on 28 October 1958, the cardinals of the Holy Roman Church chose me to assume the supreme responsibility of ruling the universal flock of Jesus Christ, at seventy-seven years of age, everyone was convinced that I would be a provisional Pope. Yet here I am, already on the eve of the fourth year of my pontificate, with an immense program of work in front of me to be carried out before the eyes of the whole world, which is watching and waiting.[34]

In a long ecclesiastical career, Roncalli had taught in a seminary in Bergamo before spending many years as a diplomat of the Vatican. He worked as a papal envoy in Bulgaria from 1925 to 1934, and then in Turkey and Greece (1935–44), and finally France (1945–52). He then became the Cardinal Patriarch of Venice (1953–58).[35] He watched the unfolding of the Second World War at close quarters. As his allocution to cardinals on 25 January 1959 indicates, he was acquainted with the significance of 'ages of renewal' in the Church's history. On the eve of Vatican II, he was convinced that he was on the brink of an historical juncture of exceptional importance which he planned to broach with a distinction: 'to define clearly and distinguish between what is sacred principle and eternal gospel and what belongs rather to changing times'.[36] John XXIII was well aware that not all aspects of the Catholic Church of his time were essential to it, and many were dispensable historical accretions of various 'changing times'.

Vatican II was held between 1962 and 1965. John XXIII died while it was under way and was succeeded by Paul VI. The Council produced 16 promulgations, which fall into three types ranked in order of authoritative status: constitutions, decrees and declarations. The four constitutions of the Council remain the most authoritative expressions of Catholic self-understanding and beliefs to date. Nothing published since by the Vatican or subsequent popes is more doctrinally substantive than this quartet of constitutions.

Ironically, collectively understood the changes that Vatican II wrought among the lives of Catholics and their improvement of relations with other Churches are profoundly traditional, not faddishly experimental. They amounted to a reversion to many practices of ancient Christians. Some of the more significant changes can be tabulated briefly. First, in the four centuries before the Council, the Church was commonly regarded as a pyramidal hierarchy. The 'Church' meant 'the Pope and the bishops'. What they say, the Church says. Vatican II made clear in its *Dogmatic Constitution on the Church* (*Lumen Gentium*) that the Church is fundamentally a people of God, within which is a hierarchy. Second, before Vatican II in Catholic theology, the kingdom of God of which Jesus spoke was simply equated with the Church. That equation ended at the Council. It concluded that the most which could be said is that the Church constitutes an 'initial budding forth' of the kingdom (*Lumen Gentium*, n. 5). Third, sin before the Council was always attributed to individuals and never to the Church. The participants at Vatican II reminded everyone that the Church is sinful as well as holy, and always finds itself in need of purification, penance and renewal (*Lumen Gentium*, n. 8). Fourth, in a daring ecumenical move, the Council taught that the Catholic Church is not coextensive with the Church of Christ. This means that Protestants can legitimately be accepted and respected as members of the Church of Christ. The most that could be said of the Catholic Church is that the Church of Christ 'subsists in it' rather than being identical with it (*Lumen Gentium*, n. 8). Fifth, in a conclusion allied with the previous one, Vatican II insisted that Christians other than Catholics are included in the Body of Christ. That Body is not inclusive of Catholics alone, as had been previously believed (*Decree on Ecumenism*, n. 3). Sixth, before Vatican II, lay Christians were regarded as the acolytes or helpers of the clergy who conducted the real mission of the Church in preaching the Gospel. The Council was explicit that lay Christians participate in the mission of the Church because they are baptized, and that they share in a threefold mission of Jesus as priest, prophet and king (*Lumen Gentium*, n. 3). Seventh, with implication for all human beings, the Council revised the dogma that salvation was only obtainable through and in the Catholic Church. The Council concluded that not only can participants in religions apart from Christianity be saved (*Lumen Gentium*, n. 16), but their religions can in themselves be instruments of salvation (*Declaration on the Relationship of the Church to Non-Christian Religions*, n. 2). Eighth, as Richard McBrien explains:

> Before the council it was also simply assumed in Catholic theology, catechesis, preaching, and teaching that the church was an absolute monarchy under the pope. Over against this view, the council taught that the governance of the universal Church devolves upon the whole college of bishops and that their pastoral authority is exercised in regional councils and in national Episcopal conferences as well as in ecumenical councils (Constitution on the Church, nn. 22–23).[37]

Ninth, error was said 'to have no rights' before Vatican II. This meant that Christians were not *free* to worship in ways that differed from the liturgies of the Catholic Church. Where the state had the power to do so, it was only to permit Catholic worship. The Council swept this away, and taught that all people may enjoy the religious freedom to worship as they wish because of their common human dignity and because faith is a free act (*Declaration of Religious Liberty*, nn. 2ff. and 9ff.). Finally, Tridentine worship operated with clergy performing the liturgy, and the laity observing it. It was conducted in Latin, with the communion cup reserved for the clergy. Preaching on scripture was frequently neglected. Four hundred years after the Reformation, Vatican II reversed all this and decreed that the assembled people of God celebrate the liturgy; that the texts of worship may be translated into vernacular languages; that the assembled people could drink from the communion cup; that the reading of scripture was to be an essential element of all worship; and that the Eucharist was to be regarded as the source and summit of the Church's life: *Ubi Eucharistia, ibi Ecclesia* – wherever the Eucharist is, there too is the Church. Such a view was entirely alien to pre-conciliar Roman theology, which was more comfortable with the idea: 'Wherever the Pope is, there too is the Church.'[38]

Much of this was entirely consonant with Protestant sensibilities and explains why Vatican II was a milestone for Catholic, Protestants, the Orthodox and all religions. More than 200 years after the French Revolution, it acknowledged the indispensability of collaborative government, and freedoms of religion, conscience and speech.

In the decades after the Council, it has become clear that errors of judgement during its course were to undo much of its work and good intentions subsequently. Pope Paul VI forbad the assembled bishops of the Council to discuss two matters that troubled them deeply: compulsory clerical celibacy and contraception. Papal authority was gravely damaged in 1968 when Paul VI condemned the use of the Pill and other forms of prophylactic contraception. This teaching was never received by the vast majority of Catholics. As for enforced celibacy, the bishops at the Council knew that for the majority of Christian history it had not been imposed on clergy, and there is no theological reason to justify it. Whether a person is married or celibate is irrelevant to the exercise of Christian ministry. The argument that a priest must be a male celibate because Jesus was falls, because he was not a priest and cannot be used anachronistically as a model for a hierachical priesthood that evolved with imperial sanction after Emperor Theodosius I (380 CE).

John XXIII made mistakes too. He allowed Cardinal Ottaviani to remain in charge of the Roman Curia as the Council progressed.

Ottaviani was no enthusiast for change and as a member of a minority of bishops at Vatican II whose views were rejected was able to collaborate with others to undermine the Council's far-reaching reforms. And so it transpired that in the early stages of the pontificate of Pope Benedict XVI, he began to enable more frequent celebration of the Tridentine liturgy around the world. Trent's view of the Church is not that of Vatican II. Of all the decrees of the Second Vatican Council, the most outstanding in its willingness to address all people of good will beyond the Church was *Gaudium et Spes* ('The joys and hopes').[39] This was one of the four constitutions of the Council, and the last to be proclaimed a day before the Council ended its fourth and final session. A cardinal involved in debates over *Gaudium et Spes* made it clear in the fourth session that he did not like its final form. His view did not prevail. His name was Joseph Ratzinger, who went on to succeed John Paul II as Benedict XVI. Before the final vote on the final draft of *Gaudium et Spes*, a dramatic stand-off developed between French and German bishops and theologians. The French, including Yves Congar and Marie-Dominique Chenu, were highly enthusiastic and supportive of the draft's optimism with regards to the world. Influential Germans, including Karl Rahner and Joseph Ratzinger, disliked the schema, thinking it overly optimistic. Representatives of the two groups met in Rome on 17 September 1965 to see if they could reach accord, which eluded them. Eventually some of them changed their minds and supported the schema, but others remained opposed to the end. A few days later, the Dominican, Chenu, delivered an impassioned lecture supporting the schema in Rome's Centro di Documentazione Olandese. His text was widely distributed among the Council's bishops.[40] Would he succeed in convincing them?

As for Karol Wojtyła, who went on to become Pope John Paul II, he too had misgivings about *Gaudium et Spes*. Representing Polish bishops, he submitted a text suggesting amendments to participants in preparatory discussions. It was considered, but not included in the final schema.[41] When it came to a deciding vote on the Council floor, hesitations did not hold sway. The constitution in its final draft was approved by a massive consenting majority.[42] There were seven invalid votes; 75 against; and 2309 in favour. Pope Paul VI duly promulgated *The Pastoral Constitution on the Church in the Modern World*.[43] Finally, on a symbolic level, the hierarchy of the Catholic Church had left the Middle Ages and entered Modernity.

Mega Media Churches

In the twentieth century, radical renewal was not an exclusive preserve of Catholics. Especially in the USA, Protestant Christians proved exceptionally daring and creative in realizing that hordes of their contemporaries never listened to Bach, plainsong or polyphony. Such people were musically moved by loud, electronically generated, dynamically pulsating, and rhythmically vibrant sounds. They relaxed by listening to woofer bass amplifiers, and carried wherever they went earphones through which they could enjoy recordings generated from tiny hand-held amplifiers. These were people who were enticed by large-screen cinema, which they began to reproduce in their homes with huge television screens and cinema sound systems.

In addition, it became obvious to many Protestant pastors that large numbers of their contemporaries were decidedly disinclined to go into buildings whose architectural style imitated medieval Gothic design or Baroque decoration. Carpeted spaces, comfortable seating, televisual images, free-wheeling music, and access to parking, all seemed to be required to motivate anyone to visit a space for worship.

Thus were born media megachurches. These buildings were 'mega' (as their designers called them) in the sense of architecturally resembling huge entertainment or sporting auditoria. They were 'media' in that their pastors innovatively introduced into worship the kinds of projected images and musical sounds they knew their visitors loved. A typical example of a megachurch is the Willow Creek Community Church of South Barrington, Illinois, USA. This church is devoid of statues and traditional religious imagery, under the conviction that these would turn away potential worshippers. It resembles a vast auditorium with the comfort of carpet and large projection screens. By the mid-1990s, up to 15,000 people were attending Sunday worship in this church.[44] Its music, as in other megachurches, can resemble styles of composition and performance common to discotheques, pop or rock concerts, with extensive use of syncopation and markedly stressed downbeats.

Megachurches are most usually found among Evangelical Christians, so-named because of their enthusiasm for celebrating and preaching the Gospel. Evangelical Protestantism during the twentieth century proved very popular in the USA, Canada, Korea, sub-Saharan Africa,

Figure 29: The megachurch in South Barrington

and on Islands in the pacific. In the USA, Evangelicals were calculated to represent 26 per cent of its population in 1996.[45] In their preaching, worship and daily living, Evangelical Protestants internationally have accentuated the necessity of undergoing a personal religious conversion, or 'new birth', so as to be committed to the Gospel. They also espouse a heightened esteem for the Bible and believe that Jesus' death on a cross redeemed humankind.[46]

Logo Christians

Enthusiasm for publicly demonstrating commitment to Christianity generated a business industry among Evangelicals in the USA to produce and market clothing and jewellery, with Christian messages or symbols displayed on them. Such market-place merchandise includes blazers, jackets, skirts, wrist watches, socks, T-shirts, leather wear, laptop cases, messenger bags, bumper stickers, purses, rings and necklaces, all bearing Christian symbols. Sporting such apparel is partly motivated by using 'the cultural trappings of the counterculture to show the counterculture a better way'.[47]

Amid the production of Christian accoutrements of countercultures, apocalypticism became popular among many North American Christians, especially those who had been 'born again' or converted anew to the Gospel. This type of apocalypticism, like any other,

Figure 30: Bracelet asking WWJD? ('What Would Jesus Do'?)

expected the imminent revelation of God at the end of history. Its distinctiveness lay in its exponents' belief in the Rapture, which they envisioned as

> an unexpected moment when all true Christians instantly and myste-
> riously disappear from the face of the earth. Those who remain
> behind then experience a seven-year period of increasing difficulties,
> war, and chaos, a period called the tribulation, in which the
> Antichrist rises to prominence, is indwelt by Satan, and persecutes all
> who do not conform to his one-world government and religion. At
> the end of seven years Jesus Christ then returns to earth in a glorious
> appearing to defeat Satan and begin a thousand-year reign of peace
> and harmony on earth, the millennium.[48]

Belief in the Rapture seized a public imagination with the publication of a series of novels, co-authored by Tim LaHaye and Jerry Jenkins, and called the Left Behind Books. The first was published in 1995, with the title *Left Behind: A Novel of Earth's Last Days*. The ninth in the series was issued in 2001 and called *USA Today: Desecration*.

Christianity and the Postmodern Age

The last four decades of the twentieth century and the opening decade of the twenty-first did not remain peaceful, either militarily or socially. This span of half a century was like an eddy with humanity adrift, swirling in a vortex of rapid and ceaseless change. The Cuban Missile Crisis strained international nerves in 1962, as did the third Indo-Chinese war in Vietnam. That conflagration dragged in Cambodia, Laos, USA, Australia and New Zealand. It was followed by genocides in Bosnia, Cambodia and Rwanda. During all this turmoil the human population trebled. The bomb of Hiroshima sounded the end of modernity, with its heady optimism about the inevitability of unstoppable humanly engineered progress. A new era was dawning as modernity ended, and it was clumsily called postmodernity. That label might have to do until it becomes clearer how the human predicament is altering.

The postmodern age is one of flux, unpredictability, randomness, chaos and confusion, but in the midst of all this, Christians continued to adapt themselves and their beliefs to new circumstances.

In terms of Darwinian evolutionary biology, Christianity is just like any other living species. It began in a simple form and mutated randomly through successful generations, so that some of its forms survived and others died out. Just as there are now 5000 different species of chameleons, similarly there is a plethora of varieties of Christianity.

A new and notable feature of Christianity over the past 60 years is that Christians who have hitherto largely been voiceless, or socially marginalized, exerted their equal dignity with their oppressor or overlords. And so it was that feminism gained widespread favour among Christians after the Second World War. The twentieth and early twenty-first centuries mark the era of female awakening in the Church. While women and girls have always been prominent and indispensable in the Church, they have often been prevented from preaching and teaching others about Christianity. Over the past six decades, for the first time in Christian history, women have followed the lead of women prime ministers and presidents around the world in exercising analogous leadership in Churches. During these decades, a large body of female theologians and biblical scholars used their skills to articulate new understandings of God and the Church.[49]

After five centuries of living under the heal of conquerors, dictators and colonizers, Christians of South America, Asia and Africa pointed out that they formed the majority of Christians, and that they are systematically exploited, robbed and demeaned by their wealthier neighbours bordering the Atlantic ocean. In the USA and Canada, Black Power and Black Theology asserted themselves and stood up to racial vilification, as well as the notion that the lives of all Christians could be determined in Europe.

Then the Twin Towers of New York were brought to the ground by two jet planes. Also attacked was the Pentagon in Washington. In two strokes, an international symbol of capitalism and another of militarism were shown to be vulnerable to attack from those who have been denigrated by military and economic might. As the twenty-first century unfolded, 'terrorism' became a household word everywhere. The date of 9/11 (the 11th day of the ninth month) in 2001 became infamous, but it occluded other dreadful events against others, enacted or influenced previously by North American Governments. Much of the following information is provided by citizens of the USA themselves, not by their detractors. On 11 September 1973, the US government orchestrated a coup in Chile which installed a violent military dictatorship led by General Augusto Pinochet, and removed from office the democratically elected President of Chile, Salvador Allende.[50] On 7 December 1975, an Indonesian Army with US weapons and consent, killed around 200,000 inhabitants in East Timor. The President of Indonesia, Suharto, met with President Gerald Ford, and his Secretary of State Henry Kissinger, in Jakarta on the evening before Indonesia's army struck. Noam Chomsky described the attack as 'the worst slaughter relative to population since the Holocaust'.[51] On the day of 11 September 2001, as about 3000 people were wrongly killed in New York, the United Nations reported that 35,615 children died of hunger internationally.[52] Terrorism is partially explained by a human psychological predisposition. When people are impotent and kept so by more economically and militarily powerful groups, they can become so desperate that they strike back *anonymously*. Their very anonymity reproduces in their perceived or real oppressors the same kind of impotent rage, because their victims cannot always find who the perpetrators of violence against them were.

In the midst of twenty-first century terrorism, Christianity continued to inspire prophets and martyrs. Martyrdom is the key to answering the question: 'Will Christianity survive in ages to come?'

Conclusion

'Why do you call me "Lord, Lord", and do not do what I tell you?'
Luke 6: 46

'If you love those who love you, what credit is that to you? For even sinners love those who love them. If you do good to those who do good to you, what credit is that to you? For even sinners do the same. If you lend to those from whom you hope to receive, what credit is that to you? Even sinners lend to sinners, to receive as much again. But love your enemies, do good, and lend, expecting nothing in return.'
Luke 6: 32–35a

Christianity's future prospects are promising. It still accounts for a third of humanity's population. If *Homo sapiens* survives another century and millennium, there is every reason for current Christians to hope that their religion will not lose its sap and wizen. It might even prove to be a *Lumen Gentium* – a light to the peoples – in a world that continues to be blighted by human misery. According to the Food and Agricultural Organization of the United Nations, the number of malnourished people in the world increased by 75 million in 2007 and 100 million in 2008. By the end of the first decade of the twenty-first century, 1 billion people could not find enough food to be happily healthy.[1] This situation is not unlike that in which Jesus lived, but his reaction to human deprivation differed starkly from that of many of those who style themselves as his disciples and devotees today. Nearly all his contemporaries lived with chronic fear of failed harvests and famine. It is easier to proclaim and chant the divinity of Christ than to emulate the lifestyle of someone who instructs: 'It is easier for a camel to go through the eye of a needle than it is for a rich person to enter the kingdom of God' (Mk 10: 25; Mt 19: 24; Lk 18: 25).

Christianity is, of course, finite, and like all contingent things will eventually expire. *Homo sapiens* in its present form may well become extinct, as did all the other of the known 22 human species that preceded it.[2] It could die by its own hand (nuclear weaponry or ecological devastation), or by a collision between the Milky Way and Andromeda galaxies, or through inevitable entropy (the gradual dissipation of the cosmos' finite amount of energy). There is another possible scenario: God might smite it for its wickedness, or transform it into a new heavenly manner of existing. Whatever the setting, in the future, Christianity, like humankind, will eventually cease to prevail in its present form.

For as long as *Homo sapiens* does endure, Christians can be expected to be among its members. As previous chapters have illustrated, Christians do not share the same beliefs. What unites them all now and over past eras has been their enthusiasm for Jesus Christ, expressed in an array of doctrines, rituals and domestic routines. No Christian thinks Jesus was or is a dodo. The historical uniqueness of Christianity stems from the way it expresses belief in Jesus as a way of believing in God. The essence of Christianity is thereby bifocal. Its attention to Jesus serves as a conduit for belief in God. Always to be remembered, though, is that faith is not primarily an intellectual assent to dicta, doctrines, propositions and theories. Faith is a way of living based on a practical decision. All human beings need to decide pragmatically at some stage in their lives whether they are going to live daily as if they are only accountable to themselves, or if they are ultimately answerable to a Creator of the Cosmos named variously as God, Allah or Adonai. The way a person spends a life and treats others flows ineluctably from this all-important, life-changing *practical* decision, which is not to assert that people unenthused by God or religion demean others horribly.

None of this explains why Christianity has splintered into 38,000 denominations, nationally and intercontinentally. The reason it is indispensable to the lives of so many diverse peoples is hopefully explained by the superintending thesis of this book. Christians give their lives to God through Jesus because in Jesus they see a combination of ordinariness and superlativeness. For his followers, Jesus encompasses in himself simplicity and excellence. In this dialectical tension between sublimity and humility lies an explanation of why he has proved to be not only one of the greatest figures of human history, but also a religious magnet of attraction, as well as a catalyst for acrimonious controversy. Just as the peasant boy Giotto has been revered since the eve of the Renaissance for being able to draw a perfect circle, the peasant Galilean boy Jesus has long since his time been adored as God in flesh. In him, for Christians, the infinite meets the finite, the transcendent enters the imminent, and the universal encounters the particular.

That might sound far too conceptually neat because it is plain that many of Jesus' plainest teachings are plainly ignored. Take, for instance, his injunction as recorded by Luke's Gospel to lend, expecting nothing in return (Lk 6: 35a). This instruction is almost 20 centuries old. In the Bible, it comes from the lips of Jesus. Christians have always known of this command, but many of them have ignored it in the past and disregard it in the present. Why? Because Jesus appeals or repels people according to what they esteem in themselves. The majority of humans in any age want to be monetarily secure if not well off, as is only to be expected. Nobody wants to waste away unto death, or be treated by others as a dispensable doormat. The guiding thesis of this book is that there have been Christians who have willingly lent and expected nothing in return. Many of them were hounded as heretics. They saw in themselves the impoverished wandering preacher, Jesus. The besmirched Cathars and Dolcinians of the Middle Ages rank among the most admirably authentic Christians who have ever lived. Others would never have dreamed of cancelling debts, lending an ear, or offering assistance without something being offered in return. It has been easy for them to think that precisely as Christians they could and ought to imitate Christ the King, the Superman and Superstar. In short, some Christians have identified themselves with Jesus' vulnerability, while others have thought they mirror him by being strong, resourceful respectable, or otherwise estimable. Christians have identified themselves with monarchs and judges who, in their own terms, are obviously excellent, like Jesus, and eminently deserving of just returns for favours bestowed on the riff-raff of the world. Many of such Christians have been met in these pages. 'Lend, and expect nothing in return' – the instruction of a lunatic, or a revelation from God about how humans ought to treat each other in their daily dealings? That is a query that has needled Christianity from its inception.

A variety of beliefs and ways of following Jesus among Christians are in themselves unlikely to ensure that Christianity will endure historically. What is far more propitious for Christianity's prospects is martyrdom. In one sense, all Christians have sought to be martyrs; that is, public witnesses to their faith. The sense in which the term 'martyrdom' is being deployed here is the willingness to be killed rather than renounce faith in Jesus Christ. There have been such martyrs throughout Christian history, and nothing is more startling or perplexing than their free decision to be killed rather than give in to their executioners. In nakedly human terms, martyrdom is inexplicable. It affronts common sense, baffles the mind, and defies easy explanation. A natural instinct of a mortally endangered human being would be to struggle to continue living by relinquishing an idea, belief or doctrine, even if only to readopt a belief once danger dissipated. Not so with martyrs. The engine of their self-sacrifice is tied to their perception of the ordinariness and excellence of Jesus. They can align themselves with him because of the humanity they share with him. They can relinquish their own lives if they recognize that his superlativeness is not of this world, or better than previously seen on Earth. That is what differentiates him from them and explains their willingness to be immolated. If Jesus is divine as well as human, if he was raised by God from death, and if he will return to judge the living and the dead, those who hope that they have been faithful to him have been emboldened to pine as well that they, like him, will survive the death of their bodies. Their martyrdom is fired not by mental assent to theories, but by their unflinching attachment to someONE. For as long as there are martyrs, there will be Christianity.

The pages of this book have wrestled to come to grips with why so many people over 20 centuries have responded in such starkly and often shockingly different ways to Jesus in their attempts to encounter God. The principal point at the book's outset was that Jesus did not devise Christianity. It arose initially over many decades as an interpretative response to who he was and what he did. Like him, his family and friends were Galileans. The more that can be known about Galilee, the more that can be deciphered of him. The more deficient is awareness of what his unique social environment was, the more fanciful and ludicrous theological theories concerning him will be. Historical delusion leads directly to theological deception. Bad history breeds bad theology.

The most difficult issue Christians have to deal with is God, or rather, how to think of, and behave in relation to, God. Many of the most astute of all human beings have struggled with the question of God, including Cicero, Augustine, Origen, Aquinas, Luther, Calvin, Descartes, Catherine of Siena, Kant, Hegel, Wittgenstein and Einstein. Who or what is God? Can God be known or seen? Does God will, command, punish or reward? Is God in or out of the universe? Could God change or evolve? There is no better or promising way for people to envisage God than to listen to an ancient writer, who is anonymous, but whose thought is captured in the Bible's First Letter of John: 'Beloved, let us love one another, because love is from God; everyone who loves is born of God and knows God. Whoever does not love does not know God, for God is love' (1 Jn 4: 7–8). John may sound like an ancient version of a modern gun-hating do-gooder, but his teaching that God is love is among the best currently available ways for humans to imagine who or what God might be. 'No one has ever seen God' (1 Jn 4: 12a), but Christians live with the conviction that love shown to others expresses concretely their love for God and God's love for the indigent of the world. And love, like faith, if it is not expressed in action, is dead. This is precisely what the Spanish missionary, Rosendo Salvado, discovered in the parched terrain of Western Australia during the nineteenth century, when he tried to win over Aborigines to Christianity:

> It is not hard to preach to a native, but it does not do much good, for he will interrupt the missionary and say: 'Everything you tell me may well be quite true; but I am hungry – are you going to give me some bread or not?' If you do not give him some, he will turn his back on you and go off into the bush to find something to eat.[3]

The principle of *faith alone* could never stand, *unless* faith is understood to include deeds for others, not practised in order to manipulate God, but to replicate God's love for creation. Matthew's Gospel couches the matter in other terms: 'You are the light of the world. A city built on a hill cannot be hidden. No one after lighting a lamp puts it under a bushel basket, but on the lampstand, and it gives light to all in the house. In the same way, let your light shine before others, so that they may see your good works and give glory to your Father in heaven' (Mt 5: 14–16). If faith is not concretely expressed in actions, it remains abstract, dead and desiccated to the point of irrelevance.

Dead is precisely how religious faith in general, including that of Christianity, was increasingly perceived over the past five centuries. That period constituted a major revolution with regard to the world's religions, but not in their favour: 'For millennia, almost all human beings believed in Gods and adhered to psychocentric religions, but then, very rapidly when measured on the scale of human history, there was an unprecedented spread of disbelief.'[4] Belief in Gods was in evidence during the Palaeolithic period, but by the late twentieth century there were about a billion atheists throughout the world, a figure that includes those who are disinterested in the notion of God.[5] By the end of the Enlightenment and throughout the nineteenth and twentieth centuries, many more people followed Immanuel Kant's advice: 'Have the courage to use your *own* understanding!'[6] And so they did, deciding that they and they alone could determine what they believed and thought, what they could do, what they wanted, and how to live. Such brazen self-determination on a widespread scale was new in human history, as was atheism on a large scale. Both were armed by a modern idea: that of inviolable *human rights* guaranteeing *freedoms*, without the inevitability of *punishments*. Most previous human generations had perceived themselves as passive victims of fate, or the recipients of divine wrath if they broke the moral strictures of their religions.

In the world of classical antiquity, people were certainly accused of atheism, but in that setting it did not mean that they had renounced Gods; only that they refused to believe in the Gods of the predominant pantheon of deities in their societies. To live in imperial Rome meant to honour the Gods of Rome. By the Middle Ages in Europe, there were no Gods according to Christendom, only one God. Medieval people did not speak of atheists, but of heretics or infidels.[7] Then, as Christendom fragmented during the Reformations of the sixteenth century, and the religious warfare of the seventeenth, bitter disputes between Christian denominations fanned acidic doubt: contradictory propositions cannot all logically be true.

In the twenty-first century, Christianity's prospects for a hopeful future are tied to the problem of doubt. There are two features of its current predicament that stymie its health. First, 38,000 rivalrous denominations illustrate that Christians themselves cannot agree on what matters most and so they *doubt each other*. Disaccord between them breeds doubt among them. Second, Christians engender *doubt among their contemporaries* by their behaviour, particularly when it is directly at odds with what is known of their lodestar, Jesus. The force of Jesus' impact on people is related to an absence of a disjunction in his life between what he said about God in relation to people, and how he lived according to what he said. This point is pivotal. Can those aspiring to be Christians now emulate him in similarly ridding their lives of such a disjunction?

In a European postmodern setting, the Flemish Dominican theologian, Edward Schillebeeckx (1914–2009), articulated an understanding of the Church that he hoped would lead Christianity into an era following the weakening of Christendom and Tridentine culture. He proposed that Christians could gather in small, prophetically and critically engaged communities to celebrate and preach the Gospel of Jesus Christ, by emulating his hankering for justice and especial love for impoverished underdogs.[8] In behaving thus, they might glimpse and refract the just love of the God of Jesus Christ.

This book has only been a glimpse of the panoply of people who have tried to live as Christians. They have included peddlers, vagabonds, lairds, lords, mercenaries and brigands. They have been rough-hewn folk, wayward youngsters and ruminating mystics. One among them was the fourth-century Christian, Basil the Great (c. 330–79). Part of his greatness lay in this counsel:

> Come now, distribute your wealth lavishly, becoming honourable and glorious in your expenditures for the needy. Let what is said of the righteous be said also of you, 'They have distributed freely, they have given to the poor; their righteousness endures forever' (Ps 112: 9). Do not enhance your own work by trafficking in the needs of others. Do not wait for a dearth of grain to open your granary: 'The people curse those who hold back grain' (Prov 11: 26). Do not wait for a famine in order to acquire gold. Do not make need a means of private gain. Do not become a dealer in human misery. Do not attempt to turn the chastisement of God into an opportunity for profit. Do not chafe the wounds of those who have already been scourged.[9]

The world today would be unrecognizable had Basil's counsel been heeded. Instead, its inhabitants are dogged by the same scourges that blighted the contemporaries of Jesus and all generations since:

violence, poverty, hunger, disease, hatred, greed and lethal injustice. Basil's comments on the way Christians should disinvest themselves of wealth for the sake of paupers are rendered all the more powerful once it is realized that he grew up pampered by the baubles of wealth. His father, Basil the Elder, was an aristocrat of Rome, and hence rich in landholdings. The boy Basil watched astutely as his parents and friends enjoyed the leisure and luxurious accoutrements that wealth can secure, while others were barely surviving.

A disturbing peculiarity of the human predicament now is that never before have there been so many people alive at the same time, and never previously has *Homo sapiens* proved to be so scientifically and technologically accomplished, while *simultaneously* the *majority* of humans live in penury. A minority population of extravagantly wealthy people has been omnipresent in history since and before the Roman Empire until the present, but the number of current destitute and starving individuals far and shockingly exceeds anything encountered in the past. It is not an accident that Basil was called 'Great'. He was a Christian who understood well the day-to-day implications of the Gospel of Jesus Christ, focused as it was on God's kingdom and divine justice. Would that the clan of such Christians grew by the hour.

List of Maps and Illustrations

Notes

Introduction

1 For the figures mentioned in this paragraph, see Martin Marty, *The Christian World: A Global History* (New York: Modern Library, 2007), 4.

2 See Martin Manser, *Scapegoats, Shambles and Shibboleths: The Queen's English from the King James Bible* (London: Hodder & Stoughton, 2009).

3 For the figures quoted in this paragraph, see Mary Farrell Bednarowski, ed., *Twentieth-Century Christianity* (Minneapolis, MN: Fortress Press, 2008), 33–4; and Marty, *The Christian World*, 4.

4 Daniel E. Bornstein, 'Living Christianity', in Daniel E. Bornstein, *Medieval Christianity* (Minneapolis, MN: Fortress Press, 2009), 1–25; 6–7.

5 Sebastian Kim and Kirsteen Kim, *Christianity as a World Religion* (London and New York: Continuum, 2008), 4.

6 On the significance of Darwin's work, see Daniel C. Dennett, *Darwin's Dangerous Idea: Evolution and the Meaning of Life* (London: Penguin Books, 1995); and Richard Dawkins, *The Greatest Show on Earth* (London: Bantam Press, 2009).

7 For an account of ancient equivalents of religion in the Mediterranean, see Paula Fredriksen, *Augustine and the Jews: A Christian Defense of Jews and Judaism* (New York: Doubleday, 2008), 6–15.

8 John Corrigan, 'Economic Change and Emotional Life', in Amanda Porterfield, ed., *Modern Christianity to 1900* (Minneapolis, MN: Fortress Press, 2007), 91.

9 Corrigan, 'Economic Change and Emotional Life', 92. see too Jane Schneider, 'Spirits and the Spirit of Capitalism', in Ellen Badone, ed., *Religious Orthodoxy and Popular Faith in European Society* (Princeton, NJ: Princeton University Press, 1990), 184. See too 182 and 188–91.

10 See Don Cupitt, *After God: The Future of Religion* (London: Weidenfeld & Nicolson, 1997), chapters 1–3.

11 On the religious life of classical Greece, see Gregory Crane, 'Appendix I: Classical Greek Religious Festivals', in Robert B. Strassler, ed., *The Landmark Herodotus: The Histories* (London: Quercus, 2007), 769–72; esp. 769.

12 Paula Fredriksen, *Jesus of Nazareth, King of the Jews: A Jewish Life and the Emergence of Christianity* (London: Macmillan, 1999), 52–4 and 65–70.

13 André Vauchez, 'Clerical Celibacy and the Laity', in Bornstein, ed., *Medieval Christianity*, 179–203; 191.

14 Elizabeth A. Clark, 'Asceticism, Class, and Gender', in Virginia Burrus, ed., *Late Ancient Christianity* (Minneapolis, MN: Fortress Press, 2005), 27–45; 28.

15 James C. Skedros, 'Shrines, Festivals, and the "Undistinguished Mob"', in Derek Krueger, ed., *Byzantine Christianity* (Minneapolis, MN: Fortress Press, 2006), 81–101; 81.

16 Peter Gardella, 'Controlling and Christianizing Sex', in Amanda Porterfield, ed., *Modern Christianity to 1900* (Minneapolis, MN: Fortress Press, 2007), 60–88; 69.

17 Margot Todd, 'A People's Reformation', in Peter Matheson, ed., *Reformation Christianity* (Minneapolis, MN: Fortress Press, 2007), 70–91; 82.

18 See Peter Marshall, 'Leaving the World', in Matheson, *Reformation Christianity*, 168–88; 178.

19 Skedros, 'Shrines', in Krueger, ed., *Byzantine Christianity*, 46, 49 and 93.

20 Krueger, ed., *Byzantine Christianity*, Plate A.

21 Bornstein, 'Relics', in Bornstein, ed., *Medieval Christianity*, 104.

22 R.N. Swanson, 'The Burdens of Purgatory', in Bornstein, ed., *Medieval Christianity*, 353–80; 362.

23 Bornstein, 'Living Christianity', in Bornstein, ed., 22.

24 Consult Mark A. Noll and Ethan R. Sanders, 'Evangelicalism in North America', in Mary Farrell Bednarowski, ed., *Twentieth-Century Global Christianity* (Minneapolis, MN: Fortress Press, 2008), 57–189 (180–7); and Colleen, McDannell, *Material Christianity: Religion and Popular Culture in America* (New Haven, CT: Yale University Press, 1995).

25 E.P. Sanders, 'Jesus in Galilee', in Doris Donnelly, ed., *Jesus: A Colloquium in the Holy Land* (London and New York: Continuum, 2001), 5–26; 9.

Chapter I

1 John P. Meier, *A Marginal Jew*, vol. III: *Companions and Competitors* (New Haven and London: Yale University Press, 2001), 646; and vol. IV: *Law and Love* (2009), 658.

2 See Jerome Murphy-O'Connor, 'Palestine', in Bruce M. Metzger and Michael D. Coogan, eds, *The Oxford Guide to People and Places of the Bible* (Oxford and New York: Oxford University Press, 2001), 225–8; 225.

3   Richard A. Horsley, *Covenant Economics: A Biblical Vision of Justice for All* (Louisville, KY: Westminster John Knox Press, 2009), 88.

4   On Abraham, see Diarmaid MacCulloch, *A History of Christianity: The First Three Thousand Years* (London: Allen Lane, 2009), 50 and 53–4.

5   Consult David Leeming, *Jealous Gods and Chosen People: The Mythology of the Middle East* (Oxford and New York: Oxford University Press, 2004), 17.

6   Details in this paragraph are indebted to the work of Paula Fredriksen, *From Jesus to Christ: The Origins of the New Testament Images of Jesus* (New Haven and London: Yale University Press, 1988), 67.

7   William W. Hallo, 'Babylon', in Bruce M. Metzger and Michael D. Coogan, eds, *The Oxford Guide to People and Places of the Bible* (London and New York: Oxford University Press, 2001), 28–30; 29.

8   Walter Burkert, *Babylon, Memphis, Persepolis: Eastern Contexts of Greek Culture* (Cambridge, MA, and London: Harvard University Press, 2004), 100; and Fredriksen, *From Jesus to Christ*, 67–8.

9   Meier, *A Marginal Jew*, vol. III, 291.

10 Maurice Sartre, *The Middle East Under Rome* (Cambridge, MA, and London: The Belknap Press of Harvard University Press, 2005), 2.

11 J. Andrew Overman, 'Syria', in Bruce M. Metzger and Michael D. Coogan, eds, *The Oxford Guide to People and Places of the Bible* (Oxford and New York: Oxford University Press, 2001), 303–4; 304.

12 Sartre, *The Middle East*, 6.

13 Sartre, *The Middle East*, 8.

14 Sartre, *The Middle East*, 8; and Fredriksen, *From Jesus to Christ*, 10 (on the culture of *paideia*).

15 Meier, *A Marginal Jew*, vol. III, 291.

16 Warren Carter, *The Roman Empire and the New Testament: An Essential Guide* (Nashville, TN: Abingdon Press, 2006), 3.

17 E.P. Sanders, 'Jesus in Galilee', in Doris Donnelly, ed., *Jesus: A Colloquium in the Holy Land* (New York and London: Continuum, 2001), 5–26; 8–10.

18 Adrian Goldsworthy, *Roman Warfare* (London: Phoenix, 2007), 107; and Philip Matyszak, *Legionary: The Roman Soldier's (Unofficial) Manual* (London: Thames & Hudson, 2009), 20.

19 Nic Fields, *The Roman Army of the Principate 27 BC–AD 117* (Oxford: Osprey Publishing, 2009), 7.

20 Carter, *The Roman Empire*, 5.

21 Sartre, *The Middle East*, 60.

22 Ekkehard W. Stegemann and Wolfgang Stegemann, *The Jesus Movement: A Social History of Its First Century* (Edinburgh: T&T Clark, 1999), 11.

23 Roman Garrison, 'Roman Government in Israel', in Craig A. Evans, ed., *Encyclopedia of the Historical Jesus* (London and New York: Routledge, 2008), 521–3; 522.

24 Thomas R. Hatina, 'Households, Jewish', in Evans, *Encyclopedia*, 293–8; 294–5.

25 Peter Richardson, *Herod: King of the Jews and Friend of the Romans* (Columbia, SC: University of South Carolina Press, 1996), 46. Herod's wives included a niece and a cousin.

26 Richardson, *Herod,* 13.

27 Richardson, *Herod,* 19.

28 Richardson, *Herod,* xx.

29 Jerome Murphy-O'Connor, *Jesus and Paul: Parallel Lives* (Collegeville, MN: Liturgical Press, 2007), 23.

30 Carolyn Osiek, 'Family Matters', in Richard A. Horsely, ed., *Christian Origins* (Minneapolis, MN: Fortress Press, 2005), 201–20; 211.

31 Peter Garnsey, *Food and Society in Classical Antiquity* (Cambridge: Cambridge University Press, 2002), 59.

32 See Carter, *The Roman Empire,* 10.

33 Osiek, 'Family Matters', 205.

34 See Carter, *The Roman Empire,* 10–11.

35 Garnsey, *Food and Society,* 1.

36 See Garnsey, *Food and Society,* 1–5.

37 Garnsey, *Food and Society,* 45–51.

38 See Horsley, *Covenant Economics,* 82–3.

39 See Carter, *The Roman Empire,* 10.

40 K.R. Bradley, *Slaves and Masters in the Roman Empire: A Study in Social Control* (New York and Oxford: Oxford University Press, 1987); and W.W. Buckland, *The Roman Law of Slavery: The Condition of the Slave in Private Law from Augustus to Justinian* (Cambridge: Cambridge University Press, 1970).

41 See Horsley, *Covenant Economics,* 83.

42 Sartre, *The Middle East,* 60.

43 Brian M. Rapske, 'Roman Rule in Palestine', in Craig A. Evans, ed., *Encyclopedia of the Historical Jesus* (New York and London: Routledge, 2008), 523–29; 525.

44 Craig A. Evans, *Fabricating Jesus: How Modern Scholars Distort the Gospels* (Downers Grove, IL: Intervarsity Press, 2006), 104 and 160.

45 Sean Freyne, *Galilee: From Alexander the Great to Hadrian, 323 BCE to 135 CE* (Edinburgh: T&T Clark, 2000), 3; and Richard A. Horsley, *Galilee: History, Politics, People* (Valley Forge, PA: Trinity Press International, 1995), 20.

46 Horsley, *Galilee,* 21.

47 Albert Lukaszewski, 'Roads and Commerce in Galilee and Judea', in Evans, *Encyclopedia*, 513–19; 514–15.

48 Horsley, *Galile*, 7.

49 John J. Rousseau and Rami Arav, *Jesus and His World: An Archaeological and Cultural Dictionary* (London: SCM Press, 1996), 248.

50 Harold Hoehner, *Herod Antipas* (Grand Rapids, MI: Zondervan, 1972), 52.

51 Bruce Chilton, 'Recovering Jesus' Mamzerut', in James H. Charlesworth, ed., *Jesus and Archaeology* (Grand Rapids, MI, and Cambridge, UK: William B. Eerdmans, 2006), 84–110; 95.

52 Rousseau and Arav, *Jesus and His World*, 214; and Craig A. Evans, 'Nazareth', in *Encyclopedia of the Historical Jesus*, 423–5; 423.

53 See Evans, *Encyclopedia*, 424.

54 Thomas R. Hatina, 'Households, Jewish', in Evans, *Encyclopedia*, 293–8; 293.

55 See Stegemann and Stegemann, *The Jesus Movement*, 10–11.

56 Consult Stegemann and Stegemann, *The Jesus Movement*, 14.

57 See Horsley, *Covenant Economics*, 87–8.

58 Meier, *A Marginal Jew*, III, 616.

59 John W. Miller, *Jesus at Thirty: A Psychological and Historical Portrait* (Minneapolis, MN: Fortress Press, 1997), 35, and Meier, *A Marginal Jew*, I, 317.

60 Meier, *A Marginal Jew*, III, 616.

61 Thomas R. Hatina, 'Households, Jewish', in Craig A. Evans, ed., *Encyclopedia of the Historical Jesus* (New York and London: Routledge, 2008), 293–7; 293–4.

62 Edward Schillebeeckx, *The Church with a Human Face: A New and Expanded Theology of Ministry* (London: SCM Press, 1985), 14.

63 James H. Charlesworth, *The Historical Jesus: An Essential Guide* (Nashville, TN: Abingdon Press, 2008), 59.

64 Gerhard E. Lenski, *Power and Privilege: A Theory of Social Stratification* (Chapel Hill, NC, and London: The University of North Carolina Press, 1984), Chapter 9, esp. 284–5.

65 James M. Robinson, 'Forward: A Down-to-Earth Jesus', in Rousseau and Arav, *Jesus and His World*, xiii–xviii; xiv.

66 Robinson, 'Foreword', xiv.

67 Robinson, 'Foreword', xiv.

68 Charlesworth, *The Historical Jesus*, 48–9.

69 On the significance of the Temple during Jesus' life, see Paula Fredriksen, *Jesus of Nazareth, King of the Jews: A Jewish Life and the Emergence of Christianity* (London: Macmillan, 2000), 51–73. On ritual purity and impurity, consult E.P. Sanders, 'Jesus, Ancient Judaism, and

Modern Christianity: The Quest Continues', in Paula Fredriksen and Adele Reinhartz, eds, *Jesus, Judaism and Christian Anti-Semitism: Reading the New Testament after the Holocaust* (Louisville, KY, and London: Westminster John Knox Press, 2002), 31–55 (36); and Fredriksen, *Jesus of Nazareth*, 51–3.

Chapter II

1 See Étienne Trocmé, *The Childhood of Christianity* (London: SCM Press, 1997), viii.

2 Edwin D. Freed, 'Christian', in Bruce Metzger and Michael D. Coogan, eds, *The Oxford Guide to People and Places of the Bible* (Oxford and New York: Oxford University Press, 2001), 41–2.

3 See Robert Doran, *Birth of a Worldview: Early Christianity in Its Jewish and Pagan Context* (Boulder, CO: Westview Press, 1995), 12.

4 This is the estimate of Trocmé, *The Childhood of Christianity*, vii.

5 Warren Carter, *The Roman Empire and the New Testament: An Essential Guide* (Nashville, TN: Abingdon Press, 2006), 3.

6 See John Dominic Crossan, *The Birth of Christianity: Discovering What Happened in the Years Immediately after the Execution of Jesus* (New York: HarperSanFrancisco, 1998), xx–xxii.

7 Ekkhard W. Stegemann and Wolfgang Stegemann, *The Jesus Movement: A Social History of Its First Century* (Edinburgh: T&T Clack, 1999), 252 and 434.

8 John W. Drane, 'Paul', in Bruce M. Metzger and Michael D. Coogan, eds, *The Oxford Guide to People and Places of the Bible* (Oxford and New York: Oxford University Press, 2001), 228–32; 228.

9 On the figure of Paul, consult Donald Harman Akenson, *Saint Paul: A Skeleton Key to the Historical Jesus* (Oxford and New York: Oxford University Press, 2000); and John Dominic Crossan and Jonathan L. Reed, *In Search of Paul: How Jesus' Apostle Opposed Rome's Empire with God's Kingdom* (London: SPCK, 2005).

10 Paula Fredriksen, *From Jesus to Christ: The Origins of New Testament Images of Christ* (New Haven and London: Yale University Press, 1988), 222.

11 Roger Haight, *Jesus Symbol of God* (Maryknoll, NY: Orbis Books, 1999), 256.

12 Maurice Sartre, *The Middle East Under Rome* (Cambridge, MA, and London: The Belknap Press of Harvard University Press, 2005), 335.

13 Warren Carter, 'Matthew's People', in Richard A. Horsley, ed., *Christian Origins* (Minneapolis, MN: Fortress Press, 2005), 138–61; 146. See too A. Scobie, 'Slums, Sanitation, and Mortality in the

Roman World,' *Klio* 68 (1986), 399–433; and C.R. Whittaker, 'The Poor', in Andrea Giarnina, ed., *The Romans*, trans. G. Cochrane (Chicago: The University of Chicago Press, 1993), 272–99; 288.

14 Sartre, *The Middle East*, 336.

15 For an historical reconstruction of the evolution of Christ-confessing assemblies after the death of Jesus, see Edward Schillebeeckx, *Jesus: An Experiment in Christology* (New York: Seabury, 1979), Part Three; *The Church with a Human Face: A New and Expanded Theology of Ministry* (London: SCM Press, 1985); and *Church: The Human Story of God* (London: SCM Press, 1990), Chapter 3.

16 On the status and activities of women among ancient Christians, see Elisabeth Schlüssler Fiorenza, *In Memory of her: A Feminist Theological Reconstruction of Christian Origins*, 2nd edn (London: SCM Press, 1994 [1983]); and Rosemary Radford Ruether, *Women and Redemption: A Theological History* (London: SCM, 1998).

17 See John Bowden, *A Chronology of World Christianity* (London and New York: Continuum, 2007), 12–21, esp. 21.

18 See Alistair H.B. Logan, 'Gnosticism', in Adrian Hastings, Alistair Mason, and Hugh Pyper, eds, *The Oxford Companion to Christian Thought: Intellectual, Spiritual, and Moral Horizons of Christianity* (Oxford and New York: Oxford University Press, 2000), 268–9.

19 Consult Martin Marty, *The Christian World: A Global History* (New York: The Modern Library, 2007), 55–7.

20 Doran, *Birth of a Worldview*, 10–11.

21 Bowden, *Chronology*, 22.

22 Bowden, *Chronology*, 31.

23 Euan Cameron, *Interpreting Christian Church History: The Challenge of the Churches' Past* (Malden, MA, and Oxford: Blackwell Publishing, 2005), 14.

24 On this point, see Morwenna Ludlow, *The Early Church* (London and New York: I.B.Tauris, 2009), 94.

25 Henry Chadwick, 'The Origin of the Title "Ecumenical Council"', *Journal of Theological Studies*, 23 (1972), 132–5.

26 See Carolyn Osiek, 'Family Matters', in Richard A. Horsley, ed., *Christian Origins* (Minneapolis, MN: Fortress Press, 2005), 201–20; 205.

27 Virginia Burrus and Rebecca Lyman, 'Shifting the Focus of History', in Virginia Burrus, ed., *Late Ancient Christianity* (Minneapolis, MN: Fortress Press, 2005), 1–23; 21.

28 Marty, *The Christian World*, 62–3.

29 Marty, *The Christian World*, 79; and Margaret L. King, *The Renaissance in Europe* (London: Laurence King Publishing, 2003), 11–12.

30 John McGuckin, 'Controversy and Councils: Greek theology, 4th–6th centuries', in Adrian Hastings, Alistair Mason and Hugh Pyper, eds, *Christian Thought: A Brief History* (Oxford and New York: Oxford University Press, 2002), 17–32; 23–4.

31 See Schillebeeckx, *The Church with a Human Face*, 141–60.

32 Dale T. Irvin and Scott W. Sunquist, *History of the World Christian Movement* (Edinburgh: T&T Clark, 2001), 225.

33 Dennis Trout, 'Saints, Identity, and the City', in Burrus, *Late Ancient Christianity*, 165–210; 179.

34 William G. Rusch, ed., *The Trinitarian Controversy* (Philadelphia, PA: Fortress Press, 1980), 17–18.

35 Norman P. Tanner, *The Councils of the Church: A Short History* (New York: The Crossroad Publishing Company, 2001), 3. See 2 as well.

36 On Church councils, see Tanner, *The Councils of the Church*, esp. 125.

37 Richard McBrien, *Catholicism*, 3rd edn (London: Geoffrey Chapman, 2000), 32, 152, 175, 179, 187, 255, 613 and 837.

38 First Council of Constantinople, 'The exposition of the 150 fathers', in Norman P. Tanner, *Decrees of the Ecumenical Councils*, vol. I (London and Washington, DC: Sheed & Ward and Georgetown University Press, 1990), 24.

39 Excerpt from the Council of Chalcedon, 'Definition of the faith', in Tanner, *Decrees*, 86–7.

40 Kallistos Ware, 'Eastern Christianity', in Richard Harries and Henry Mayr-Harting, *Christianity: Two Thousand Years* (Oxford and New York: Oxford University Press, 2001), 65–95; 68.

41 Ware, 'Eastern Christianity', 78.

42 Ware, 'Eastern Christianity', 79.

Chapter III

 1 Averil Cameron, 'Late Antiquity', in Richard Harries and Henry Mayr-Harting, eds, *Christianity: Two Thousand Years* (Oxford and New York: Oxford University Press, 2001), 9 and 242, n. 9.

 2 Henry Mayr-Harting, 'The Early Middle Ages', in Harries and Mayr-Harting, *Christianity*, 44–64; 45.

 3 See Martin Marty, *The Christian World: A Global History* (New York: The Modern Library, 2007), 75.

 4 Daniel E. Bornstein, 'Living Christianity', in Daniel E. Bornstein, ed., *Medieval Christianity* (Minneapolis, MN: Fortress Press, 2009), 1–22; 5.

 5 Bornstein, 'Living Christianity', 4.

 6 See Bornstein, 'Living Christianity', 3–5.

 7 See Marty, *The Christian World*, 87–8.

 8 Marty, *The Christian World*, 83.

9   Margaret Truran, 'Benedictine thought', in Adrian Hastings, Alistair Mason and Hugh Pyper, eds, *The Oxford Companion to Christian Thought* (Oxford and New York: Oxford University Press, 2000), 68–9; 68.

10 Bornstein, 'Living Christianity', 2.

11 Margaret R. Miles, *The Word Made Flesh: A History of Christian Thought* (Malden, MA and Oxford: Blackwell Publishing, 2005), 136.

12 F.L. Cross and E.A. Livingstone, eds, 3rd edn, *The Oxford Dictionary of The Christian Church* (Oxford and New York: Oxford University Press, 1997), 984.

13 John Bowden, *A Chronology of World Christianity* (London and New York: Continuum, 2007), 74.

14 Marty, *The Christian World*, 88–9.

15 Bornstein, 'Living Christianity', 5.

16 See Yitzhak Hen, 'Converting the Barbarian West', in Daniel E. Bornstein, ed., *Medieval Christianity* (Minneapolis, MN: Fortress Press, 2009), 29–52 (42–4); *Culture and Religion in Merovingian Gaul, A.D. 481–751* (Leiden: Brill, 1995); and Richard Fletcher, *The Conversion of Europe: From Paganism to Christianity, 371–1386 AD* (London: HarperCollins, 1997).

17 Marty, *The Christian World*, 88.

18 Mayr-Harting, 'The Early Middle Ages', 46–7.

19 Einhards' 'Life of Charlemagne,' in Einhard and Notker the Stammerer, *Two Lives of Charlemagne*, trans. Lewis Thorpe (Harmondsworth: Penguin, 1969), 79. See too Bornstein, 'Living Christianity', 6–7.

20 See Diana Webb, 'Domestic Religion', in Bornstein, *Medieval Christianity*, 303–28; 303.

21 See Richard Kieckheffer, 'The Impact of Architecture', in Bornstein, *Medieval Christianity*, 109–46; 109.

22 Kieckheffer, 'The Impact of Architecture', 114.

23 Kieckheffer, 'The Impact of Architecture', 116.

24 Chris Brazier, *No-Nonsense Guide to World History* (Oxford: New Internationalist Publications, 2001), 43.

25 Marty, *The Christian World*, 43.

26 Derek, 'The Practice of Christianity in Byzantium', in Derek Krueger, ed., *Byzantine Christianity* (Minneapolis, MN: Fortress Press, 2006), 1–15; 4–5.

27 Sharon E.J. Gerstel, 'The Layperson in Church', in Derek Krueger, ed., *Byzantine Christianity* (Minneapolis, MN: Fortress Press, 2006), 103–23; 105.

28 Miles, *The Word Made Flesh*, 120.

29 Miles, *The Word Made Flesh*, 121.

30 Miles, *The Word Made Flesh*, 134.
31 Richard P. McBrien, *The Church: The Evolution of Catholicism* (New York: HarperOne, 2008), 71.
32 David Levine, *At the Dawn of Modernity: Biology, Culture, and Material Life in Europe after the Year 1000* (Berkeley, CA: University of California Press, 2001), 22.
33 Edwin Mullins, *In Search of Cluny: God's Lost Empire* (Oxford: Signal Books, 2006), 8–9.
34 Edwin Mullins, *In Search of Cluny*, 1.
35 Mullins, *In Search of Cluny*, 13–15.
36 Mullins, *In Search of Cluny*, 15.
37 Mullins, *In Search of Cluny*, 15–17.
38 For details in this and the previous paragraph, see Mullins, *in Search of Cluny*, 18, 24, 26–7 and 28.
39 Mullins, *In Search of Cluny*, 145.
40 Mullins, *In Search of Cluny*, 11.
41 Bowden, *Chronology*, 146.

Chapter IV

1 Euan Cameron, *Interpreting Christian History: The Challenge of the Churches' Past* (Malden, MA, and Oxford: Blackwell Publishing, 2005), 5.
2 See Cameron, *Interpreting Christian History*, 24.
3 George Herring, *An Introduction to the History of Christianity: From the Early Church to the Enlightenment* (London and New York: Continuum, 2006), 130.
4 See Cameron, *Interpreting Church History*, 24.
5 André Vauchez, 'Clerical Celibacy and the Laity', in Daniel E. Bornstein, ed., *Medieval Christianity* (Minneapolis, MN: Fortress Press, 2009), 179–203 (184); Anne L. Barstow, *Married Priests and the Reforming Papacy: The Eleventh-Century Debates* (New York: Edwin Mellen, 1982); and Michael Frassetto, ed., *Medieval Purity and Piety: Essays on Medieval Clerical Celibacy and Religious Reform* (New York: Garland, 1998).
6 Vauchez, 'Clerical Celibacy', 185.
7 Vauchez, 'Clerical Celibacy', 186. See too R.N. Swanson, 'Angels Incarnate: Clergy and Masculinity from the Gregorian Reform to Reformation', in Dawn Hadley, ed., *Masculinity in Medieval Europe* (New York: Addison Wesley Longman, 1999), 160–77.
8 Vauchez, 'Clerical Celibacy', 182.
9 Alexander Murray, 'The Later Middle Ages', in Richard Harries and Henry Mayr-Harting, eds, *Christianity: Two Thousand Years* (Oxford and New York: Oxford University Press, 2001), 96–131; 111.

10 Herring, *An Introduction*, 137–8; and Margaret R. Wiles, *The Word Made Flesh: A History of Christian Thought* (Malden MA, and Oxford: Blackwell Publishing, 2005), 134 and 143.

11 David Levine, *At the Dawn of Modernity: Biology, Culture, and Material Life in Europe after the Year 1000* (Berkeley, CA: University of California Press, 2001), 25.

12 For a lucid account of Anselm and the English translation of *Cur Deus Homo?* above, see Gerald O'Collins, *Jesus Our Redeemer: A Christian Approach to Salvation* (Oxford and New York: Oxford University Press, 2007), 134–5.

13 See Dale T. Irwin and Scott W. Sunquist, *History of the Christian Movement* (Edinburgh: T&T Clark, 2001), 395.

14 Translation of Robert of Rheims, *Historia Iherosolimitana*, in *The Crusades: Idea and Reality*, L. and J. Riley-Smith (London: Edward Arnold, 1981), 44.

15 Martin Marty, *The Christian World: A Global History* (New York: The Modern Library, 2007), 90.

16 Irvin and Sunquist, *History of the Christian Movement*, 397.

17 Irwin and Sunquist, *History of the Christian Movement*, 403. See too 402 on Nur ad-Din and Salah ad-Din.

18 Irwin and Sunquist, *History of the Christian Movement*, 391–92.

19 On flagellants, see Gary Dickson, 'Medieval Revivalism', in Daniel E. Bornstein, ed., *Medieval Christianity* (Minneapolis, MN: Fortress Press, 2009), 147–76; 155–60.

20 Wiles, *The Word Made Flesh*, 154.

21 Dickson, 'Medieval Revivalism', 160.

22 Wiles, *The Word Made Flesh*, 156.

23 Wiles, *The Word Made Flesh*, 156.

24 Herring, *An Introduction*, 182–3; C.H. Lawrence, *Medieval Monasticism: Forms of the Religious Life in Western Europe in the Middle Ages*, 3rd edn (Edinburgh: Longman, 2001), 69–70.

25 Herring, *An Introduction*, 190; and David H. Williams, *The Cistercians in the Early Middle Ages* (Leominster: Gracewig, 1998), 78.

26 Herring, *An Introduction*, 189.

27 John A. Thomson, *The Western Church in the Middle Ages* (London: Arnold, 1998), 111–12.

28 F. Donald Logan, *A History of the Church in the Middle Ages* (London and New York: Routledge, 2002), 142.

29 Wiles, *The Word Made Flesh*, 174 (on cathedrals) and 219 (on paintings).

30 See Irvin and Sunquist, *History of the World Christian Movement*, 412–13.

31 From the anonymous *Chronicon universale*, cited in Frances Andrews, *The Early Humiliati* (Cambridge: Cambridge University Press, 1999), 39.

32 See Grado G. Merlo, 'Heresy and Dissent', in Daniel E. Bornstein, ed., *Medieval Christianity* (Minneapolis, MN: Fortress Press, 2009), 229–64; 238–56.

33 Edward Norman, *The Roman Catholic Church: An Illustrated History* (London: Thames & Hudson, 2007), 93.

34 Merlo, 'Heresy and Dissent', 263.

35 Fourth Lateran Council (1215), *De fide catholica*, 1, trans. Norman Tanner, ed., *Decrees of the Ecumenical Councils*, vol. 1 (London, Sheed and Ward, and Georgetown, WA: Georgetown University Press, 1990), 230–31.

36 David Stancliffe, *The Lion Companion to Church Architecture* (Oxford: Lion Hudson, 2008), 109–66.

37 On organum and its different kinds, see Leo Treitler, ed., *Strunk's Source Readings in Music History* (New York and London: W.W. Norton, 1998), 221.

38 Cameron, *Interpreting Christian History*, 29 and 30.

39 John Bowden, *A Chronology of World Christianity* (London and New York: Continuum, 2007), 246.

Chapter V

1 Margaret L. King, *The Renaissance in Europe* (London: Laurence King Publishing, 2003), viii–ix.

2 King, *The Renaissance*, 66–7.

3 Virgil, *Aeneid*, 2. 40–56, 199–231; David Adams Leeming, *The World of Myth: An Anthology* (New York and Oxford: Oxford University Press, 1990), 319–20; and Simon Price and Emily Kearns, eds, *The Oxford Dictionary of Classical Myth and Religion* (Oxford and New York: Oxford University Press, 2003), 312.

4 King, *The Renaissance*, 53.

5 Dante Alighieri, *The Inferno*, trans. John Ciardi (New York: New American Library, 1954), 76.

6 David Levine, *At the Dawn of Modernity: Biology, Culture, and Material Life in Europe after the Year 1000* (Berkeley, CA: University of California Press, 2001), 325–6.

7 King, *The Renaissance*, 54. See too Gene Bruckner, *The Society of Renaissance Florence* (New York: Harper & Row, 1971).

8 Giovanni Boccaccio, *The Decameron*, trans. Mark Musa and Peter Bondanella (New York: New American Library), 437; and Roberto Rusconi, 'Hearing Women's Sins', in Daniel E. Bornstein, ed., *Medieval Christianity* (Minneapolis, MN: Fortress Press, 2009), 205–25; 220–1.

9   See Francesco Petrarch, *Letters*, trans. M. Bishop (Bloomington, IN: Indiana University Press, 1966); King, *The Renaissance*, 56; and John Larner, *Italy in the Age of Dante and Petrarch, 1216–1380,* (London: Longman, 1980).

10 John W. Coakley, 'Renaissance', in John Bowden, ed., *Encyclopedia of Christianity* (Oxford and New York: Oxford University Press, 2005), 1026–9; 1027.

11 See Coakley, 'Renaissance', 1026.

12 Michelle P. Brown, *The Lion Companion to Christian Art* (Oxford: Lion, 2008), 195.

13 Consult the Renaissance work of Leon Battista Alberti, *On Painting*, trans. John R. Spencer (New Haven, CT: Yale University Press, 1956).

14 Brown, *Lion Companion to Christian Art*, 200.

15 King, *The Renaissance*, 106.

16 King, *The Renaissance*, 171.

17 King, *The Renaissance*, 129–30.

18 Leo Treitler, ed., *Source Readings in Music History*, rev. edn; originally ed. Oliver Strunk (London and New York; W.W. Norton, 1998), 373.

19 Diana Webb, 'Domestic Religion', in Daniel E. Bornstein, ed., *Medieval Christianity* (Minneapolis, MN: Fortress Press, 2009), 303–28; 317. This domestic penitential ritual is depicted in greater detail by R.C. Trexler in *Public Life in the Renaissance Florence* (Ithaca, NY: Cornell University Press), 176–85.

20 Webb, 'Domestic Religion', 319. See too Christiane Klapisch-Züber, *Women, Family and Ritual in Renaissance Italy* (Chicago, IL: Chicago University Press, 1985), 114–15 and 310–29.

21 Thomas Aquinas, *Summa Theologiae*, I–II, 88, 2.

22 Fourth Lateran Council, Norman Tanner, trans. and ed., *Decrees of the Ecumenical Councils*, vol. I (London, Sheed & Ward, and Georgetown University, Washington, DC: Georgetown University Press, 1990), 245. See too P.A. Kirsch, *Der sacerdos proprius in der abendländischen Kirche vor dem Jahre 1215*, Archiv für katholisches Kirchenrecht 84 (1904), 527–37.

23 *Le costituzioni per il clero (1542) di Gian Matteo Giberti vescovo di Verona*, ed., Roberto Pasquali (Vicenza: Istituto per le ricerche di storia sociale e religiosa, 2000), 436 and 438 (tit. VI, cap. XXII).

24 *Rituale Romanum Pauli 5. Pont. Max. Iussu editum* (Rome: Stamperia Camerale, 1614).

25 Roberto Rusconi, 'Hearing Women's Sins', in Daniel E. Bornestein, ed., *Medieval Christianity* (Minneapolis, MN: Fortress Press, 2009), 205–25; 223. Consult, as well, Thomas N. Tentler, *Sin and Confession*

on the Eve of the Reformation (Princeton, NJ: Princeton University Press, 1977).

26 J.D. Mansi, ed., *Sacrorum conciliorum nova et amplissima collection*, vol. 24 (Graz: Akademische Druck, 1961 [1903]), 70–1.

27 See R.N. Swanson, 'The Burdens of Purgatory', in Daniel E. Bernstein, ed., *Medieval Christianity* (Minneapolis, MN: Fortress Press, 2009), 353–80; 355; and Jacques Le Goff, *The Birth of Purgatory* (Chicago, IL: University of Chicago Press, 1984).

28 Consult R.N. Swanson, ed., *Promissory Notes on the Treasury of Merits: Indulgences in Late Medieval Europe* (Leiden: Brill, 2006).

29 David Arnold, *The Age of Discovery: 1400–1600* (London: Routledge, 1994), 16.

30 Teofilo F. Ruiz, 'Jews, Muslims, and Christians', in Daniel E. Bornstein, ed., *Medieval Christianity* (Minneapolis, MN: Fortress Press, 2009), 265–99; 296–7; and Benjamin R. Gambel, *The Last Jews on Iberian Soil: Navarrese Jewry, 1479–1498* (Berkeley, CA: University of California Press, 1989).

31 Arnold, *The Age of Discovery*, 12 and 17.

32 Arnold, *The Age of Discovery*, 19 and 23–4.

33 Gustavo Gutiérrez, *Las Casas: In Search of the Poor Jesus Christ*, trans. Robert R. Barr (Maryknoll, NY: Orbis Books, 1995), 22 and 471, n. 1.

34 Gutiérrez, *Las Casas*, 3.

35 Gutiérrez, *Las Casas*, 23.

36 Bartolomé de Las Casas, A *Short Account of the Destruction of the Indies*, trans. Nigel Griffin (London: Penguin Books, London, 1992), 3.

37 Las Casas, *A Short Account of the Destruction of the Indies*, 22.

Chapter VI

1 Enrique Dussel, *Von der Erfindung Amerikas zur Entdeckung des Anderen: Ein Projekt der Transmoderne*, Theologie Interkulturell 6 (Düsseldorf: Patmos, 1993), 10.

2 Joerg Rieger, 'Theology and the Power of the Margins in a Postmodern World', in Jeorg Rieger, ed., *Opting for the Margins: Postmodernity and Liberation in Christian Theology* (Oxford and New York: Oxford University Press, 2003), 179–99; 189.

3 James M. Stayer, 'The Dream of a Just Society', in Peter Matheson, ed., *Reformation Christianity* (Minneapolis, MN: Fortress Press, 2007), 191–211; 192.

4 Carlos Eire, 'New Ways of Confronting Death', in Amanda Porterfield, ed., *Modern Christianity to 1900* (Minneapolis, MN: Fortress Press, 2007), 31–59; 36.

5   Margaret R. Wiles, *The Word Made Flesh: A History of Christian Thought* (Malden, MA, and Oxford: Blackwell Publishing, 2005), 245.

6   Johann Tetzel, quoted in Roland H. Bainton, *Here I stand: A Life of Martin Luther* (New York: Abingdon, 1950), 78.

7   George Herring, *An Introduction to the History of Christianity: From the Early Church to the Enlightenment* (London and New York: Continuum, 2006), 226.

8   Consult F.L. Cross and E.A. Livingston, *The Oxford Dictionary of the Christian Church*, 3rd edn (Oxford and New York: Oxford University Press, 1997), 131.

9   Diarmaid MacCulloch, *Reformation: Europe's House Divided 1490–1700* (London: Allen Lane, 2003), 115.

10 MacCulloch, *Reformation*, 116.

11 *The Oxford Dictionary of the Christian Church*, 1338.

12 Wiles, *The Word Made Flesh*, 244.

13 MacCulloch, *Reformation*, 117.

14 Craig C. Hill, 'Romans', in John Barton and John Muddiman, eds, *The Oxford Bible Commentary* (Oxford and New York, 2007), 1083–198; 1198.

15 On God's righteousness, see P. Stuhlmacher, *Paul's Letter to the Romans: A Commentary*, trans. S.J. Hafemann (Louisville, KY: Westminster John Knox Press, 1994), 29–32; and James D.G. Dunn, *Romans*, i. chs 1–8, chs 9.16, World Biblical Commentary, 38A–B (Dallas, TX: Word, 1988), i. 41.

16 See Hill, 'Romans', 1089–90; Karl Barth, *The Epistle to the Romans*, trans. E.C. Hoskyns (London: Oxford University Press, 1933), 41; and J.R. Edwards, *Romans*, New International Bible Commentary (Peabody, MA: Hendrickson, 1992), 42–3.

17 Cited in H.G. Haile, *Luther: An Experiment in Biography* (Princeton, NJ: Princeton University Press, 1980), 177.

18 See Wiles, *The Word Made Flesh*, 245–6.

19 Herring, *An Introduction*, 238.

20 C. Scott Dixon, 'Luther, Martin', in John Bowden, ed., *Encyclopedia of Christianity* (Oxford and New York: Oxford University Press, 2005), 716–19; 717.

21 MacCulloch, *Reformation*, 127–8 and 131.

22 Wiles, *The Word Made Flesh*, 243.

23 MacCulloch, *Reformation*, 122.

24 See Wiles, *The Word Made Flesh*, 241.

25 See Margaret L. King, *The Renaissance in Europe* (London: Laurence King Publishing, 2003), 271.

26 Hans Küng, *Christianity: Its Essence and History*, trans. John Bowden (London: SCM Press, 1995).

27 King, *The Renaissance*, 271.

28 Consult Euan Cameron, *Interpreting Christian History: The Challenge of the Churches' Past* (Malden, MA, and Oxford: Blackwell Publishing, 2005), 32.

29 See Küng, *Christianity*, 551–2.

30 'Erasmus', in Richard L. DeMolen, ed., *Erasmus* (London: Edward Arnold, 1973), 134.

31 Quoted in Leo Treitler, ed., *Source Readings in Music History*, rev. edn of Oliver Strunk's first edn (New York and London: W.W. Norton, 1998), 363.

32 Dixon, 'Luther, Martin,' 717.

33 Wiles, *The Word Made Flesh*, 257.

34 C. Scott Dixon, 'Calvin, John', in John Bowden, ed., *Encyclopedia of Christianity* (Oxford and New York: Oxford University Press, 2005), 194–7; 194.

35 Herring, *An Introduction*, 244.

36 Herring, *An Introduction*, 245.

37 Raymond A. Mentzer, 'The Piety of Townspeople and City Folk', in Peter Matheson, ed., *Reformation Christianity* (Minneapolis, MN: Fortress Press, 2007), 23–47; 26–7.

38 Mentzer, 'The Piety', 27.

39 Margo Todd, 'A People's Reformation', in Peter Matheson, ed., *Reformation Christianity* (Minneapolis, MN: Fortress Press, 2007), 70–91; 71.

40 Consult A.G. Dickens, *The English Reformation*, 2nd edn (University Park, PA: Pennsylvania State University Press, 1991); Eamon Duffy, *The Stripping of the Altars: Traditional Religion in England, c. 1400–c. 1580* (New Haven, CT: Yale University Press, 1992); and Christopher Haigh, *English Reformations: Religion, Politics, and Society under the Tudors* (Oxford: Clarendon Press, 1993).

41 Todd, 'A People's Christianity', 82.

42 Todd, 'A People's Christianity', 82.

43 Consult Margo Todd, *The Culture of Protestantism in Early Modern Scotland* (New Haven, CT: Yale University Press, 2002).

44 Norman P. Tanner, *The Councils of the Church: A Short History* (New York, NY: Crossroad, 2001), 86.

45 John Gribbin, *Companion to the Cosmos* (London: Phoenix Giant, 1997), 105.

46 Holmes Rolston, III, *Environmental Ethics* (Philadelphia, PA: Temple University Press, 1988), 230.

47 See Paul Brockelman, *Cosmology and Creation: The Spiritual Significance of Contemporary Cosmology* (New York and Oxford: Oxford University Press, 1990).

48 John and Mary Gribbin, *How Far is Up? Measuring the Size of the Universe* (Duxford, Cambridge: Icon Books, 2003), 103.

49 King, *The Renaissance*, 333.

50 Victor J. Stenger, *God the Failed Hypothesis: How Science Shows That God Does Not Exist* (Amherst, NY: Prometheus Books, 2007), 48.

Chapter VII

1 Romanld G. Asch, *The Thirty Years War: The Holy Roman Empire and Europe, 1618–48* (London: Macmillan, 1997), 27–8 and 56–65; and Euan Cameron, *Interpreting Church History: The Challenge of the Church's Past* (Malden, MA, and Oxford: Blackwells Publishing, 2005), 38.

2 See John Corrigan, 'Economic Change and Emotional Life', in Amanda Porterfield, ed., *Modern Christianity to 1900* (Minneapolis, MN: Fortress Press, 2007), 89–112; 101.

3 For the characterization of Quakers in this chapter, see Peter Day, *A Dictionary of Christian Denominations* (London and New York: Continuum, 2003), 415–16.

4 Ava Chamberlain, 'Domestic Piety in New England', in Amanda Porterfield, ed., *Modern Christianity to 1900* (Minneapolis, MN: Fortress Press, 2007), 233–57; 249.

5 Chamberlain, 'Domestic Piety', 249–50.

6 Chamberlain, 'Domestic Piety', 251. See 250 as well.

7 Rosemary Radford Ruether, *Christianity and the Making of the Modern Family* (London: SCM Press, 2001), 85.

8 Chamberlain, 'Domestic Piety', 235.

9 David B. Barrett, George T. Kurian and Todd M. Johnson, eds, *World Christian Encyclopedia: A Comparative Survey of Churches and Religions in the Modern World*, vol. 1 (Oxford and New York: Oxford University Press, 2001), 776.

10 Barrett and others, eds, *World Christian Encyclopedia*, vol. 1, 496.

11 Howard J. Wiarda, *The Soul of Latin America: The Cultural and Political Tradition* (New Haven, CT: Tale Divinity Press, 2001), 104.

12 Sebastian Kim and Kirsteen Kim, *Christianity as a World Religion* (London and New York: Continuum, 2008), 140.

13 Kim and Kim, *Christianity*, 140–1.

14 John L. Kater, Jr, 'America, Christianity in Latin', in John Bowden, ed., *Encyclopedia of Christianity* (Oxford and New York: Oxford University Press, 2005), 19–31; 19.

15   See Virgil Elizondo, *Guadalupe, Mother of a New Creation* (Maryknoll, NY: Orbis, 1997), 5–22, esp. 8; and Kim and Kim, *Christianity*, 144.

16   Kim and Kim, *Christianity*, 145. See 144 as well.

17   Barrett and others, eds, *World Christian Encyclopedia*, vol. 1, 131–2.

18   Consult Enrique Dussell, *A History of the Church in Latin America*, trans. Alan Neely (Grand Rapids, MI: Wm B. Eerdmans, 1981), 60.

19   Enrique Dussel, 'Sobre la Historia de la Teología en América Latina', in *Liberación y cautiverio: Debates en torno al método de la teología en América latina* (Mexico City: Comité Organizador, 1976), 19–68, esp. pp. 35–7.

20   Consult E.J. Stormon, ed. and trans, *The Salvado Memoirs* (Melbourne: Melbourne University Press, 1977).

21   Barrett and others, eds, *World Christian Encyclopedia*, vol. 1, 594 and 596.

22   Council of Trent, 'Decree on Justification' (13 January 1547), in Norman P. Tanner, ed., *Decrees of the Ecumenical Councils*, Vol. II (London: Sheed & Ward, and Washington, DC: Georgetown University Press, 1990), 672.

23   Council of Trent, 'Decree on Justification', 675.

24   John Bowden, *A Chronology of World Christianity* (London and New York: Continuum International, 2007), 297–8.

25   Margaret L. King, *The Renaissance in Europe* (London: Laurence King Publishing, 2003), 244.

26   David Stancliffe, *The Lion Companion to Church Architecture* (Oxford: Lion Hudson, 2008), 179.

27   James Byrne, *Glory, Jest, and Riddle: Religious Thought in the Enlightenment* (London: SCM Press, 1996), 16.

28   Byrne, *Glory, Jest, and Riddle*, 92 and ch. 6.

29   See Janet Broughton, *Descartes's Mehod of Doubt* (Princeton, NJ, and Oxford: Princeton University Press, 2002), 13, n. 13.

30   For a massive reservoir of detail on the Enlightenment, consult Alan Charles Kors, Editor in Chief, *Encyclopedia of the Enlightenment*, 4 vols (New York and Oxford: Oxford University Press, 2003).

31   Day, *Christian Denominations*, 306–7.

32   Hilary M. Carey, 'An Historical Outline of Religion in Australia', in James Rupp, ed., *The Encyclopedia of Religion in Australia* (Cambridge: Cambridge University Press, 2009), 5–21; 5.

33   Carey, 'Historical Outline', 8.

34   E.J. Stormon, trans. and ed., 'Introduction', in Dom Rosendo Salvado, *The Salvado Memoirs: Historical Memoirs of Australia and Particularly of the Benedictine Mission of New Norcia and the Habits and Customs of the Australian Natives* (Nedlands, WA: University of Western Australia Press, 1977), ix–xix; x–xi.

35 Stormon, 'Foreword', in Salvado, *Salvado Memoirs*, xi.

36 Salvado, *Salvado Memoirs*, 43.

37 Salvado, *Salvado Memoirs*, 47–8.

38 Salvado, *Salvado Memoirs*, 48.

39 Salvado, *Salvado Memoirs*, 115.

40 Salvado, *Salvado Memoirs*, see 116.

41 Salvado, *Salvado Memoirs*, 116.

42 Bowden, *Chronology*, 352.

43 Recorded in Jeremy Morris, *The Church in the Modern Age* (London and New York: I.B.Tauris, 2007), 57.

44 Morris, *The Church*, 57.

45 Consult Owen Chadwick, *A History of the Popes: 1830–1914* (Oxford: Clarendon Press, 1998), 161–214; and Nicholas Atkin and Frank Tallett, *Priests, Prelates and People: A History of European Catholicism since 1750* (London and New York: I.B.Tauris, 2003), 130–41, esp. 139–41.

46 First Vatican Council, 'First Dogmatic Constitution on the Church of Christ' (18 July 1870), ch. 4, in Norman P. Tanner, ed., *Decrees of the Ecumenical Councils*, vol. II (London: Sheed & Ward, and Washington, DC: Georgetown University Press, 1990), 816.

47 Norman P. Tanner, *The Councils of the Church: A Short History* (New York: Crossroad, 2001), 92.

48 On the origin and nature of the Salvation Army, see Pamela J. Walker, *Pulling the Devil's Kingdom Down: The Salvation Army in Victorian Britain* (Berkeley, CA: University of California Press, 2001), chs 1–4.

49 Peter Day, *A Dictionary of Christian Denominations* (London and New York: Continuum, 2003), 432.

50 For a fine account of life in its origin and development, see Richard Southwood, *The Story of Life* (Oxford and New York: Oxford University Press, 2003).

51 Consult John F. Haught, *God after Darwin: A Theology of Evolution* (Boulder, CO, and Oxford: Westview Press, 2000).

52 Thomas Chubb, *The True Gospel of Jesus Christ Asserted* (London: Tho. Cox, MDCCXXXVIII [1738]). The emphases in the text are Chubb's. All subsequent page references to this text will be indicated within parentheses at the end of quotations.

Chapter VIII

1 David B. Barrett, George T. Kurian and Todd M. Johnson, eds, *World Christian Encyclopedia: A Comparative Survey of Churches and Religions in the Modern World*, 2nd edn, vol. 1 (New York and Oxford: Oxford University Press, 2001), 3.

2 Barrett and others, *World Christian Encyclopedia*, 3.

3   Kathleen Dugan, 'Shavuot', in Orlando O. Espín and James B. Nickoloff, eds, *An Introductory Dictionary of Theology and Religious Studies* (Dublin: The Columba Press, 2007), 1270–1; 1270.

4   See Allan Anderson, *An Introduction to Pentecostalism* (Cambridge: Cambridge University Press, 2008), 33.

5   Anderson, *Pentecostalism*, 39.

6   Anderson, *Pentecostalism*, 39.

7   William D. Faupel, *The Everlasting Gospel: The Significance of Eschatology in the Development of Pentecostal Thought* (Sheffield: Sheffield Academic Press, 1996), 194–7 and 200–2.

8   David Martin, *Pentecostalism: The World Their Parish* (Oxford: Blackwell, 2002), 1.

9   David B. Barrett and Todd M. Johnson, 'Annual Statistical Table on Global Mission: 2003', *International Bulletin of Missionary Research*, 27: 1 (2203), 24–5; 25.

10 Patrick Johnstone and Jason Mandryk, *Operation World: 21st Century Edition* (Carlisle: Paternoster Press, 2001), 3. In addition, see 21, 755, 757 and 762.

11 See Donald E. Miller and Tetsunao Yamamori, *Global Pentecostalism: The New Face of Christian Social Engagement* (Berkeley, CA: University of California Press, 2007), 20.

12 Miller and Yamamori, *Global Pentecostalism*, 26.

13 Paul Gifford, *Ghana's New Christianity: Pentecostalism in a Globalizing African Economy* (Bloomingdon, IN: Indiana University Press, 2004), 56.

14 Miller and Yamamori, *Global Pentecostalism*, 27.

15 See Miller and Yamamori, *Global Pentecostalism*, 27 and 28.

16 Anderson, *Pentecostalism*, 1–4.

17 Norman A. Hjelm, 'Ecumenical Movement', in John Bowden, ed., *Encyclopedia of Christianity* (Oxford and New York: Oxford University Press, 2005), 363–6; 364. Delegates attended from 44 countries. The only major group not represented was the Catholic Church of the Roman Rite. See too Evelyn A. Kirkley, 'World Council of Churches', in Espín and Nickoloff, eds, *Dictionary*, 1496; and Harold E. Fey, ed., *A History of the Ecumenical Movement: 1948–1968* (Geneva: WCC Publications, 1993).

18 Consult John Wijngaards, *The Ordination of Women in the Catholic Church* (London: Darton, Longman & Todd, 2001); and *No Women in Holy Orders? The Women Deacons of the Early Church* (Norwich: Canterbury Press, 2002).

19 Mark Chaves, *Ordaining Women: Culture and Conflict in Religious Organizations* (Cambridge, MA: Harvard University Press, 1997), 16–17.

20 John Bowden, *A Chronology of World Christianity* (London and New York: Continuum, 2007), 412.

21 Paul Mojzes, 'Orthodoxy Under Communism', in Mary Farrell Bednarowski, ed., *Twentieth-Century Global Christianity* (Minneapolis, MN: Fortress Press, 2008), 131–56; 141.

22 Mojzes, 'Orthodoxy', 138–9. See, as well, Dimitry Pospielovsky, *The Russian Church under Soviet Regime, 1917–1982*, 2 vols (Crestwood, NY: St Vladimir's Seminary Press, 1984).

23 Consult Michael Haynes and Rumy Husan, *A Century of State Murder?: Death and Policy in Twentieth-Century Russia* (London, and Sterling, VA: Pluto Press, 2003), 211–12.

24 Mojzes, 'Orthodoxy', 145; and Paul Mojzes, *Religious Liberty in Eastern Europe and the USSR* (Boulder: East European Monographs, 1997), 66–7.

25 Mojzes, 'Orthodoxy', 140–2.

26 Victoria J. Barnett, 'Ordinary Christians and the Holocaust', in Dednarowski, *Twentieth-Century Global Christianity*, 265–79; 266.

27 Gavin I. Langmuir, *History, Religion, and Antisemitism* (Berkeley, CA: University of California Press, 1990), 284.

28 See, Langmuir, *History*, 285.

29 Langmuir, *History*, 295.

30 Jermey Morris, *The Church in the Modern Age* (London and New York: I.B.Tauris, 2007), 13.

31 R. Hilberg, *Die Vernichtung der europäischen Juden: Die Gesamtgeschichte des Holocaust* (Frankfurt am Main: Fisher Taschenbuch Verlag, 1997), 15f.; and Hans Küng, *Judaism*, trans. John Bowden (London: SCM Press, 1992), 232–40.

32 Morris, *The Church*, 14.

33 John XXIII, cited in Giuseppe Alberigo and Joseph A. Komonchak, eds, *History of Vatican II, Vol I: Announcing and Preparing Vatican Council II Toward a new Era in Catholicism* (Maryknoll, NY: Orbis, and Leuven: Peeters, 1995), 2. A translation of the Pope's allocution on 25 January is contained in *The Pope Speaks*, 5 (1958–59), 398–401.

34 Pope John XXIII, *Journal of a Soul*, Trans. D. White, rev. edn (New York: Image/Doubleday, 1980), 325.

35 For details of his diplomatic work, see his *Journal of a Soul*.

36 Pope John XXIII, 'Allocution to the Franciscan Order' (16 April 1959), in *Discorsi Messaggi Colloqui del S. Padre Giovanni XXIII*, 6 vols (Città del Vaticano, 1960–67), I, 250.

37 Richard P. McBrien, *Report on the Church: Catholicism after Vatican II* (New York, NY: HarperSanFrancisco, 1992), 22. The list of points in this paragraph is largely based on McBrien, 21–22.

38 See Adrian Hastings, 'The Key Texts', in Adrian Hastings, ed., *Modern Catholicism: Vatican II and After* (London: SPCK; and New York: Oxford University Press, 1991), 56–67; 58–9.

39 Norman Tanner, *The Church and the World: 'Gaudium et Spes, Inter Mirifica'* (Newyork, Mahwah, NJ: Paulist Press, 2005), xii.

40 Giovanni Turbanti, 'Il ruolo del P.D. Chenu nell'elaborazione della costituzione Guadim et Spes', in *Marie-Dominique Chenu: Moyen Âge et modernité* (Paris: Le Centre d'études du Saulchoir, 1997), 173–212.

41 See Yves Congar, *Mon Journal Concile*, vol. II (Paris: Les Édition du Cerf, 2002), 308–9.

42 John O'Malley, *What Happened at Vatican II* (Cambridge, MA, and London: The Belknap Press of Harvard University Press, 2008), 258–9.

43 Tanner, *The Church and the World*, 37.

44 Mark A. Noll and Ethan Sanders, 'Evangelicalism in North America', in Bednarowski, *Twentieth-Century Global Christianity* (Minneapolis, MN: Fortress Press, 2008), 157–89; 179.

45 Noll and Sanders, 'Evangelicalism', 162.

46 Consult David Bebbington, *Evangelicalism in Modern Britain* (London: Unwin Hyman, 1989), 2–17.

47 Noll and Sanders, 'Evangelicalism', 181. See too 183.

48 Noll and Sanders, 'Evangelicalism', 214. See 212–14 as well.

49 See Elisabeth Schlüssler Fiorenza, *In Memory of Her: A Feminist Theological Reconstruction of Christ Origins*, 2nd edn (London: SCM Press, 1995).

50 Jack Nelson-Pallmeyer, *Is Religion Killing Us? Violence in the Bible and Quran* (Harrisburg, PA: Trinity Press International, 2003), 115.

51 Cited in Nelson-Pallmeyer. *Is Religion Killing Us?*, 116. See 115 as well.

52 United Nations, Food and Agricultural Organization (FAO), quoted in Nelson-Pallmeyer, *Is Religion Killing Us?*, 116.

Conclusion

1 Food and Agricultural Organization of the UN (FAO), *Reaching the Marginalized EFA Report* (Oxford: Oxford University Press, 2010), 24.

2 G.J. Sawyer and Vicktor Deak, *The Last Human: A Guide to Twenty-Two Species of Extinct Humans* (New Haven and London: Yale University Press, 2007).

3 Rosendo Salvado, *The Salvado Memoirs*, trans. and ed. E.J. Stormon (Nedlands, W.A.: University of Western Australia Press, 1997), 55.

4 Gavin I. Langmuir, *History, Religion, and Antisemitism* (Berkeley, CA: University of California Press, 1990), 306–7.

5 Michael J. Buckley, *At the Origins of Modern Atheism* (New Haven, CT: Yale University Press, 1987), 311.

6 Immanuel Kant, 'An Answer to the Question: What Is Enlightenment?', in James Schmidt, *What Is Enlightenment? Eighteenth-Century Answers and Twentieth-Century Questions* (Berkeley, CA: University of California Press, 1996), 58–64; 58.

7 Langmuir, *History*, 309.

8 Edward Schillebeeckx, *The Church with a Human Face: A New and Expanded Theology of Ministry*, trans. John Bowden (London, SCM Press, 1985); *God Is New each Moment: In Conversation with Huub Oosterhuis and Piet Hoogeveen* (Edinburgh: T&T Clark, 1983); and *For the Same of the Gospel*, trans. John Bowden (London: SCM Press, 1989), ch. 9, esp. 79–84.

9 St Basil the Great, *On Social Justice*, trans. C. Paul Schroeder (Crestwood, NY: St Vladimir's Seminary Press, 2009), 63–4. Biblical references added.

Further Reading

Anderson, Allan, *An Introduction to Pentecostalism* (Cambridge: Cambridge University Press, 2004)

Bowden, John, ed., *Encyclopedia of Christianity* (Oxford and New York: Oxford University Press, 2005)

Feuerbach, Ludwig, trans. George Eliot, *The Essence of Christianity* (New York, NY: Prometheus Books (1989) [1841])

Fiorenza, Elisabeth Schlüssler, *A Critical Feminist Ekklēia-logy of Liberation* (London: SCM, 1993)

Harnack, Adolf, *What Is Christianity? Sixteen Lectures delivered in the University of Berlin during the Winter-Term 1899–1900*, trans. Thomas Bailey Saunders (London, Edinburgh and Oxford: Williams and Norgate, and New York: G.P. Putman's Sons, 1901)

Hastings, Adrian, *A World History of Christianity* (Grand Rapids, MI: Eerdmans, 1999)

Herring, George, *An Introduction to the History of Christianity: From the Early Church to the Enlightenment* (London and New York: Continuum, 2006)

Janz, Denis R., General Editor, *A People's History of Christianity*, 7 vols (Minneapolis, MN: Fortress Press, 2005–2009)

Küng, Hans, *Christianity: The Religious Situation of Our Time*, trans. John Bowden (London: SCM Press, 1995)

Ludlow, Morwenna, *The Early Church* (London and New York: I.B. Tauris, 2009)

MacCulloch, Diarmaid, *Christianity: The First Three Thousand Years* (London: Allen Lane, 2009)

Marty, Martin, *The Christian World: A Global History* (New York: The Modern Library, 2007)

McGrath, Alister E., *Christianity: An Introduction*, 2nd edn (Malden, MA: Blackwell Publishing, 2006/2009)

McManners, John, *The Oxford Illustrated History of Christianity* (Oxford: Oxford University Press, 1990)

Miles, Margaret R. *The Word Made Flesh: A History of Christian Thought* (Malden, MA: Blackwell Publishing, 2004/2008)

Miller, Donald E. and Tetsunao Yamori, *Global Pentecostalism: The New Face of Christian Social Engagement* (Berkeley, CA: University of California Press, 2007)

Morris, Jeremy, *The Church in the Modern Age* (London and New York: I.B.Tauris, 2007)

Ratzinger, Joseph, trans. J.R. Foster, *Introduction to Christianity* (San Francisco: Ignatius Press, 2004; 1968 [German original])

Schillebeeckx, Edward, *Church: The Human Story of God*, trans. John Bowden (London: SCM Press, 1990)

Woodhead, Linda, *An Introduction to Christianity* (Cambridge: Cambridge University Press, 2007)

Index

I.B.TAURIS INTRODUCTIONS TO RELIGION

Daoism: An Introduction – Ronnie L Littlejohn
HB 9781845116385
PB 9781845116392

Jainism: An Introduction – Jeffery D Long
HB 9781845116255
PB 9781845116262

Judaism: An Introduction – Oliver Leaman
HB 9781848853942
PB 9781848853959

Zoroastrianism: An Introduction – Jenny Rose
HB 9781848850873
PB 9781848850880

Confucianism: An Introduction – Ronnie L Littlejohn
HB 9781848851733
PB 9781848851740

Sikhism: An Introduction – Nikky-Guninder Kaur Singh
HB 9781848853201
PB 9781848853218

Islam: An Introduction – Catharina Raudvere
HB 9781848850835
PB 9781848850842

Christianity: An Introduction – Philip Kennedy
HB 9781848853829
PB 9781848853836

Hinduism: An Introduction – Will Sweetman
HB 9781848853270
PB 9781848853287

Buddhism: An Introduction – Alexander Wynne
HB 9781848853966
PB 9781848853973